Queering the Redneck Riviera

UNIVERSITY PRESS OF FLORIDA

Florida A&M University, Tallahassee
Florida Atlantic University, Boca Raton
Florida Gulf Coast University, Ft. Myers
Florida International University, Miami
Florida State University, Tallahassee
New College of Florida, Sarasota
University of Central Florida, Orlando
University of Florida, Gainesville
University of North Florida, Jacksonville
University of South Florida, Tampa
University of West Florida, Pensacola

QUEERING THE REDNECK RIVIERA

SEXUALITY AND THE RISE OF FLORIDA TOURISM

Jerry T. Watkins III

UNIVERSITY PRESS OF FLORIDA
Gainesville / Tallahassee / Tampa / Boca Raton
Pensacola / Orlando / Miami / Jacksonville / Ft. Myers / Sarasota

Printed in the United States of America on acid-free paper

This book may be available in an electronic edition.

23 22 21 20 19 18 6 5 4 3 2 1

LIBRARY OF CONGRESS CATALOGING-IN-PUBLICATION DATA
Names: Watkins, Jerry T. III, author.
Title: Queering the Redneck Riviera : sexuality and the rise of Florida tourism / Jerry T. Watkins III.
Description: Gainesville : University Press of Florida, 2018. | Includes bibliographical references and index.
Identifiers: LCCN 2017040582 | ISBN 9780813056913 (cloth : alk. paper)
Subjects: LCSH: Gays—Travel—Florida—History. | Tourism—Florida—History. | Gay travelers—Florida—History.
Classification: LCC HQ75.26.F6 W38 2018 | DDC 910.86/640759—dc23
LC record available at https://lccn.loc.gov/2017040582

The University Press of Florida is the scholarly publishing agency for the State University System of Florida, comprising Florida A&M University, Florida Atlantic University, Florida Gulf Coast University, Florida International University, Florida State University, New College of Florida, University of Central Florida, University of Florida, University of North Florida, University of South Florida, and University of West Florida.

UNIVERSITY PRESS OF FLORIDA
15 Northwest 15th Street
Gainesville, FL 32611-2079
http://upress.ufl.edu

CONTENTS

FIGURES

ACKNOWLEDGMENTS

This book has been a journey, to say the least. Growing up in Panama City was in many ways idyllic, though I didn't really understand that until much later in life after I moved away. Like so many youngsters, I believed my hometown was too small, too provincial, and I longed for something more. I began to have a sense that I was gay in the early 1990s though I wouldn't have used that word then. I was a devout Southern Baptist, so that made the rest of the decade rather complicated, especially when my Christian elementary-school principal said that boys couldn't wear earrings because they "didn't want fags in their school." I spent all of high school in the closet trying desperately to "pray the gay away" while at the same time engaging in some of the activities at some of the places I describe in this book.

After coming out in August 1998, I walked into the Fiesta Room late one summer night. The journey to this book really began there. I spent the late 1990s and early 2000s at the Fiesta Room Lounge. When I was eighteen I thought the old men sitting around the bar were "tired old queens" at best and creepy at worst. Little did I know that they would become my greatest teachers. Then when my family moved to Atlanta I spent many nights dancing in the discos and partaking of everything the gay life had to offer. I had precious little consciousness of the weight of the past on me at that time. After the aimless years, I returned to school to study marketing, but it turns out I was too much of a commie-pinko-fag even at that young age to be happy in the corporate world. I returned to my first love: history.

I've had some phenomenal mentors over the years of study. Alecia Long's History of Sexuality class at Georgia State University showed me that sex and sexuality had a history and that they constituted an important area of study. Cliff Kuhn taught me the importance of oral and community history, and he also introduced me to John Howard. Early on in my studies, I was interested in LGBTQ history mainly to understand myself, but I was still focused on the metropolitan gay experience. While we were having drinks at a now closed gay bar in London, John Howard convinced me that my small town had an LGBTQ history and that it was important. Naïvely, I thought the Fiesta Room "looked old," so I decided to start there. Those older men around the bar became my teachers. Mike Krall and his partner Bubba Gilbert, along with Jim Smith, Butch McKay, and others, made up much of the oral history that informed my master's thesis. I was lucky to have such caring mentors who took the time to shepherd me through academic history and the gay history of my hometown. I will be eternally grateful to those individuals for their guidance over the last decade. They have helped make me the historian that I am today.

One cannot undertake, let alone finish, a book without a great deal of support. My family has loved and supported me in these endeavors well beyond anything I could have hoped for. Along the way, numerous friends have read drafts, commented on ideas over tea or around conference tables, and others have supplied coffee and love. They all helped keep me sane and dragged me out of the library when I needed some fresh air. My husband has been something of a rock these last few years as I struggled with job hunting, writing, and the travails of academic life. I love him more than words can express.

My PhD from King's College London would not have been possible without Polly Penter, whose guidance through the Kafkaesque UK Home Office's student-visa process allowed me to finish my studies. Uli and Jim at London's Gay's The Word (the greatest bookshop in the world in my humble opinion) provided support and guidance for all things related to my reading needs over the course of my time in London. Seriously, when you are in London, stop in and say hi to these guys!

Archivists and librarians are the backbone of my profession. In many ways they are the unsung heroes because without them we could not do our work. The Bay County Public Library Local History Room has been invaluable in uncovering things and even supplying me with information when I was back in London. The Pensacola Historical Society and Special Collections at the University of West Florida as well as the staff at the State Archives of Florida in Tallahassee have always gone above and beyond the call of duty. The Atlanta History Center and the Georgia LGBTQ Archives Project have both provided much-needed assistance for materials beyond the Gulf Coast. I'm also incredibly grateful to ONE National Gay and Lesbian Archives for letting me in early, allowing me to stay late, and inviting me to lunch when I didn't realize just how challenging twenty-seven boxes of letters would be. All of these institutions are staffed by people who love what they do and care about helping preserve the past and present it to the public.

I'm grateful to Georgia State University for employing me and allowing me to finally get some teaching experience during the process of writing this book. The History Department welcomed me back with open arms. My colleagues at the College of William and Mary have provided moral support as well as sounding boards in the home stretch of this book. The William and Mary LGBTIQ Research Project and the Tyler Funds have provided financial support along the way. Working with Leisa and the students on the William and Mary LGBTIQ Research Project has been a joy.

Gay Grassroots in Pensacola and the Prime Timers in Tallahassee have put me in touch with more than a few men willing to speak about the project. Gay Grassroots invited me to give a talk about my work in 2015, and it was through that event that I met Kurt Young. He is a fount of knowledge and always willing to help. He also provided the photo albums that Ray and Henry collected over their years of running the Emma Jones parties. Without him, chapter 5 would have been much less fun since my words can only do so much when it comes to describing the events. In addition, Tom Baker was quite generous with his time and his memories, and indeed much of chapter 2 would not have been possible without him opening the door.

Publishing a book was brand-new territory for me and involved a substantial reorganization of the chapters. I was overwhelmed by the challenge on more than one occasion, but my editor, Sian Hunter, the two reviewers that agreed to read my manuscript, and my copy editor have been invaluable. They helped me turn an unruly manuscript into a focused final product. Stacy Braukman served as one of the reviewers and, despite personal struggles, her comments were insightful and challenging, always pushing me to say exactly what I mean and to clarify my argument. She also helped me to think through some of the issues I had with connecting the Gulf Coast to larger events. The other anonymous reviewer's critique felt biting at times, especially when pointing out that I might have a proverbial darling I was unwilling to kill. I had several, and I was glad to have them pointed out. I was too lost in telling the LGBTQ story and trying to include everything. This reviewer waded through disjointed chapters to help me find my way back to my argument about capitalism and sexuality. I hope one day this person introduces himself or herself so I can thank the reviewer properly.

This work is dedicated to the men and women who lived it, the vast majority of whom I will never know. On more than one occasion I cried when reading the interrogations conducted by the Florida Legislative Investigation Committee or hearing the stories shared during the course of research. They had to endure things I cannot today imagine, and I know that my life is easier because of the work many of them did. These days, I'd much rather sit with the older guys at the bar than anywhere else. In the immortal words of ACT UP: Silence = Death. Despite attempts to erase us and our history, we are here, and we will continue to be here.

INTRODUCTION

The legislators, the judges, the Chambers of Commerce in Florida, are interested in one thing only: TOURIST TRADE! Tourist money and the state and local taxes levied on the tourist and the winter resident keep the state solvent. Therefore, anything which might offend or alienate the visitor is banned. Florida has nothing to offer but grief for the flamboyant, the flaunting homophile. On the other hand, as in most other places, the quiet, the self-respecting are lost in the crowd.

—J.R.

In March 1963, "J.R." wrote to the Los Angeles–based homophile organization ONE, Inc., publishers of *ONE* magazine, to report on the state of homosexual/homophile life in various parts of Florida.[1] His letter included descriptions of Miami, Jacksonville, and Pensacola, among others, and ultimately concluded that Florida "has nothing to offer but grief for the flamboyant, the flaunting homophile," but the "quiet and self-respecting" are safer because they more easily blend into the crowd. On some levels, his assertions are accurate for this moment in Florida's history. A variety of surveillant authorities, bureaucrats, local boosters, and ordinary citizens *were* primarily interested in increasing the tourist trade across the state. Looking around, J.R. would have seen various advertisements for local attractions, stories about the Florida Showcase in New York City, and his newspaper would have been daily filled with stories about tourism. He is also correct when he asserted that there was much grief for those men and women whose homosexual desires became known. Like so much of the country after the Second World War, Florida changed rapidly, and a variety of individuals, behaviors, and identities were unwelcome in the hologram of paradise known as "The Sunshine State."

Through so many brochures, colorful maps, bus tours, welcome stations, and glasses of orange juice, Florida became "The Sunshine State"—the imagined tropical paradise with perfect, sunny weather that promised a release from cares and worries. This title was both fiction and fact. It was a deliberate creation, but also reflected a real possibility of experience for a certain part of the vacationing public. This book uses the full official title, in ways that might feel awkward, because it evokes everything beyond a description of the weather or what was possible in Florida. "The Sunshine State" was an intentional, aspirational, carefully constructed, tightly managed, and heavily policed version of Florida that was packaged and sold on the increasingly competitive open market. Florida was a brand, and "The Sunshine State" was clever branding, to use marketing jargon. Salespersons, government officials, local boosters, and advertising agencies sold this vision to the outside world while local and state law enforcement policed the boundaries of respectability within Florida.

The decades surrounding the middle of the twentieth century were a time of intense and dynamic change in Florida. As common knowledge holds, South Florida became the North and northern Florida remained culturally identified with the Deep South. As pensioners, migrants, and wealthy vacationers from the U.S. Northeast made up an ever-increasing percentage of South Florida's population, the region's politics came to reflect the change. This led to many struggles between the northern rural counties, whose representatives formed the "Porkchop Gang," and southern urban counties because of Florida's malapportioned legislature.[2] Added to this conflict were anxieties over the civil rights movement, Cold War anti-Communist hysteria, increasing homosexual visibility in cities such as Miami, and the increasing percentage of budgets based on the shifting sands of tourism.

This work focuses on the northern part of the state, the area between Pensacola in the west and Tallahassee in the east, and the changes wrought by postwar capitalist expansion. Though Pensacola, with its deepwater port, has enjoyed a long history as a hub of activity and circulation, and Tallahassee, because of its role as Florida's capital city, has enjoyed a similar status, most of the Panhandle remained rural and agrarian until World

War II. Some realized the potential of the beach and began to capitalize on it in the first years of the century. However, many of the smaller municipalities along the coast were based around fishing villages or timber farms until military installations and defense industries, such as shipbuilding, brought tens of thousands of people to the Panhandle during the country's mobilization for war. It was not until after the war that tourism and the business of selling the region's patch of "The Sunshine State" began in earnest on the Panhandle.

After fighting ceased and the country settled into the Cold War, another shift in population occurred. Many war workers relocated to other parts of the country in search of employment. Former soldiers, laborers, and their families settled along the Gulf Coast. Still more people traveled to the coast for vacation thanks to increased automobility, better roads, and that new American civic virtue: leisure spending. Beginning in the early 1950s, this net population growth (both permanent and vacationing) inaugurated fierce competition on the free market for tourist dollars as motels, amusements, and restaurants replaced sand dunes at an ever-increasing rate. Even beyond the spaces immediately adjacent to the sand, the quest for tourists had dramatic impact inland as county governments, state-level commissions, agencies, and politicians grappled with maintaining a favorable public image in the search for increased revenue.

J.R. was incorrect when he asserted, "anything which might offend or alienate the visitor is banned." At this time in the United States, the politics of exposure meant that naming and shaming wrongdoers, especially those deemed subversive to the "American way," became everybody's duty. Interested parties in Florida constructed threats to carefully crafted "family-friendly" images as threats to livelihood, which were to be dealt with publicly. Newspapers became arbiters of the increasingly rigid public morality and an essential part of constructing, selling, and enforcing local slices of "The Sunshine State" as racially moderate, good for business, and family friendly. In 1962, R. J. Strickland, lead investigator for the Florida Legislative Investigation Committee (FLIC) stated, "we should not overlook the newspapers and if the newspapers would get in back of this program the job would be much easier for the law enforcement officers and other groups in the problem."[3] Whether reminding readers to treat visitors as guests, pick up trash along the roadways, or report any suspected homosexual activity to law enforcement, newspapers went a long way toward shaping and reinforcing particular images in their parts of the Panhandle and the entire state.

At mid-century much of the Panhandle lacked the glitz and glamour of Miami—but that was intentional. As historian Harvey H. Jackson III asserts, "along this coast folks from the lower South found a way of life, a culture, and context, much like the one they left back home—segregated (where blacks existed at all), small town, provincial, self-centered, and unassuming. Only the landscape was different."[4] Summer vacationers from around the South did not travel far either physically or culturally for their vacation—part of the reason that part of Florida became known as the Redneck Riviera. Many southerners newly raised to the working or middle class had only one to two weeks' vacation per year and so wanted to maximize their time. Though they found an environment much like that back home, it was far enough from prying eyes. At the beach they could do things they would not necessarily do back home in front of the neighbors. Sociologists as early as the 1920s called this phenomenon a "moral holiday."[5]

The three cities that feature most prominently—Panama City, Pensacola, and Tallahassee—are the largest cities in the area. Their populations ranged from 50,000 to 200,000 residents. They had bars, restaurants, and coffee houses. All three cities had cinemas, theaters, and various levels of an art scene. The populations of Pensacola and Panama City Beach swelled dramatically over the summer months in this period. On the surface, they seem miles away, both literally and figuratively, from the smaller towns inland, the kind with one traffic signal and a boiled-peanut stand on every corner. These cities occupy spaces between rural and urban life, trading on their association with the nebulous concept of "small-town values." It is tricky to define just what those values are geographically or temporally. For this reason I use "rural" and "small town" not as physical descriptors or pejoratives but as shorthand for a set of ideas (imaginaries) that have come to be associated with the small-town South: conservatism, patriotism, heteronormativity, free-market capitalism, nationalism, Protestant Christianity, family, faith, and folk communalism.

The Panhandle was a place of seeming contradictions after demobilization from the Second World War. *Miami Herald* reporter Robert Shaw described Pensacola as like a gangly teenager suddenly unsure of what to do with itself.[6] This was true for much of the Panhandle as well. Conflicts over how best to capitalize on tourism and sell their part of "The Sunshine State" frequently erupted as municipalities sought to purge from their midst, and discourage from coming, an ever-shifting array of undesirables. Nothing exemplified this more than the changes in name for the Panhandle from "Redneck Riviera" to the aspirational "Miracle Strip" or "Emerald Coast" during the last half of the twentieth century. At certain times, there was plenty of room in North Florida for the weird, the kitschy, the madams, the gamblers, the promoters, and "all the infections of Western life."[7] Yet there was precious little room for the sexually queer as mid-century morality hardened the boundaries of acceptable behavior. Even scholarship on the Redneck Riviera and the politics of the coastal South fails to address LGBTQ contributions and presence in the region. This book, therefore, is a start to queering the Redneck Riviera.

Words have meaning and carry weight. All of the terms used throughout this work perform different types of conceptual labor. Each comes with its own baggage, and some readers will approach words differently from how I have used them. "Gay," "lesbian," "homosexual," "homophile," "queer," "pansy," "fairy," and "faggot" have all been used at various times to describe people both pejoratively and as reclaimed self-identifiers. It is difficult to read identities onto another person accurately. It is downright dangerous to read identities, labels, desires, or their meanings onto individuals in the past. This book endeavors to use the terms that individuals used or that were in general use at particular moments. "Homosexual" and "homophile" are mainly used in the early parts of the book while "gay," "lesbian," and "LGBTQ" are used later to connote the shift in identity politics.

I use "queer" as both an adjective and a verb. Men and women who *liked that* (same-sex sexual activity or homosex) but were not necessarily *like that* (out, gay, or lesbian) confound neat definitional boundaries, and so far "queer" is the best word scholars have come across to describe these individuals. This strategy grew out of groups such as Queer Nation and ACT UP in their attempts to reclaim and thereby remove the stigma from these words. As a verb, "to queer" means to transcend, play with, or confound definitional boundaries or assumptions. "Queering the Redneck Riviera" means to play with assumptions about the beliefs and behaviors of people (transient and local) in this part of Florida.

The term "redneck" also comes with cultural baggage. According to the *Oxford English Dictionary,* the term originated in the early nineteenth century to define white agricultural workers from the rural South, "typically considered as holding bigoted or reactionary attitudes."[8] One can still use the term in that way, but it has also been used as a self-identifier detached from its original class distinctions to push back against liberal derision and "big-city values." Much like "rural" and "small-town values" have come to describe a mindset, so too has "redneck"—illustrated by a redneck-pride sticker on a $75,000 truck or the Rednecks With Paychecks off-road mud crawl. At mid-century, "Redneck Riviera" was not an identity descriptor that many in region were proud of, as evidenced by the constant attempts to rebrand, but it is what many people called the beaches of North Florida. When proud rednecks started taking their new money elsewhere, they were again courted. There is now space for them in this part of Florida. I use the term not as a pejorative, but as the descriptor in use at the time. Just as "homosexual"/"homophile" gave way to "gay," "lesbian," and "LGBTQ," so did "Redneck Riviera" give way to "Miracle Strip" and "Emerald Coast." Unqueering and un-rednecking went hand in hand for much of the period under discussion, though queer folks fared much worse.

So much activity I describe was about removing from view, or even removing from the state, anything queer. Scholar Carol Mason uses the term "unqueering" to refer to the process of flattening out sexual difference through the active oppression, exclusion, or erasure of queer people. Unqueering is a process with myriad expressions. It is state authority arresting men for cruising (chapters 2 and 3). It is moral/ideological entrepreneurs seeking to foreclose queer visibility through legislation or public shame in service of economic gain (chapters 5 and 6). Many of the people that populate this narrative were locals or recent transplants who came to make their home in the land of sunshine either because of opportunity or simply out of a desire for warmth. In Panama City, discourses of shame surrounding the series of arrests at a public restroom sent one man back into the closet and propelled another out of it (chapter 2). In Pensacola, the gay social group that called itself the Emma Jones Society held beach parties and conventions beginning in 1965 that were known to local politicians and businesses. These were early indications of the transition from closet economy to liberation economy.[9] With regime change and the growth of conservative moralizing (that is, Anita Bryant, the "silent majority," the "moral majority"), the gay and lesbian gatherings were beyond the pale. Officials arrested dozens of people while seeking to shut down gay bars (chapter 5). Unqueering, then, is a useful way to frame and understand the dialectical relationship between sexuality and "The Sunshine State."[10]

John D'Emilio's pioneering essay "Capitalism and Gay Identity" sets out that gay and lesbian identity in the United States grew out of the specific societal changes wrought by capitalism.[11] Drawing on D'Emilio's fundamental but problematic urban-centered assertion, early historians of sexuality often articulated LGBTQ history as a coming-out narrative. The evidence seemed to show that men and women with homosexual desires moved to cities for expanded economic opportunity. There they articulated an identity through contact with others like themselves at illicit social institutions (bars, bathhouses, tea rooms). From there, communities (ghettos) coalesced into politics (Stonewall, Gay Liberation Front). This was the experience for many, but not for all.

What D'Emilio's work did not explain, but later historians have endeavored to demonstrate, was how manifestations of American capitalism created openings for LGBTQ identities in historically and regionally specific ways—that is, outside of the metropolis. Scholars working on the Deep South such as John Howard, Donna Jo Smith, and James Sears sought to rectify this metro-normative, bicoastal bias in scholarship.[12] They produced work that argued for a queer experience that was distinct, though not necessarily unique, because of American capitalism's hegemony.

As scholarship progressed, historians such as David Johnson, Margot Canaday, and others articulated a link between the persecution of alleged sexual deviants after the Second World War and America's vigorous defense of the capitalist system (freedom, free markets, free enterprise) and containment of communism. Conformity to the ideal of a home stocked with new appliances and inhabited by the nuclear family was one of the central pillars of this containment. Of course, capitalism is inherently unstable, as the regular booms and busts make clear. Many at mid-century imagined that the "American way of life" was constantly under siege from without. At times of social stress, the system must always find scapegoats to obscure its own culpability. Whether immigrants, homosexuals, or a variety of "others," anything but capitalism must be blamed for undermining the family.[13]

Within this period of scapegoating was the earliest period of LGBTQ economy. Writing in the early 1990s, Jeffrey Escoffier articulates what he saw then as four phases of gay and lesbian economy: closet, liberation, territorial, and AIDS.[14] The closet economy was one in which great pains were taken to keep one's identity hidden because the consequences of disclosure could be extreme. It was characterized by bars, bathhouses, private parties, and coded mail-order services that operated on the margins of legality. Escoffier locates the liberation economy as largely post-Stonewall and characterized by economic institutions that had emerged from the confines of semi-legality and were more out. Next came the territorial economy characterized by "gayborhoods" that proceeded into the AIDS economy where the dominant institutions were those that provided services to the dying. This should not be read as a narrative of linear progress since much overlap and cycles of change occurred between phases, as reflected on the Florida Panhandle. For instance, Pensacola has a sizeable gay and lesbian population but never had a "gayborhood." It is not stuck in liberation economy waiting to move into territorial economy. Rather, gay and lesbian life on the Gulf Coast is better characterized by a de-territorialized economy/community.

As historian John Howard argues in his work on queer Mississippi, circulation rather than congregation marked LGBTQ experiences of the South because the sense of space was more expansive than in densely populated urban areas.[15] Tourism in Florida adds another layer to Howard's findings. As this part of Florida joined "The Sunshine State," it was subject to the vagaries of an economy built around service-sector and moral/ideological entrepreneurialism, federal largess, and the fickle tourist dollar. This profoundly affected the LGBTQ experience at mid-century as individuals and small groups navigated ever more hostile waters. The reality of postwar capitalism meant that better roads and more cars could take men and women to more tolerant spaces as long as business owners could benefit and they were not *too* visible. When queer presence and visibility threatened that image and livelihood, moral panics and attendant repression were swift and severe, as evidenced by the Florida Legislative Investigation Committee's (FLIC) investigation of perversion, and a variety of local law-enforcement activities. Along the Panhandle, both on the sand but also in the state capital, postwar capitalism and available spaces/ places shaped gay, lesbian, *and* queer sexualities.

"Under capitalism," as economic historian David Harvey argues, "there is, then, a perpetual struggle in which capital builds a physical landscape appropriate to its own condition at a particular moment in time, only to have to destroy it, usually in the course of a crisis, at a subsequent point in time."[16] Though hurricanes sometimes caused the physical destruction, the built environment and the moral horizon continually shifted like waves and sand dunes in search of increasing revenue. In a place that was distinctly southern, governed by people who were trying to sell "The Sunshine State" as distinctly not southern, and where moral entrepreneurs constructed threats to reputation as threats to livelihood, queer locals and visitors intermingled and even thrived. Gay men, lesbians, and the otherwise queer were an essential part of "The Sunshine State," where they used the burgeoning tourist economy and their spending power to create a queer political economy, ultimately leading to a very queer Redneck Riviera. Placing the queer at the center of this story exposes the unique interactions of capitalism, tourism, sexuality, and space.

Why Florida? Why did Florida "suddenly" see an increase in homosexual "shenanigans"—a term that implies both secret and high-spirited behavior? One doctor recruited by the FLIC theorized in 1962, "You get people who are dissatisfied and unhappy and the wonderful land of the future opens up for you. You see people moving to new opportunities for positive reasons. They move to Florida to get away from the smog, snow, etc. Also, Florida is a booming country. A study will indicate an area in which there is change. It is going to be an area of unrest which will provide a fertile ground for them."[17] Gay men, lesbians, and the otherwise queer moved to Florida for a variety of reasons, even the same reasons as non-LGBTQ people. The "booming country" provided untold opportunity for men and women at mid-century. The "problem" of homosexuality was not actually new in Florida despite what the committee believed. They were not outside agitators; many were Floridians.

State- and local-level official oppression figures prominently in this narrative. Historian Gary Mormino asserts in *Land of Sunshine, State of Dreams: A Social History of Modern Florida* that, to average Floridians, "Tallahassee and Washington were distant places, largely indifferent to their lives."[18] This indifference was the privileged position of conformists.

The state was in fact very interested in certain lives—especially queer or subversive individuals' lives. Much of my source material comes from the Johns Committee, or FLIC, who turned their attention to Florida's "homosexual problem" after failing to link Florida's NAACP with communist subversion. Scholars such as Stacy Braukman, Judith Poucher, Jim Schnur, and others have written extensively about the FLIC, its mission, and its tactics.[19] This book builds on their work and attempts to go beyond a history of criminality; my interrogations serve as a guide, a map, to a queer geography. Reading against the grain and between the lines, I make arguments about spaces, practices, and travels. Because so many of these individuals have been lost to the past, the only way to recover their voices was to rely on transcripts, which I have used extensively.

These interrogation transcripts, though produced by an agency set on exposing and punishing homosexuals, provide valuable insight into the movements and social lives of queer men and women across Florida in the early 1960s. Indeed, this project would not be possible without access to those transcripts. However, they are not without problems. The records exist because of a brush with the legal system. The behavior of the people interrogated was exposed, often for the first time, to surveillant authorities. Historian Stacy Braukman writes, "the very nature of the furtive, anonymous bathroom encounter meant that the committee often ended up interrogating men who were deeply conflicted about their sexual desires."[20] As historian Matt Houlbrook writes in *Queer London: Perils and Pleasures in the Sexual Metropolis 1918–1957*, "this dissonance means that we must understand the records of official agencies . . . as being produced at the point where public and private, pain and pleasure, intersect."[21] The dissonance, the gulf between behavior, identity, and what one actually admitted to, could be great. Some transcripts are heart-wrenching as the individual under interrogation steadily realizes the gravity of the situation upon the evaporation of cognitive dissonance. Others evidence an inner strength as individuals deflect questions and defy the interrogator's expectations.

The second major problem is the inability to name. One of the conditions for opening the records was that names of suspects and others mentioned be redacted. Use of individuals' real names in connection with their interrogation, except where given permission, is a criminal offense. I therefore chose pseudonyms for many FLIC interrogations for ease of readability. Because of wider legal and ethical concerns, some names not connected with the FLIC in this project are also pseudonyms. I have used the real names of public officials and some people when given permission. I have chosen pseudonyms for others, which are culturally appropriate, and of roughly equal prevalence. I do not mean to malign anyone's good name, but I do mean to show that "we" are part of every community. Pseudonyms are not distinguished in the text or the notes. Further, I have spoken with a variety of narrators for different reasons beyond whatever sexual identity they chose.[22]

This book is heavily dependent on the actions of white men in this era, and so is not an all-inclusive LGBTQ history. There were distinct differences in how men and women were able to access the queer Redneck Riviera. The access to paid work outside the home and the freedom to travel unaccompanied was still a largely male privilege although, as I show in chapter 4, certain industries and the U.S. military allowed women a higher level of economic freedom in Pensacola. Lesbians owned property near Tallahassee; some started a secretive organization in Pensacola named the Women's Social Organization of the South, Inc. A lesbian-owned bookstore, Rubyfruit Books, opened in Tallahassee in 1983, and Bella Books and Naiad Press are both headquartered in Tallahassee.

The system of Jim Crow segregation meant that the tourist experience for people of color was markedly different. The walls of segregation were high and stretched all the way to the Gulf. The struggle for equality of gay and lesbian African Americans along the Gulf Coast deserves full scholarly attention. Trying to tell that story was beyond the scope of this book, so I chose to focus my intervention on tourism, "The Sunshine State," and queering the narrative surrounding the Redneck Riviera. It is my hope that this early work will inspire future scholars to write the histories of queer African Americans and lesbians in this time and place.

This book is an exploration of the ways that queer people, though mostly men, experienced the spaces around them. It proceeds roughly chronologically, and the chapters build upon each other. I begin with "Selling 'The Sunshine State'" to set up the ways that postwar capitalist expansion created "The Sunshine State." I look at how the product came to be packaged and sold and the various ways it was policed. Chapter 2 uses a series of arrests in Bay County to show the confluence of state and local forces brought to bear on men engaged in illicit sex that went a long way in unqueering "The Sunshine State." The next two chapters use cruising for sex and the connections made in bars and house parties to make arguments about mobility, sex(uality)-based networks that blurred the lines between acts and identities, and the transition to a liberation economy. The final two chapters use the Emma Jones Society beach parties in Pensacola and the growth of recognizable sites of community such as bars to show how gay men and lesbians used the continually expanding tourist economy to stake their claim on the sand and to craft the Gay Gulf Coast and then Gay Riviera. The gay men, lesbians, and the otherwise queer were an essential part of the region, thereby confounding expectations and queering the Redneck Riviera.

I

SELLING "THE SUNSHINE STATE"

> If it could be defined as a salable product, the State of Florida would be the hottest-selling item on the world market today. And if Governor LeRoy Collins could be classed as a salesman, he would be the luckiest man alive in having over a million and a half prospective customers beating a path to his door.
>
> —*PANAMA CITY NEWS-HERALD*, 1957

Little along the Gulf Coast makes sense without the concept of "The Sunshine State." Politicians, local boosters, and businesses were aware that, to reap the benefits of postwar capitalist expansion, they must conceive of "The Sunshine State" as a product and actively sell the attractions of their state or particular locality on the increasingly competitive free market. Florida's number-one salesman was Governor LeRoy Collins, who led the state from 1955 until 1961 and set the style for later governors by embodying the role of chief executive as promoter.[1] Beyond the physical space of North Florida's beaches, where seemingly unregulated development reigned for most of the early twentieth century, so much government policy (both local and state) and so many business decisions were made with an eye toward capitalizing on tourists. Visitors came to Florida because they were sold on the tropical paradise, beach lifestyle, or the variety of inland entertainments and attractions. As one British man observed, "to most Americans Florida is not a state but a state of mind, not a place to live at all but a place to work off a year's inhibitions in a few determined weeks of pleasure."[2]

Historian Harvey H. Jackson III writes of the immediate postwar era

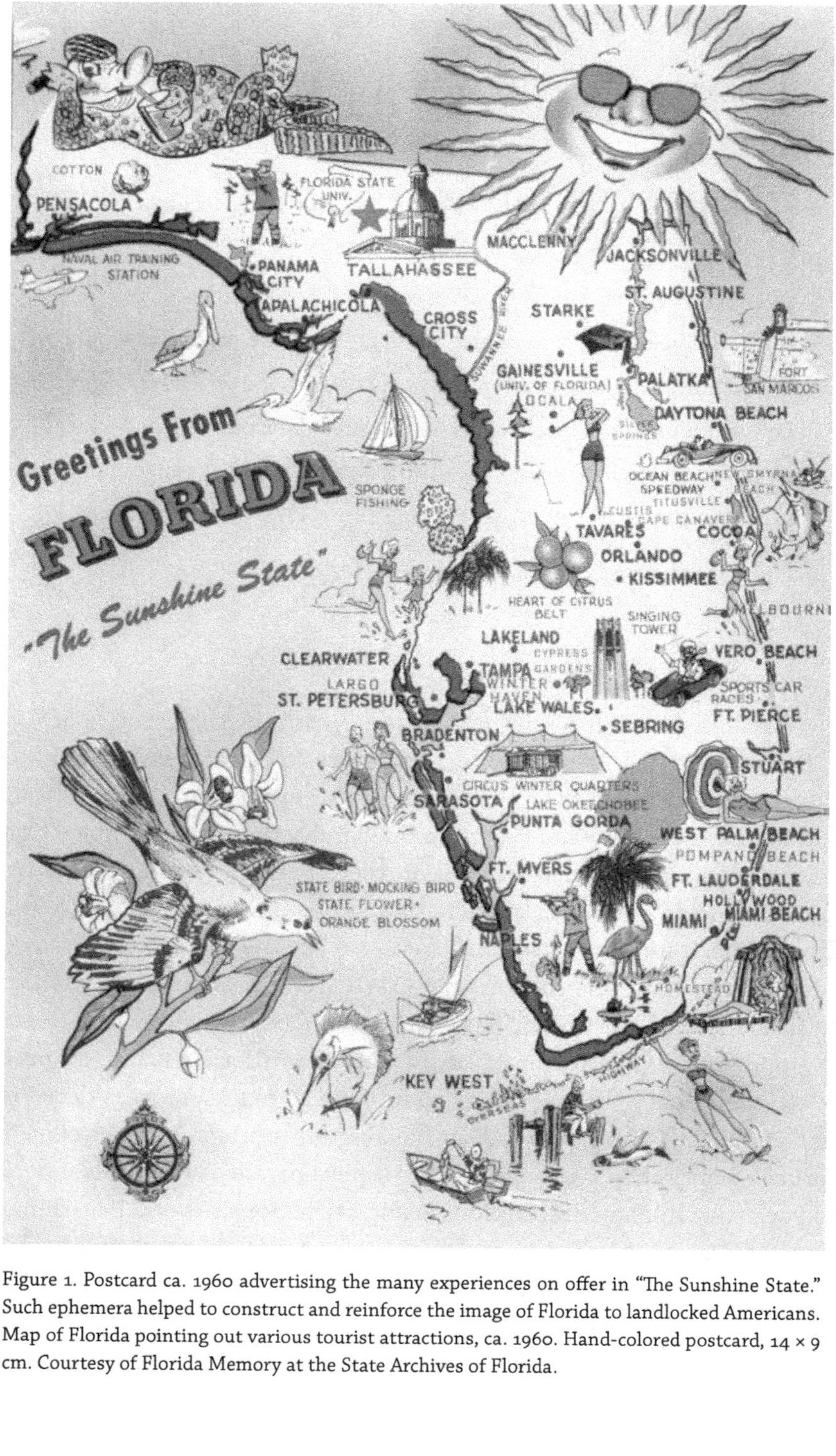

Figure 1. Postcard ca. 1960 advertising the many experiences on offer in "The Sunshine State." Such ephemera helped to construct and reinforce the image of Florida to landlocked Americans. Map of Florida pointing out various tourist attractions, ca. 1960. Hand-colored postcard, 14 × 9 cm. Courtesy of Florida Memory at the State Archives of Florida.

in *The Rise and Decline of the Redneck Riviera: An Insider's History of the Florida-Alabama Coast,* "Thus the seeds of a future were sown. Prosperity would come to the coast if locals could attract more visitors with promises that they could leave their cares (and maybe their inhibitions) behind, while they fished, surf-bathed, and relaxed."[3] Developers, business owners, and politicians realized early on that their prosperity depended on tourists and they could capitalize on the natural beauty of the coast. The image of South Florida and its beaches as a paradise for a particular kind of tourist—namely white and affluent—was cultivated and continually reinforced through tourist brochures, zoning regulations, and the selective enforcement of morality through face-saving crackdowns on a variety of "social ills."[4] In the same way, folks along Florida's northern Gulf Coast cultivated an image for a particular kind of tourist—namely southern, white, and working class—hence the "Redneck Riviera" moniker, a name highly contested from the very beginning.

A vacation along Florida's Panhandle was a different experience for African Americans at mid-century. The civil rights movement was never far from the minds of lawmakers, especially as statehouses in Mississippi and Alabama recorded dramatic depressions in their sales-tax revenues when tourists became afraid of unrest.[5] Jim Crow segregation practices reached all the way to the Gulf Coast by tradition and law. Much of the black population of coastal counties worked inland or in the service of beach business. Most beaches were whites-only, though Escambia in the west and Bay County in the east leased private beach space to African Americans at certain times. Until 1956, when Escambia County canceled the leases at Johnson and Wingate beaches, African Americans from as far away as Tennessee traveled to Pensacola for a vacation on the beach. For much of the Gulf Coast's past, histories of colonization, creolization, and tanning complicated strict racial categorizations.[6]

As the civil rights struggle intensified throughout the South, cities blocked beach access for African Americans in places like Johnson Beach in Pensacola. Stories of civil disobedience, physical violence, and harassment swirled around the discussion of closure. Jackson argues, "it is also possible that officials canceled the lease simply because they could—one more way to show restive blacks who was in charge."[7] Access to public accommodations and facilities was a key part of the civil rights movement, and beach access was an essential component of the larger movement in

Florida, in particular by the early 1960s when wade-ins took place along the coast.[8]

Much of the tourist boom of the 1960s was the result of the active sales campaign begun in the late 1940s and then continuously refined throughout the 1950s. In 1951, after a successful advertising campaign, Governor Fuller Warren met with a group of industry leaders in Tallahassee. He reminded them that, despite the success of the earlier campaign, "we cannot rest upon our oars. Tourism is bitterly competitive. Once we had only to think of California and Arizona as competitors for tourists. Now every state, and the territories too, think of themselves as tourist centers. If we let up for one minute, we may find it difficult to keep those visitors we have, let alone bring new people here."[9] The economic benefits of increased tourism could not be understated as the economic security of the state increasingly relied on tourist expansion. According to a publication by the Florida Development Commission, for every dollar spent on tourism advertising in 1956, $122 came back to the state in the form of tax revenue.[10] As more and more Americans gained access to the American dream and increased leisure spending, competition among tourist-centered businesses only grew tougher.

As competition between municipalities in North Florida quickly escalated, the varieties of ways to advertise became increasingly diverse. Developers and chambers of commerce realized that "you do not grow people on the coast, you bring them in," a strategy that relied increasingly on promotion. With the help of "promoter extraordinaire" Jim Sumter, the promotion of the coast and the lifestyles possible there became more and more about spectacle and getting the public's attention.[11] Local boosters sold a coastal lifestyle through tourist brochures, advertising campaigns in various newspapers, and other direct marketing. Once the variety of interested parties created this image of a tropical paradise, it was consistently impressed on residents and business owners that they played a part in making "The Sunshine State" a reality.

"The Sunshine State" as a concept, a slogan, and an idea was malleable enough to accommodate a variety of tourists over the last half of the twentieth century. To return to David Harvey's observation, capitalism's profit drive must continually renew the landscape, both physical and mental.[12] Time and time again, the built environment and the ideological horizon shifted in North Florida. As successive generations threw off the redneck label and then reclaimed it as an identity rather than a class descriptor, developers replaced kitschy motels and mini-golf courses with scenery-destroying and barely distinguishable condominium units. Beyond the built environment, the moral horizon shifted to attract visitors—sometimes expanding and at other times contracting the limits of acceptable or tolerable behaviors.

At mid-century, there was something for everyone, as long as "everyone" was white, heterosexual, and able-bodied. In order to capitalize on local particularities, there was no single blueprint for selling Florida; rather, each area sought out its "thing" that made it special. Across the state, from travel writers to government agents, "The Sunshine State" was about promotion and selling Florida as a vacationland for a wide range of tastes and desires.[13] The name is used here to describe the constellation of forces at work in Florida. It is both a physical description and an imagined possibility where the advertisement and the product are one. Gamblers, drinkers, civil rights "agitators," homosexuals, and the otherwise queer were not welcome in "The Sunshine State" at various times. Rather than quietly move them along, interested authorities practiced a politics of exposure to ensure compliance with mid-century norms and unqueer "The Sunshine State." The image and the support/enforcement structure show how "The Sunshine State" was deliberately crafted through promotion to outsiders, advice on good citizenship to residents, and selective enforcement of morality through agencies such as the Johns Committee. "The Sunshine State" was a product, a destination, and a dream, but queer men and women were not welcome.

"Florida Welcomes You"

Though Florida's history is intimately tied to flows of water, via both the saltwater that surrounds it as well as the freshwater streams that flow through it, after World War II, Pensacola and indeed the entire northern section of the state were confronted with a different sort of flow. The automobile tourist who drove from land-locked parts of the South (and later the North and Canada) became an integral component of the region's development. As people drove to and through Pensacola—the "western gate to the Sunshine State"—in their cars, developers and city planners encountered the changing needs of people from inland.[14] What better way to welcome

Figure 2. "Florida Welcomes You!" Francis P. Johnson, "Tourists at the Florida Welcome Station," 1955. Black-and-white photoprint, 4 × 5 in. Courtesy of Florida Memory at the State Archives of Florida.

those entering the state by car than with a glass of orange juice (made from Florida oranges) and a large sign that read "Florida Welcomes You"?

The sudden explosion of tourists made up by the newly mobile southern working class grew from seeds sown before the Second World War in Roosevelt's New Deal. According to Historian Harvey H. Jackson III, "children of the Depression and of conflict, more hopeful, indeed optimistic, than they had been in a decade, drove down on New Deal–paved, military-improved roads in automobiles they bought on easy credit or with cashed-in war bonds. They came on vacations from jobs that they were trained and educated for under the GI Bill. They left behind homes financed through that same program."[15] Without the benefit of New Deal programs that put so many to work before the war, and the government assistance that lifted so many veterans into the middle class and agrarians into the working class upon demobilization, tourism as it came to be on the Gulf Coast would have looked markedly different. The newly enlarged, though not necessarily coherent, classes (and their values) shaped tourism practices and local policies as cities sought an ever-increasing share of this market. The automobile irrevocably altered the landscape along the Panhandle as drive-in cinemas, drive-through restaurants, motels, and parking lots dotted the landscape and replaced the sand dunes at alarming rates.

The car created a new class of tourist and new spaces for tourism along Florida's northern Gulf Coast. Rather than utilizing trains or buses, which were subject to schedules and designated routes, individuals or a single family could use their private automobile to take a weekend at the beach on their own time and at their pace or take their business elsewhere if the roads were not sufficient.[16] In 1960, 82 percent of the almost eleven million visitors to Florida came in their cars.[17] How best to help them?

In 1945, Florida began an official program to test the feasibility and utility of welcome stations. The first station opened in 1949 on US Highway 17 north of Jacksonville to greet drivers traveling along the East Coast.[18] The State Road Department conceived of the strategically located stations as a way to welcome visitors who entered Florida in their automobiles, as well as to guide and assist guests in mapping out the remainder of their journey.[19] Large parking lots surrounded the stations, and knowledgeable volunteers (usually women) armed with maps and travel guides—often sponsored by hotels or tourist boards—were on hand to answer travelers' questions.[20] The buildings had a spacious, open room with a central desk as well as public restrooms and picnic tables. And, of course, some even offered drive-up services.

Initially, the State Road Department was unsure if these stations would prove helpful, but Pensacola boosters could see the potential from the beginning and early on requested that the Road Department consider them for the program. In a letter to Sanderford Jarman, of Pensacola's Municipal Advertising Board, dated October 4, 1946, F. Elgin Bayless, chairman of the State Road Department, wrote that a welcome station in Pensacola would be considered if "the reception given our initial unit justifies an expansion of the program."[21] The department planned the first station so that a highway patrolman and his wife could act as hosts. The traffic soon became so constant that officials added other hostesses.[22]

The program proved very successful, and by the close of the 1950s every major highway possessed a welcome station. When the interstate highways opened, the state installed welcome stations at those entrances to Florida as well.

Pensacola's station was constructed in 1954 to greet those entering the state from the west. Located on U.S. Highway 90, just two miles from the border with Alabama along a section of road that would eventually become part of Interstate 10, the small and unassuming building greeted motorists with a large sign that read "Florida Welcomes You." According to the morning *Pensacola Journal,* "three hostesses will be on hand to provide visitors with free orange juice and to aid them in mapping out their trips throughout the state."[23] Of course, if those trips included Pensacola beaches and businesses, that would be even better.

Beyond simply greeting tourists as they entered the state, some welcome station volunteers served as ambassadors to promote and sell "The Sunshine State" throughout the United States on the variety of promotional tours that took place in the 1950s and 1960s. In 1955, Helen Costopolos, a volunteer at the Pensacola Welcome Station, was selected by boosters to travel to New York on a "propaganda campaign for the Sunshine State" and Pensacola specifically.[24] In addition to her knowledge of Florida and her winning smile, her accent was "typically Florida." Unlike cities further along the coast or inland, Pensacola was advantageously located to piggyback on the promotion of the welcome stations and Florida generally.

Managing Impressions

The maps, brochures, coupon books, and guides available at welcome stations and beyond played an essential role in crafting visitor expectations. According to scholars James Brock and Gerri Reeves, photographs on maps, brochures, and other forms of advertising "embody models of possibility for tourists; they define the safely known horizon of experience."[25] Florida boosters created and actively sold a vision of "The Sunshine State" through nationwide advertising campaigns and tours. At the welcome stations, customers no longer needed to be sold a Florida vacation, but they just might need help emptying their wallets on a variety of attractions when they arrived at their destination. It was important, therefore, that the environment be as close to the postcard image as possible, lest disappointment garner a negative review.

Florida has an abundance of charming scenery. However, more tourists meant more trash. Carelessly disposed-of trash threatened to sour a visitor's impression of the natural environment, which could lead to disappointment and then to a negative review and then no more tourists—or so panicky promoters' reasoning went. In a letter to the editors of the *Pensacola News-Journal* in April 1961, Ruby Parker expressed the sentiments of many Pensacola residents, and indeed many Floridians: "When visitors return home and show snapshots and movies, the loveliness of this spot [the Bluffs] is marred by the litter."[26] Parker explicitly links visitor perceptions, literally through photographs and film, with their likelihood to return. The most valuable kind of advertising was the testimonial of a satisfied customer, especially if that customer had beautiful photographs.

Further along the coast, the aesthetic appeal of Bay County's built environment was imagined as crucial to maintaining the city's reputation. The editors at the *Panama City News-Herald* recognized this and consistently reminded citizens and lawmakers, "Any city such as Panama City, which relies heavily on transient traffic for much of its economy, and which proclaims itself as a tourist center, must have an attractive community."[27] Through the long 1950s, when the guiding principle seemed to be "build it faster, longer, and bigger, paint it colors that never appeared in nature, and you'd get their attention—and their money," the definition of "attractive" caused much contentious debate.[28] The focus, and in particular situations one could say hypervigilance, on visitor perception fed into the low-level anxiety that led to moral panics across North Florida.

In cities so dependent on first impressions, struggles over how best to allocate funds to embellish what nature provided were inevitable.[29] Projects such as "Great White Way" lighting in Panama City, or the planting of palm trees along highways that led to the coast, competed for finite resources with basic road construction, maintenance, and paving. These conflicts consistently played out through a never-ending stream of articles and editorials in newspapers such as the *Panama City News-Herald* Pensacola's *News-Journal,* and Tallahassee's *Democrat*. Bay County resident Olan Volner wrote in 1962, "Improvement of the city's streets is badly needed and glad to see that work is in progress to improve them. Since the tourist trade is a contributing factor to the city's economy, the city has to maintain a certain standard of modernization if we are to attract new tourists and to get the old ones to come back year after year."[30] In the rush to build accommodations and amusements, basic road construction was essential. Without adequate roads, visitors would drive to other beaches that were easier to reach, and they would tell their friends, who would then drive to other beaches.

Beyond the built environment, officials and local promoters believed that it was necessary for the "right" kind of tourist to populate the beaches. Editor and Pensacola promoter Earle Bowden wrote in 1962 that "the island [Pensacola Beach] has become a quiet vacation spot, suitable for family groups, although lacking somewhat the flamboyance of other beach and resort areas catering to the teens and young bloods. . . . This rightly should be our image, clean, wholesome recreation. This is the best in promotion of tourism and pays off considerably as opposed to the all-night beach parties and rowdy behavior."[31] This intense focus on wholesome, heterosexual, and family-centered recreation portended trouble for Pensacola's queer residents and those visitors looking to take a "moral holiday" on Pensacola's beaches. Bowden's statement exposes the economic motivations behind the reputation-management campaigns and moral panics that marked the period after 1960.

The affordability of the Panhandle put a beach vacation within reach of a large segment of the white southern population. Because the beaches of Bay County were more affordable even than Pensacola, they became the destination of choice for many working-class southerners.[32] Panama City and its beaches were not trying to be Miami, and in many ways defined itself in opposition to the glitz and glamour of South Florida. Its boosters wanted to maintain the small-town southern feel and level of affordability. According to reporter William Gober in a 1950 article, "it is a myth about Florida being a playground for the rich alone. People in the middle and low-income groups are promised they'll be surprised how far a dollar will go."[33] Florida had something for everyone. The *Panama City Herald* published a letter written to the Chamber of Commerce from a particularly satisfied New Englander named Andrew Broun. The chief benefit of the state's northern beaches was "the prices compared to the prices 400 to 600 miles down the East and West coasts, beautiful beaches, good stores, churches of all denominations, friendly people—

what more could one want?"[34] He and his wife were satisfied customers and became two more Panama City promoters in New England after their recent pleasant experience.

More than natural beauty, low prices, and warm temperatures, the general friendliness of the people served to draw vacationers to Bay County and the larger Gulf Coast year after year. In numerous articles and remembrances, visitors spoke of the welcome provided by the residents of Bay County. In a poll of soldiers at Fort Rucker, Alabama, the overwhelming majority selected Panama City as their favorite leave destination because "it has wonderful beaches—its people are friendly, and it has good restaurants."[35] Sometimes these soldiers came back to live after their tours. A Chamber of Commerce publication quoted Johnny Weaver, who recalled, "After my discharge from the military in early 1944, my mind was made up to make this my home."[36]

Advertisers and boosters could not let up on the pace of their efforts to attract visitors. Though the beaches of the Gulf Coast continued to grow year by year, chambers of commerce, business leaders, and promoters launched newer and flashier campaigns to keep the number of visitors on the increase. The welcome station's Helen Costopolos went on tour in the 1950s, and then came 1962's Florida Showcase in New York City.[37] The showcase, like other promotional tours and events, brought together a collection of images, artifacts, and products from Florida all designed to promote the state to tourists and business interests. Florida became "The Sunshine State" through the repetitions of these showcases. Here, the idea of Florida as a product and "The Sunshine State" as a brand was made clear through the careful crafting of window displays. Florida had become a saleable product.

In 1968, the seventh annual Miracle Strip Caravan left Panama City bound for destinations throughout the South. What began seven years earlier as a tentative cooperation between the Gulf's municipalities had grown into a "four-day, 1,300-mile, five-state safari to sell people on coming to the Gulf resort areas on their vacations." Boosters armed members of the traveling show with brochures and other descriptive literature for points of interest along the Gulf Coast from Pensacola to Panama City. The caravan even included local beauty queens such as Miss Panama City, and Miss Miracle Strip Park.[38] Unlike the stationary welcome stations built at major entry points that relied on visitors to come to them, this

Figure 3. In 1962, Florida was on display in New York City's Rockefeller Plaza. In this image, the state is a collection of items in a shop window, enticing passersby to consume "The Sunshine State." Storefront of Florida showcase, 1960s. Black-and-white photoprint, 4 × 5 in. Courtesy of Florida Memory at the State Archives of Florida.

tour took the brochures and maps to targeted destinations. It was a mobile sales campaign.

While friendliness first attracted some to the beaches of North Florida, editorialists routinely reminded locals that maintenance of a favorable impression was necessary to bring people back yearly. According to one *Panama City News* editorial, "We firmly believe one of the main reasons for the increase in popularity of this area is the word-of-mouth praise of people who have visited here and wanted to return."[39] Managing visitor perceptions, as shaped by both tourist brochures and the informal conversations of satisfied customers and their pictures, were essential ingredients in the continued growth of the entire region as a tourist destination. Managing the behavior of Floridians and visitors alike was also one of the essential ingredients.

A Politics of Exposure

An essential component of "The Sunshine State" generally was the crafting of a positive image outside of Florida, especially when negative publicity threatened to drive away tourists. Historian Stacy Braukman writes that economic considerations influenced many actions taken by Florida's governing bodies. From the statehouse in Tallahassee to local council chambers across the state, many lawmakers recognized the need to maintain the state's positive national image for the sake of attracting seasonal tourists, year-round residents, and new businesses.[40] This was especially true when it came to race relations, crime, and communism. The politics of exposure practiced by the FLIC, in conjunction with local newspapers, was part of this larger effort to assure residents and visitors that Florida was a safe place to visit and spend one's money by continually reminding them that "this community has enough law-abiding citizens to recognize evil conditions and DO SOMETHING ABOUT THEM" (emphasis in original).[41]

The competing interests around how to best improve a tourist destination's image could all unite around the idea that wholesomeness and obeying the law were imperative, though just what those terms meant was a source of contention between state and local authorities. Many believed that cities had to foster a "tough on crime" reputation to attract visitors and dissuade criminals; otherwise, the community would suffer because of lost income.

Collaborations between churches and law enforcement could go a long way in mobilizing citizens. In 1948 W. J. Hughes, the pastor of St. Mark Methodist Church in Pensacola, wrote a letter to Judge Earnest Mason urging him to remain conscious of the message sent to lawbreakers if his sentence of the recently arrested owner of an illegal gambling establishment was too lenient.[42] This minister was the head of Pensacola's "Good Citizenship League," which billed itself as "composed of 100 men selected from our various churches to act as a unit in behalf of law enforcement. We are desperately in earnest about conditions being improved in our county." This blurring of the line between church and state was not uncommon in the South and was part of the religious public revivals at midcentury. Bringing the country "back to God" meant that "good Christian folk" across the country were taking it upon themselves to root out sin. The very soul of the nation and God's financial blessings were at stake.[43]

In 1950, the State of Florida launched an unprecedented advertising and public-relations campaign to combat the negative publicity that linked the state and Miami with national crime syndicates.[44] One of Florida's first televised moments, according to historian Gary R. Mormino, was the 1950 Kefauver hearings, which linked Florida with crime in the minds of Americans who tuned in.[45] This was not the image that promoters wanted to project. Lou Wolfson, a businessman from Jacksonville, stated, "It hurts me to see Florida get such bad publicity. Pick up a paper anywhere on the outside, and you see Florida linked with crime. People are afraid to come here."[46] The article challenged everyday Floridians to participate in rehabbing Florida's image: "every citizen can and must play a part."[47] Reporter William Gober wrote, "Florida must throw out the racketeers and polish up its Southern courtesy if its $825,000,000 a year tourist business is to keep growing. That's the view of civic and business leaders who are trying to bring to a swift end the bad publicity Florida has been getting."[48] According to historian Fred Fejes, advertising campaigns and national publicity around Florida's toughness on crime served to assure the nation that Florida was a safe place to visit and, more importantly, spend one's money.[49]

Beverly Grizzard, a member of the State Advertising Commission, admonished Floridians in the same article by William Gober, "Florida's hospitality should be as popular as its matchless climate and a part of it. In creating and maintaining Florida hospitality, every citizen can and must play a part. Let's treat our visitors like invited guests deserve to be treated—as you would want to be treated if you were visiting in their hometown. Let's make them want to come back, bring their friends, and live."[50] This article explicitly charged Floridians to polish their hospitality skills and reminded them to make visitors feel at home. Residents were an essential part of selling "The Sunshine State" because, without friendly locals, the beauty of the sand or the warmth of the sun was almost meaningless.

The politics of exposure seems counterintuitive to many, as J.R. reminded us: "Anything which might offend or alienate the visitor is banned."[51] Would it not make more sense to hide things so as not to damage reputations? In 1950 W. A. Shands, chairman of the Florida Senate Committee on Crime and Corruption, told reporters that "the Senate Committee is not after scandal for the sake of sensational headlines, but at the same time he emphasized that the committee's long-range objectives can best be attained by arousing public opinion through putting the spotlight on evils."[52] Twelve years later R. J. Strickland, the lead investigator for the FLIC, echoed this when he told a meeting that newspapers were an essential part of cleaning up the "homosexual problem" because exposure made the job of law enforcement that much easier.[53] Charley Johns called it "shock treatment" whereby locals who were accustomed to sticking their heads in the sand or reticent to "speak ill" needed to be shocked into action.[54] With newspapers exposing immorality, the good citizens of Florida could participate in getting rid of it. As with anti-Communist campaigns nationally, exposing homosexuals became public spectacles designed to both frighten and reassure audiences.[55] They should, therefore, be seen as part of advertising and selling "The Sunshine State."

Early in the 1950s the strategy of exposure proved successful against illegal gambling across Florida. According to one report, "In the wake of Governor Fuller Warren's 'get tough' letter to all sheriffs, constables, county solicitors and law enforcement agencies, a survey of the state shows that the 'lid' is truly on."[56] To suppress illegal gambling, Florida's governor Fuller Warren announced a plan in 1950 to toughen enforcement of gambling laws. Projecting a tough-on-crime image would go a long way in assuring potential tourists that Florida was safe for the average American. It seems from this article that the mere threat was enough to drive illegal gambling out of business as Warren stated that gambling had decreased dramatically. Exposure could only go so far and was only the first step. Warren urged Floridians to "rally behind him" and watch their neighbors.[57]

Unqueering

As the 1950s wore on, national events had profound consequences for Floridians. The 1954 *Brown v. Board* decision declared racially segregated schools unconstitutional. The walls of Jim Crow began to crack, and intransigent southerners sought to stem the tide of cultural change. The queer history of Florida and the white backlash against the civil rights movement must be located within postwar defenses of capitalism. The pro-capitalist, anti-communist discourses of "the American way of life" gave context and flesh to arguments against a variety of subversions. Scholar Stacy Braukman argues that this "allowed southern conservatives to construct other enemies in those terms: homosexuals as secret infiltrators, polluters and corruptors, and integrationists as secret race mixers and statists."[58] Freedom to travel, freedom to associate, and freedom from interference were pillars of America's free-enterprise system. In the increasingly bifurcated thinking of Cold War Americans, anti-communism proved a useful tool against other changes.

While other states in the Deep South sponsored Citizens' Councils to block integration, Florida sponsored "a body forged in the heat of the South's resistance against integration, a forerunner in the modern culture wars"—the Florida Legislative Investigation Committee.[59] The committee was unique in the ferocity with which it went well beyond its original anti-NAACP remit to tackle the "problems" of homosexual teachers, pornography and indecent literature, student peace and civil rights groups, and even academic freedom in the guise of "liberal professors."[60] Headed by a man with frustrated political aspirations, the committee set about its mission with zeal.

The FLIC began in 1956 as a response to and method by which Florida politicians, especially the intransigent segregationists of North Florida, hoped to forestall integration by linking civil rights groups with communism. Rather than simply blocking integration with the use of violence and grandstanding on school steps (though interracial violence happened in Florida), Charley Johns and a handful of others sought to use anti-subversion statutes to legally slow or block integration and the granting of rights to African Americans. If Johns and his committee could prove that the NAACP was funded by, and a front for, communist organizations, then surely Floridians would want this "menace" stopped. The committee spent nine years engaged in this effort; however, by 1960 its primary mission shifted to what it saw as the homosexual problem. It is not that gay men and lesbians were suddenly present in the state. Rather, the coding of homosexuals as subversive meant they would no longer be quietly tolerated and could be treated like every other enemy of the state.

The FLIC was one of many official, state-sanctioned manifestations of Florida's desire to clean up and maintain its image for the purpose of attracting tourists and businesses. Just as the 1950 hearings, bad publicity, and subsequent advertising campaigns were an essential part of protecting "The Sunshine State," so too was the FLIC. They all came from the same impulse. Though often cloaked in the moral entrepreneurial language of "protecting children" and general morality, the committee was part of the larger effort to enforce a certain vision of "The Sunshine State" that grew out of the necessities of postwar capitalist competition.

The FLIC did not exist in a vacuum. It was not an aberration dreamed up by a handful of power-hungry politicians. Rather, those who held power in the government, as well as those who supported the broader segregationist agenda, wholeheartedly supported the FLIC in its mission. Braukman contends that "it is best understood as an instrument of state power that was at once aggressive in its attacks on integrationists and responsive to the concerns of those Floridians nervously watching the exploding civil rights movement, the escalating Cold War, and the emergence of an urban gay subculture."[61] The committee fits within the broader culture of containment and conformity that took shape after World War II. Rather than looking back on the committee as an aberration, it is more helpful to historicize it by recognizing its continued support by Florida's citizens and politicians. The legislature granted all of the FLIC's requests for continued funding until its demise in 1965.

The FLIC then was a turning point, or even an escalation, in the unqueering of "The Sunshine State." Though local efforts in Miami and smaller cities tried to push back against the rising gay and lesbian visibility, the FLIC was the first state-level coordinated effort. The committee centralized and coordinated the response to Florida's queer presence. By 1960 plans were in the works to coordinate a statewide fingerprint database so that teachers fired for homosexual behavior or other forms of subversion could be tracked across the state. FLIC officials traveled around the state conducting investigations and helping local law enforcement. They set the tone and parameters of the discussion around homosexuality in Florida. They should therefore be seen as the primary driver in the state's effort to unqueer "The Sunshine State."

. . .

The economic expansion of the postwar era meant that Florida was in competition with other Sunbelt states to keep tourists coming back. It also meant that rising incomes opened entirely new markets and increased automobility as previously landlocked southerners drove down to the coast. Welcome stations, brochures, and advertisements all served to create the image of Florida as a tropical paradise. Also, the remembrances and photographs from satisfied customers were the best kinds of advertisement. Ideas of how best to sell Florida competed across the state as business owners' desire to make money sometimes conflicted with ideas about what was "family friendly." The success of the tourist industry opened spaces for queer socializing, yet the defense of "the American way of life"—that nebulous term that is usually just short for white, patriarchal, capitalist, and nationalist—brought severe backlash against queer residents and visitors. The FLIC, local law enforcers, and others in the web of surveillant authorities in "The Sunshine State" set about unqueering in earnest after 1960.

2

QUEER CIRCULATION AND THE ECONOMICS OF A MORAL PANIC

From just across the borders of Alabama, Georgia, and Mississippi, white tourists, pensioners, and migrants came to the Gulf Coast in droves by bus and by car. Whether because of their limited means or the Gulf Coast's proximity, these white southerners helped craft what was becoming the Redneck Rivera, with Bay County as its Florida epicenter. African Americans participated in the tourist culture in other areas of the Panhandle and the state; however, racially segregated accommodations and beach access meant that in the 1950s the tourist boom in Bay County was an almost exclusively white phenomenon.[1]

Bay County was a nexus of activity as locals, visitors, strangers, and friends circulated and congregated. Some of these visitors were lesbian, gay, bisexual, transgendered, or otherwise queer. Some articulated those identities while others did not, even as they participated in queer worlds and sex(uality)-based networks—that is, networks based around shared desires for sexual acts and/or shared conceptions of sexual identity—which were dramatically expanding in this era thanks to the very increases in automobility that helped Bay County generally. The burgeoning tourist economy, which supposedly needed such protection from harm, concurrently created spaces for queer socialization.

In the context of this dynamic regional economy rapidly retooling towards tourism, queer men circulated, congregated, made contact, and had sex—and were at times punished for it. Yet, they were more than simply punished. Thanks to the confluence of forces at work in Florida at this time as part of "The Sunshine State," the men arrested in October 1961 were the victims of a campaign of public shame. The rapidly changing economy and

Figure 4. Aerial view of pier—Panama City, 1960. Black-and-white photoprint, 4 × 5 in. Courtesy of Florida Memory at the State Archives of Florida.

population created opportunities for queer connection even as it created the backlash against queer visibility. The communication networks (television advertising, newspapers, magazines) and advancements in transportation (better roads, wider availability of the automobile) that made Florida so attractive to visitors also made it attractive to queer men. Information networks, from national magazines to local graffiti, pointed the way to queer hot spots while better roads and vehicles made them easier to reach. Selling "The Sunshine State" and the policies that went along with it made this time in Florida a perfect storm that swept up the residents of Bay County.

The experiences of two local men, Tom Baker and Jeffrey Durant, serve to personalize and foreground the lived experiences of homosexual men in Bay County at this time. Their stories represent opposite ends of the spectrum of reactions to an increasingly homophobic atmosphere in Florida as well as the particular circumstances in Bay County. Rather than exhibiting archetypes, the contrast of their stories serves to illuminate the variety of experiences that were possible and to show the serious consequences of Florida's unqueering.

The story of Jeffrey Durant's migration is typical in some respects of many others who made their homes in Panama City after World War II. A native of Ohio, Durant migrated south to warmer climates in the mid-1930s and graduated from Florida Southern College in Lakeland in 1940. Whether for employment opportunities, the friendliness of the people, or just a change of scenery, Durant arrived in Panama City just after the war and began teaching at a local school. He spent the rest of his life in Panama City, eventually retiring from education in the middle of the 1970s.[2] It seemed that Durant loved the area, given his choice to stay in Bay County to make a career and a home. White and middle class, unattached by family or spouse, Durant was free to go anywhere. He chose Panama City even though Florida became a dangerous place for homosexual men and women as the quiet accommodation of queer eccentrics was foreclosed by "The Sunshine State." Aside from his sexual identity, Durant's story was typical among those who relocated to Bay County as the country settled into the 1950s and the age of white American prosperity.

Tom Baker most likely never met Jeffrey Durant, though their paths would have crossed frequently in postwar Panama City. Born before the war, both came of age just after it; Durant was a transplant and Baker a local. Both participated in queer cultures organized around new and improved technologies of communication and transportation, the very technologies that aided the broader Florida tourist boom. Durant, a subscriber to national homophile magazines, edited and published outside of Florida, briefly participated in the increasingly nationalized homophile discourses before retreating from the queer culture on offer. Baker, conversely, participated in the emergent bar culture and utilized a more local homosexual discourse in conjunction with his automobile to frequent local sites for recreational homosex.

The events of October 1961 radically altered the lives of Baker and Durant, although they reacted in markedly dissimilar ways. After that month, they would become ever less likely to bump into each other. Though publicly disgraced and encouraged to leave Bay County, Baker became out and proud (in the classic formulation of gay identity politics) and spent several nomadic years traveling the United States and then returning to his home city until finally settling down later in life in his family's home. Durant, on the other hand, remained in Panama City, devoting himself to his work as an educator and his church, retreating from the increasingly diverse opportunities on offer on Florida's "Gay Gulf Coast."

The Context

In October 1961, surveillant authorities charged with growing the region's reputation for "good clean fun" in order to assure the benefits of postwar capitalism for all, began a crackdown on the most obvious site of queer socialization—a downtown public restroom. Newspaper editors, law enforcers, and city boosters conspired not only to arrest men engaged in consensual, albeit illegal, sexual activity but also to humiliate them as part of a larger effort to demonstrate vigilance to potential tourists and migrants to assure the benefits of capitalist commerce. Whereas restroom busts occurred throughout the South and the nation in this era, this particular operation demonstrates the distinctive constellation of forces at work in Bay County.[3]

This operation reveals a moral panic led by reporters, real estate developers, and law enforcement who believed, and continually reminded the public, that threats to image were threats to livelihood. The rapidity with which the area retooled its economy to one based on tourism created an underlying current of anxiety/excitement alongside the ever-present anxieties of the Cold War. Further, state-government officials in Tallahassee, already engaged in witch hunts of their own, intervened in Panama City politics.

Inundated for over a decade with messages linking visitor perception with increased tourist dollars, local newspapers, not surprisingly, initiated the campaign to clean up Bay County. Also, given the ways that alleged sexual deviants (in this case queer men) are frequently made scapegoats during periods of high social stress, it is evident why Bay County's queer population became such public targets.[4] However, homosexuals were not the only targets in this cleanup campaign. The operation in October 1961 was part of a larger effort to rid the area of vice, corruption, moonshine, and gambling that went public with the removal of Sheriff Doc Daffin in May 1961.

The *Panama City News* and *Herald*—a single editorial organization, morning and afternoon editions, with a combined edition on Sunday—took seriously its role as arbiter of social conduct. In addition to featuring stories about safeguarding Florida's image, the papers routinely carried stories and editorials aimed at nurturing Bay County's image throughout the 1950s and into the early 1960s. It was the staff of the *Panama City News-Herald* who brought about the investigation that ultimately led to the removal of Sheriff Daffin, for which they received the Pulitzer Prize in 1962.

In the autumn of 1959, the *Panama City News-Herald* received a tip from Duke Newcome, at the time a local police officer who would later become a reporter for the newspaper, about illegal bolita lottery and moonshine operations. By the end of 1960 the wave of editorials by Edwin Callaway, executive editor, and Bob Brown, managing editor, failed to generate sufficient local response. The two contacted the governor's office in Tallahassee. Newly sworn-in Governor Farris Bryant, a Democrat and segregationist who was keenly aware of and interested in Florida's reputation, convened a task force in conjunction with the State Beverage Department to investigate the situation in Bay County.[5] The removal of Sheriff Daffin by the governor's order in May 1961 was the ultimate result of the task force's investigations.[6] Bryant's removal of Daffin helped create the atmosphere that fed the flames of moral panic and drives to clean up Bay County.

Gubernatorial intervention in a Panhandle municipality's politics to cleanse a city was not without precedent. In 1950 Governor Fuller Warren suspended Okaloosa County Sheriff H. Isle Enzor for failure to uphold laws against gambling. Some said that this was an effort to shift attention away from gambling and organized crime in South Florida that came to light as the result of the Kefauver Commission.[7] The removal of Sheriff Enzor initiated a period of moral panic and municipal cleanup as locals scrambled to reconstruct their city's reputation after the open secret was revealed to the wider world. This was the same trajectory of events as a decade later.

The staff at the *Panama City News-Herald* faced an uphill battle in their crusade to end corruption in Bay County. In an unattributed trade-journal article about the decision to award the Pulitzer Prize, the author wrote, "working to expose a popular sheriff, the newspaper found public sentiment against it. Unable to disclose facts that could have changed public opinion, staff members were forced to continue to accept criticism, open hostility and a certain amount of verbal abuse from the public."[8] Throughout the month of May 1961, the newspaper ran articles and editorials aimed at quieting public outrage at the governor's intervention in local affairs while also avoiding anything that might jeopardize the investigation.

The governor installed Sheriff Charlie Abbott after Daffin's removal. Abbott took the reins of law enforcement in Bay County in a tumultuous time; he faced a city that was fractured beyond simply pro-Daffin versus pro-Abbott. Some people realized huge profits in the moonshine business and stood to lose vast sums of money if Abbott fulfilled his mandate from the governor. Beyond the moonshine trade, the public was divided over whether Panama City needed to be cleaned up or was "just fine as it was."[9] Some were unaware of the crimes, while others were aware but resented the outside interference in local affairs.

The expectations placed on Abbott by Governor Bryant and the *News-Herald* were high. The newspaper supported Abbott and the larger drive to clean up Bay County. One editorial stated, "Now, with Charles H. Abbott as sheriff, Bay County can look with assurance for clean, honest, sincere, and diligent law enforcement,"[10] the implication being that the previous administration had failed to live up to that list. Abbott lived up to those expectations throughout the summer by systematically and publicly addressing issues raised against Doc Daffin and other major crimes in Bay County.[11] The breakup of a prostitution ring at the Dixie Sherman Hotel and the Marie Hotel and a raid on a moonshine operation were all reported prominently on the paper's front pages.[12] It was in this state of heightened awareness and publicity that Durant, Baker, and other queer men of Bay County found themselves in the autumn of 1961.

The Restroom

On Saturday September 30, 1961, Tom Baker finished his shift at the Bud Davis Drive-in Theater. Because his parents were out of town and there was no one to check in with, he decided to visit the public restroom downtown on his way home. Baker had regularly visited during the daytime, though never at night because of parental curfew restrictions. This attractive, athletic, and popular high-school student had no idea as he sat down in the first stall for a bit of voyeurism that life as he knew it was over.[13] Baker remembers his arrest vividly: "I went to the bathroom

Figure 5. Public bathroom at the corner of Jenks Avenue and Oak Avenue, Panama City, 1942. Photo by Jackie Hogan. Bay County Digitized Photo Archive, Digital6930. Courtesy of the Local History Room, Bay County Public Library, Panama City.

to check it out. . . . I went in the first stall. The lights were off. But the streetlights was shining, and you could see. There was people in both the other stalls and three people at the urinals playing with each other. Then whamo, the lights came on, and there were lots of police screaming at everyone. Dragging them outside under arrest. They carried us to the City jail."[14]

At the time, Baker was unaware that, the day before, the Panama City Police Department and the Bay County Sheriff's Office in conjunction with the FLIC launched the operation. By week's end, a series of stakeouts and raids culminated in the arrests of over twenty men connected with a supposed "homosexual ring" in Panama City. Though the FLIC's mandate was to remove homosexuals from the educational system, they routinely assisted local law-enforcement agencies with investigations as their efforts broadened to ridding "The Sunshine State" of homosexuals. Panama City law enforcement kept the story out of the newspapers until Sheriff Abbot and Police Chief Tom McCauley made a public statement on October 5; however, once broken, the story became very public.[15] It was, quite literally, the talk of the town.

Though cruising and illicit public sex were well known to law-enforcement agencies across the country and even in Bay County, the Bay County sheriff and the Panama City Police Department failed to act on this information until the FLIC applied pressure from above. R. J. Strickland, the lead investigator for the FLIC, contacted Sheriff Abbott in early September to advise him of the "homosexual problem" and requested that he begin collecting evidence.[16]

The broader campaign to clean up Panama City played a role in shaping the official law-enforcement response to men cruising in public spaces. Sheriff Abbot and other local law enforcement needed to appear shocked and active in combating the supposedly newly discovered "menace." However, as the *Panama City News* asserted at the time: "Homosexual activity centered around the public toilet on Jenks Avenue is not new. We have in our files letters dating well over a year back and recommending that the public toilet either be closed or policed at night."[17] In August 1961, the morning *News* reported on the case of Herman Knight, who pled guilty to vagrancy and was sentenced to thirty-five days in jail after he was arrested for performing a sexual act with an unnamed airman.[18] The report indicated that he and other homosexuals spent a great deal of time in that restroom. Detective Chief D. L. Barron stated in response to the arrest that law-enforcement officers "have a lot of trouble with homosexuals" at that location.

When it was made public in the newspaper after the October arrests that the problem was far more extensive, Barron attempted to deflect criticism. He admitted, "Over a period of years, we've averaged arresting two or three perverts each month. There was never an indication that this huge ring existed."[19] Barron's language speaks to the changing conception of homosexuals at the time. He and others in Bay County had conceived of individual "perverts." Now, within the larger discourses of Cold War subversion, there were imagined networks of perverts just as there were networks of communists. The available sources do not indicate the extent of use by men, though anecdotal evidence shows that the restroom served a single function at night—as a public cruising ground. Certain members of government and law enforcement were aware of the problem even if they were unaware of the extent until approached by the FLIC.

The kind of reporting that surrounded this event was not without precedent. Historian Fred Fejes documents a similar unqueering campaign that occurred in Miami in 1954 in response to increasing homosexual visibility.

The *Miami Herald*'s revelation of gay bars and queer cruising grounds in Miami was part of a drive to enforce new cultural standards while placing boundaries on behaviors and identities previously tolerated. Homosexuals had become too public, too visible, too queer. The newspaper articles and arrests were "part of an overall campaign by the city's media and civic leaders to redefine the image of Miami as a major, respected urban center, free of the vice and flamboyance which characterized its short history."[20] Panama City was not trying to redefine itself as an urban center like Miami, yet it wanted to define itself as a tourist destination. Exposure of the city's "homosexual problem" and the efforts to clean it up went a long way in achieving that goal. Also, queer men became the victims of larger state and national discourses of mid-century conformity.

Economic Shifts Create an Ideal Location

Situating the restroom both in its physical location as well as this specific moment in time is key to understanding the arrests and the wider public response. The restroom was in a unique space at the intersection of the local and the nonlocal where residents and visitors crossed paths. While Tom Baker felt it was mostly locals who utilized the restroom for illicit sex, interrogations and the addresses of the men arrested indicate that the space drew men from beyond the borders of Bay County.

Unlike the beach, which drew scores of seasonal or short-term visitors, downtown Panama City was not significantly affected by the tourist season. It was the business district and the center of Bay County's government. A steady stream of statewide and regional conventions kept the area busy throughout the year. The eleventh annual convention of the Southern Motel Exposition occurred just days after the arrests, attesting both to the growth of southern tourism generally and the ascent of Panama City in particular.[21]

The center of the increased tourist presence was the Dixie Sherman Hotel. It was Panama City's grandest hotel and at the time was the tallest building in the county. Located one block from the restroom, the upper floors gave one an unobstructed view of the downtown area. Given its proximity to the Marina Civic Center, it was also the hotel of choice during conventions held at the auditorium. The constant influx of tourists provided a steady stream of men into and out of downtown Panama City. Though the claim might have been a diversionary tactic, each man interviewed in connection with sexual activity in the toilet "only had acts with tourists."[22]

Tourists were not the only people to make use of the Dixie Sherman. The hotel bar was a popular spot for locals, who could mingle with tourists, exchanging information or glances, making new business contacts, or making new sexual contacts. It was a popular cruising ground in its own right. Henry Python recalled an experience at the Dixie Sherman's bar with a salesman and a "Frenchman." He told investigators that "we met these two characters in there—tried to get us to go up there [to their room] with them. . . . I have seen this other guy several times since."[23] Knight hints at a larger network of men who sought sex in the downtown area.

Located beside the Dixie Sherman Hotel was the Greyhound Bus Station. The presence of the bus station meant increased movement in, around, and through downtown Panama City. In the early 1960s air travel into and out of Panama City was still in its infancy, so the primary modes of transportation for the vast majority of visitors were the automobile and the bus. Whether the city was their destination, or if they were just passing through, men in transit would have made use of both the bus-station restroom and probably the public restroom only one block away. This significant nexus of movement provided a stream of people in downtown Panama City.

Across the corner from the Dixie Sherman stood another building that drew people to the downtown area, the main branch of the U.S. Post Office in Bay County. Adjacent to the post office was the Bay County Public Library. While a library would not necessarily draw a heavy amount of tourist traffic, it did draw locals to the area. The building had its own toilet facilities, though these were apparently quite small and not conducive to sexual activity, according to Tom Baker.[24]

Across the street from the restroom, library, and post office stood the offices of the *Panama City News-Herald*. Cruising the area around the public toilet took place immediately in front of the very people who were so invested in cleaning up such activity in Panama City. The newspaper's possession of letters about the activity at the restroom from years previous, and the fact that it was right outside their window, hint at the ways that homosexual activity could be at least grudgingly tolerated until the open secret became known on the outside. Managing the perceptions of outsiders in service of "The Sunshine State" influenced the timing and pace of this particular moral panic.

The location of the restroom, at the heart of movement and circulation in downtown Panama City, made it an ideal location for illicit semipublic sex. The increased numbers of tourists and locals downtown meant a greater number of potential sexual contacts. For those men unable to read the complex signs of cruising—furtive glances, winks, and nods—nothing would appear out of the ordinary. As scholar Laud Humphreys discovered in the process of collecting data for his *Tearoom Trade: Impersonal Sex in Public Places*, activity in a public toilet stopped when strangers entered the facility.[25]

The layout of the restroom was also conducive to anonymous sex. According to Tom Baker, the room contained three stalls with glory holes on one wall with four urinals on another wall.[26] This layout was much like public restrooms around the country, as described by other scholars.[27] The "glory hole" is a hole cut through the partition, usually at a height that would allow an average-sized man to stand with his penis through the hole.[28] The use of the glory hole offers a degree of anonymity. Neither side sees the other during the act, and unless the two men departed at the same time, they would not be known or recognized. This level of anonymity was essential to some men who needed to shield their behavior in the public restroom from their identities outside of the sex act.[29]

This particular restroom was a place of abandon or caution, depending on the time of day. At night, when the first arrests took place, some men considered this restroom a safe place to act upon their homosexual desires. The sexual behavior engaged in at the public restroom was, according to the sheriff, so unabashed as to be shocking. Tom Baker's report of his arrest also indicates that the activity was blatant. Duke Newcome reported, "Upon entering the building [the two officers] were accosted by several men offering to commit acts with them. . . . The acts in the restroom were committed so openly that those involved in the sordid activity inside the building failed to stop when a stranger walked inside."[30] This statement refers to Friday September 29, 1961, the first night of the operation. The men were arrested late in the evening after nearby businesses were closed, which speaks to the restroom's singular function at night.

The public restroom as facilitator of homosexual activity has its limits. In the South, public toilet facilities were segregated by race, with African Americans forced to use separate facilities until well into the 1960s in some places. However, this particular restroom did not have facilities for African

Americans; the entire building was designated "white only."[31] This created a racially segregated experience, which cannot be used to generalize about all queer experiences in Bay County, though the publicity surrounding this operation likely affected African American queer men.

The men involved in this sting operation came from both the middle and the working classes: four students, two members of the Air Force, five teachers (one of whom was also in the Air Force), three ministers, five general laborers, one merchant, one scientist, three involved in sales, and two whose occupation is unknown.[32] Two traveled from Tallahassee, and one lived in Montgomery, Alabama. The three men in the Air Force were all recent transplants to Bay County, and the others listed addresses in Bay County, though some were rural postal routes. This facility was a space of contact, congregation, and circulation, which brought together geographically diverse men.

One man arrested in this operation, Stanley Martin, exemplifies the ways that this restroom facilitated contacts between the local and the visitor and speaks to the wider networks available to mobile men. Martin lived and worked in Atlanta at the Internal Revenue Service until his arrest in 1953 as part of what was called the Atlanta Public Library Perversion Case.[33] After his dismissal from the revenue service, he became a salesman for Vulcan Paper and later moved to Montgomery, Alabama. Martin's travels as a paper salesman likely took him to Panama City frequently. Authorities arrested Martin in the public restroom in October 1961. Knowing the potential for homosex in public restrooms, it is not surprising that Martin found his way to this particular facility in Panama City.

This restroom played a major role in the homosexual activities of Bay County, situated as it was at the intersection of the local and the nonlocal. The changing nature of the region's economy and the increased numbers of people visiting the county created an ideal space for semi-anonymous sexual activity. Though cruising happened throughout Bay County, this restroom was situated perfectly to facilitate such activity.

Beyond the Stalls

Outside of the public restroom, affective ties materialized, creating sex(uality)-based networks that spanned the Panhandle. Men cruised the streets and the restroom for anonymous sexual encounters, *and* they established relationships outside of the public restroom in a variety of ways. However, the arrests and attendant publicity also show the consequences for those not part of sex(uality)-based communication networks.

Historians have documented that cruising in public spaces was often the first and sometimes the only available entry to a wider queer world for men. Because of the warmer climate in Florida, more people spend time outside and men have a history of making these outdoor spaces into cruising grounds. For many they become a "vital form of community initiation, imitation, and belonging."[34] Contacts that began in the restroom, or other sites of congregation throughout the city, held the potential to morph into something greater. Several men in Panama City attempted to move beyond the strict anonymity practiced by many in public sexual encounters. Some only wanted to repeat encounters in the restroom, while others were able to form a network based around shared sexual preferences and availability, though not necessarily identity.

In the public restroom, cruising could be more blatant and overt than on public streets. Once they established mutual interest, men could quickly cast subtlety aside. David Maguire stated that he "went in to use the restroom and when I walked out he was standing in the door, and I asked him if he wanted a blowjob, and he said yes."[35] The way a man stood, his position and the length of time spent in the facility were important signs to men experienced in the art of cruising. Noticing the man "loitering with intent" in the restroom alerted Maguire to his potential as a sexual partner, given that men simply using the toilet do not usually loiter.[36] In the queer-appropriated space of the public restroom, Maguire felt some degree of comfort, which allowed his rather blunt approach.

Queer men were not the only ones who knew the signs that indicated homosexual desires. The man Maguire propositioned for oral sex was a plainclothes police officer planted in the restroom to entrap men. This practice of entrapment was widespread, and a number of scholars have documented the practice across the country.[37] Law-enforcement agencies such as police departments, sheriffs' departments, and the Federal Bureau of Investigation shared information across state lines and across agencies about methods to entrap homosexuals, ever refining their techniques.

Many tourists visited Panama City's beaches and downtown area. Over 250,000 tourists visited Panama City in 1960, according to the *News-Herald*.[38] Cruising and arrests for public sex happened across the country in small towns and large cities alike. However, the high numbers of tourists gave Panama City a level of anonymity and increased sexual choice akin to that enjoyed by men in larger cities such as Atlanta, reflecting the broader impact of movement, mobility, and expansion of the postwar tourist economy. This anonymity was such in Panama City that most men interrogated claimed to have sex only with tourists and never with the same person twice. According to Karl Schmidt, "I don't know their names. They were people, mostly tourists."[39] The possibilities for that kind of anonymity and increased choice were not necessarily attainable in other places where people were more familiar with each other.

Some beachgoers and tourists, far from home, are more likely to engage in behaviors that they would not necessarily enjoy in their normal environs. Sociologist Norman Hayner argues that some tourists take a "moral holiday" when they are far from home and far from the prying eyes and prevailing community standards.[40] Eric Zuelow in his *History of Modern Tourism* writes that "many working-class American beachgoers believed in 'abandoning limits'" when they were on a beach vacation.[41] Some men who came to Bay County for business or pleasure certainly engaged in recreational homosex because they were far from home and beyond the normal community standards and strictures. The lure of the beach and the exponentially increasing economic activity drew men to the area, and the idea that they might never see someone again helped them shed some of their inhibitions.

It must be noted that claiming to have acts solely with tourists could have been a diversionary tactic employed to avoid implicating other locals. Tom Baker believed that "you would just about have to be a local even to know it [the restroom] was there."[42] Dale Maguire told interrogators that he regularly saw men he had acts with "walking around the streets. I've seen them come up around the library, the restrooms."[43] Tourists were prevalent in the area around the toilet facility, but many of the men arrested in this operation lived in the area—though some were very recent transplants. The truth lies somewhere in between. The anonymous nature of sex in this restroom, coupled with a desire to protect others, meant that men arrested could truthfully say they did not know anything about the men with whom they had sex.

While some men were comfortable engaging in sex acts within the confines of the restroom, others were not and, through various means, formed networks beyond its walls based on a shared desire for homosex.

According to the sheriff, 90 percent of the men arrested admitted using the restroom as their "major contact point."[44] However, it must be remembered that Sheriff Abbott wanted to assure the residents of Bay County that their county was safe. By focusing attention on this restroom operation, Abbott could assure the citizens of the county that the "problem" was under control. For this reason, it is hard to know fully just how many men used this particular restroom as their major contact point.

Luke Harvey told investigators, "Yes, sir, I have met several people, but you couldn't have any relationships down there."[45] For him, the restroom provided only a meeting, and sex had to be taken elsewhere due to the fear of being caught. Some had sex in cars while driving, others parked in secluded spots, while still others took their sex partners home. It is evident from the testimony that activities in this restroom facilitated contacts elsewhere. These contacts became a sex(uality)-based network for the men involved. Taking the sexual activity beyond the restroom hints at the desire for more than anonymous release—that is, the men desired both sex and company with others who shared their identities.

The experience of David Maguire and Karl Schmidt illustrates the ways in which contacts that began in the restroom could spread beyond it—in this instance, the telephone-facilitated contacts among men who met in the public restroom and desired the safety of sex(uality)-based networks. Despite the risk of eavesdropping by nosy neighbors as a result of the party-line system, whereby several homes shared a single line, and any telephone on a line could be used to listen to any conversation on that line, several men in Panama City utilized the telephone to expedite sexual gratification.

On the night of September 29, 1961, police arrested the two men on different sides of town. Maguire and Schmidt arranged a date earlier in the day, which was to occur at Maguire's house that night. Though he was young, Schmidt was already a practicing homosexual. He admitted to cruising the downtown restroom "sometimes twice a month, sometimes oftener," in addition to having previously arranged dates with other men.[46] After a lengthy series of questions about Schmidt's previous sexual experiences, interrogators asked, "Is that the type of acts that you've described here that were going to happen tonight. . . . You went there for the purpose of having a sexual act, is that true?"[47] Schmidt was well aware of what Maguire expected in the encounter they had planned.

Schmidt and Maguire had not previously exchanged contact details. Schmidt theorized, "a guy that I'd known before told him about it, how he could reach men."[48] According to Maguire, "a mutual—a friend of his [Schmidt's], I guess they had had acts together before gave me his phone number."[49] Karl Schmidt's telephone number was shared not by Schmidt himself, but by a third man. Both men trusted this third man enough to give him their respective contact details. This confidence is a major investment since responding favorably to a cold call from a complete stranger could prove disastrous. Local police sometimes used arrested men to telephone other men they suspected of homosexual activity, as was the case after Tom Baker's arrest.[50] Schmidt indicated that several people possessed his phone number and shared that information among other interested parties: "Someone that I met in the restroom told him about me and he called me on the telephone."[51] Schmidt admits previous attempts to arrange dates with other, unnamed men. On one of these occasions, the attempt resulted in his arrest for solicitation. The man he called initially agreed to meet but later backed out and called the police.

Using the telephone to arrange a date represented an attempt to move sexual acts from the potentially dangerous public arena to an ostensibly safer private one. Men ran the risk of violent rejection or arrest when approaching a stranger in a public toilet, whereas possessing a few reliable telephone numbers provided a type of guarantee. In our postmodern era of smartphone apps where men can meet each other, indicate preferences, and block unwanted advances with the touch of a button, it is hard for many privileged young men to imagine the threat (some would say thrill) posed by the public sphere. This sex(uality)-based network could provide a level of safety but came with its own risks of exposure as the case of Maguire and Schmidt illustrates. The more one is known, the more one's identity is exposed.

Another practice of queer communication involving the restroom came in the form of graffiti. According to Tom Baker, graffiti littered the walls. Some messages were simply "for a good time call . . ." while others were invitations to take sexual activity beyond the walls of the restroom.[52] Tom Baker remembers one message that read "man in black shirt here last Friday, if you are around, get in touch." These scribbles invited men to move beyond the walls of the restroom and make contacts beyond public sex. Anyone could write a note on a wall, and it is highly likely that hoaxes or jokes made up much of the writing. Yet, among those notes were genuine attempts at connection. Though in this instance no evidence exists for the efficacy of this form of communication, this absence of evidence should not be read as an evidence of absence.

Graffiti, just like the telephone, was a significant attempt to reach beyond the immediacy and anonymity of particular encounters to create sex(uality)-based networks. The men writing may not have conceived of their missives as anything more than trying to repeat a pleasurable encounter, but in an era before apps or even openly gay personals ads, this scribbling serves as a textual link between the men and points the way to encounters beyond anonymous sex through a hole in a wall.

A Queer Discourse of Sexuality

Jeffrey Durant was not involved directly in the cleanup operation at the public restroom. It is unknown if any of his friends or acquaintances were involved or whether he ever utilized the space. However, Durant could not escape the discourses surrounding homosexual behavior that swirled around Panama City in the early 1960s. He was a white, well-educated, literate, middle-class teacher. He subscribed to *ONE* and other homophile publications, which carried stories about the witch hunts in Florida, and he most certainly read the newspaper every morning.[53] Durant could see what was happening to those around him whose sexual proclivities became known, including fellow teachers across the state.

The residents of Panama City became keenly interested in sexuality as a result of the public discussion of homosexual behavior in the newspaper. After the arrests and publicity surrounding the public restroom, the numbers of people inquiring about books on sexuality at the library increased dramatically.[54] There is no indication of the kinds of information patrons requested, but the simple fact that this event sparked an increased interest in knowledge of sexuality is significant. As scholar Martin Meeker writes in *Contacts Desired,* "The circulation of information happens in the immediate surroundings of everyday life: on the street, in the church, in the classroom, at the kitchen table, in the lunchroom, on the couch, and under the sheets."[55] It is hard to gauge the amount of discussion in everyday life, but people were certainly talking. Newspaper coverage indicates that Bay County's "homosexual ring" was a topic of conversation at all levels of public discourse. Bay County residents would have likely welcomed early versions of the FLIC's proposed information program, which eventually resulted in the publication of the infamous "purple pamphlet" in 1964.[56]

In 1962, the FLIC met with academics, psychiatrists, and other interested parties to discuss the homosexual situation in Florida. The notion that a whole community must be involved is echoed throughout the report. Rather than hiding the issue or allowing offenders to resign quietly, publicity and education "will get the mothers and fathers and school teachers aware of this problem. It will let people take legitimate measures. . . . we should give our main attention to thinking about what we can do on the community level. We should accept the community as our locale for education, and make it clear to every community that it is a community problem."[57] The men in attendance at the meeting acknowledged that many areas had ignored the problem for too long. This ignorance led to unnecessary shock, disbelief, and erroneous ideas about outside corruption. At mid-century the newspaper was one of the best ways to reach a community and was therefore an essential part of the politics of exposure.

The increased traffic at the public library was just one way that Panama City's residents showed a concern over the discovery of homosexual men. The newspaper's coverage illustrates the extent of panic and concern brought on by the revelation of homosexual activity. In his analysis of a similar though earlier scandal in Idaho, John Gerassi writes of the ways that the local newspaper influenced public responses: "Boiseans, who were used to the *Statesman*'s habit of covering local crime news in inside pages, were now convinced that the newspaper was really alarmed—proof that all decent Boiseans should be even more alarmed."[58] In the same way, the *Panama City News-Herald* had the power to shape the public opinion and response to this incident. Only one other controversy in the months surrounding this story garnered as much newspaper coverage in Bay County: the removal of Sheriff Daffin in May of 1961, which ultimately led to this cleanup operation.

The *Panama City News-Herald* published every story relating to the homosexual ring on the front page and used bold headlines above stories filled with alarming language. Headlines such as "Homosexual Ring Rounded Up by City, County, State Officers" were splashed across the front page in one-inch letters.[59] That initial story began at the top of the page, continued down the page past the fold, and onto page 2. Duke Newcome, now a reporter, along with Edwin Callaway and Bob Brown, the editors, wanted and encouraged people to stand up and take notice. The inflammatory language of the *Panama City News-Herald* used by Newcome, Brown, and Callaway was not incongruent with the terms used by other papers around the country for similar events. Examining the newspaper coverage from cities in the area suggests that the Panama City editors placed a higher level of importance on this story and others like it.

The *Pensacola News-Journal* reported the arrests in Panama City on the afternoon of October 5 on page 14A. The story was titled "3 Church Figures—20 Men Arrested on Sex Charges," and the story contained less than 150 words.[60] While the story in the *Panama City News-Herald* treated all of the men arrested equally, giving names, addresses, and occupations for each, the *News-Journal* named only the three churchmen and two teachers. Singling out the churchmen and educators implies that their transgressions were perceived as more egregious than those of the other men involved. In Tallahassee, the coverage was only slightly more in-depth than in Pensacola. The *Tallahassee Democrat* broke the story on Friday October 6, 1961, on its second page, with the only follow-up being a report the following day concerning the dispositions of those tried that morning.[61] Just as in Pensacola, the paper named only the teachers and churchmen.

It is not that Pensacola and Tallahassee were uninterested in the region's homosexuals. Rather, the editors of the *Panama City News-Herald* seemed more zealous in their campaign against certain things (homosexuals, gambling, and moonshine) than were editors of the other cities' newspapers. The editors in Panama City likely took their cue from the *Miami Herald*'s drive to expose sexual deviants.[62] It would be inaccurate to write off the editors as simply homophobic, though that perhaps played a part. It is more productive to remember where and when these editors were writing. They had a deep love for their city and genuinely wanted to clean it up. Also, to many people, this was, in fact, a very big deal. Historicizing their actions helps to put them in the broader context of "The Sunshine State" at that time and to show just how successful moral entrepreneurial campaigns could be. Whipping the public into a panic over a variety of immoralities could go a long way toward rehabbing an image.

The Panama City papers were also interested in publicly shaming men arrested elsewhere on the Gulf Coast. This practice was in line with FLIC guidelines and the more general politics of exposure practiced at mid-century. According to one committee member, "homosexuals dreaded exposure more than anything else. Exposing homosexuals is the best way to show a community that there is a problem."[63] R. J. Strickland recognized the value of newspaper participation. He advised the committee in January 1962, possibly as a result of the operation in Panama City, "we should not overlook the newspapers and if the papers would get in back of this program the job would be much easier for the law enforcement officer."[64] Panama City newspapers had certainly been proven essential in exposing not only homosexuality, but also the operations against prostitution, moonshine, and gambling. They were so successful and their coverage so in-depth that they won the Pulitzer Prize.

More than simply reporting events or responding to letters, the *News-Herald* took an active role in constructing the response to the situation. One editorial called for education when it stated that "the challenge to the community thrown out by Strickland was this: 'Educate!' Educate the public, educate the parents, educate the children."[65] Throughout the next several months, the *News-Herald* placed stories that dealt with homosexuality on its front pages. In an effort to reassure the residents of Bay County, the papers kept them abreast of the progress with Governor Bryant and the FLIC's plans for an education program. Headlines such as "Bryant Mapping Anti-Lewd Plan," "Gov. Bryant Has Plan to Deal with Homos," and "Funds to Fight Homos, Trashy Literature," litter the front pages of the *News-Herald* in the first six months of 1962.[66]

Letters printed in the editorial sections of the *News-Herald* indicated that the ministers and teachers had hurt the community in ways that the others involved in the incident could not. One anonymous resident wrote, "Concern is all the greater because churches and schools, both dear to the hearts of all, are involved."[67] The actions of the ministers and teachers had violated the public trust. However, it was more than that. If homosexuality was a contagion, and ministers as well as teachers had fallen victim, then who was safe?

The *Panama City News* published a letter by Mary Benedict, a local mother, who proposes to speak for the entire community. The following highlights from her letter indicate that she was having a crisis of faith and wrote the letter in a state of shock. "Perhaps I can speak for many mothers today . . . with a troubled heart and reddened eyes. . . . And my children? What do I tell them tonight when they come home asking 'Mama what does all this mean?' What shall I say? How can I tell them that the teachers they have been taught to respect have succumbed to temptations? How can I tell them or explain a reason why their loved church leaders have failed them? A good example . . . is tremendously important in the formation of good character and good citizenship . . . previously good examples have now been shockingly shattered."[68] This mother's emotional appeal to the newspaper and other parents shows the distress she is feeling. This incident shook her beliefs as well as the faith and trust in her ministers and her children's teachers. It is not surprising that this mother experienced such a crisis. Much of society views educators as the vanguard of culture, the transmitters of morality and societal stability. They are also expected to lead the next generation and in certain culturally and legally proscribed ways challenge the status quo. They often must walk a fine line, or minefield, depending on the moment.[69]

It must be remembered that the average citizens of Panama City at this time were genuinely shocked by the revelation of the extent of homosexuality in their town. Despite the restroom's notoriety among municipal authorities, newspaper editors, and law enforcement, the general population was likely unaware of what went on there. Given what lawmakers, law enforcers, and so-called experts told Americans about homosexuals throughout the 1950s, coupled with the undercurrent of anxiety over the Cold War and the health of Bay County's tourism industry, it is unsurprising that citizens such as Mary Benedict expressed these sentiments. The residents of Bay County were a product of their time, and this particular incident helps us understand the intersections of sexuality and the region-specific effects of postwar capitalism through the impact on queer folks.

Another letter to the editor, published on Wednesday, October 18, 1961, asked, "What is to become of Panama City?"[70] The text reads as if from someone having a crisis of faith: "Our schools and churches have become so contaminated that our citizens do not know whom to trust, much less respect."[71] This could be seen as an aberration, one man's dire outlook on the situation, but the editorial response pointed out that it reflected the sentiment of many such letters written to the paper. The editorial reply attempted to address the anonymous letter writer's questions and concerns. As in other such articles and opinion pieces, law enforcement was highly praised for their swift and thorough investigation. Also, it was pointed out again that "we must not look askance at all our clergy, all our teachers, all our neighbors . . . tarring all groups with the pitch deserved by a few."[72] These constant reminders indicated that the anxiety level in Panama City had reached a fever pitch and threatened to devolve into a full-scale witch hunt.

This particular editorial differs from most in that it does not resurrect the threadbare banner of "protecting children," but rather kept its focus on "good citizens" more generally whose responsibility it was to assist law enforcement. This letter and the response explicitly state that Panama City's reputation was at stake and the city would be judged based on the severity and thoroughness of the response to illicit sexuality. Without a harsh and swift response, thereby demonstrating toughness on crime, tourists and businesses just might take their dollars elsewhere—or so it was feared.

The anonymous letter writer might not have fully grasped just what was at stake should Panama City's reputation be tarnished. However, law enforcement and beach developers were very aware and therefore concerned. And, as Fred Fejes shows concerning Miami, cleaning up Panama City in general was of high importance, especially as it related to the area's reputation throughout the South as a family-friendly tourist destination. Few editorials were as blatant as the following one when discussing the impact of public perception on the health of the tourist industry: "The initial publicity of such repugnant cases has had terrific impact, not only in this community but in distant places. The only way to counteract such publicity is for thorough investigations to be continued. Let the world know that Panama City is determined to clean up."[73] It could be added to this, "let the world know that Panama City is a safe city for you and your family to visit and spend your money." Protecting the area's reputation was essential to increasing the number of tourist dollars, for which all municipalities along the Gulf Coast were competing.

In July 1961, the *Panama City News* published an editorial titled "No Time For Leniency." From the statehouse to the local paper, residents of tourist destinations were continually reminded that they must be ever vigilant in keeping their part of "The Sunshine State" in order. The editorial ends with the admonition, "If we are to keep our beaches attractive for tourist families, we must discourage, through strict law enforcement and strong penalties, such disgraceful occurrences."[74] The concern over vacationers and their dollars was on the minds of many.

The very public nature of this operation indicated Panama City's desire to appear to respond swiftly and harshly to the supposed homosexual problem. City leaders, developers, law enforcement, and residents seemed to believe that, if Panama City did not provide a response promptly and harshly to the situation after it became known, the possible damage to the city's reputation was irreparable. More than a simple desire to make Panama City safe for locals, there was a desire to make Panama City safe for tourists. Every city official wants their city to be a safe city. What makes Panama City and the wider Redneck Riviera distinct is the role of tourism in the local economy and the impact that the desire for tourist dollars (governed by their perceptions) had on local politics.

The gossip in the public domain and the damaging reports in the newspapers had a profound effect on queer locals. Jeffrey Durant is one example of the way certain individuals chose to practice self-silencing and further closet themselves rather than risk exposure as homosexual. In 1957, Durant subscribed to *ONE*, the nationally circulated homophile magazine published by ONE, Inc. He renewed his subscription in 1958 with additional funds earmarked as "a donation toward furthering the splendid work your organization is doing."[75] In December 1959, he ordered several books from ONE, Inc.'s book service. The surviving records do not reveal any details regarding how he became aware of the organization, but the course of his life after his last communication in December 1959 is telling.

Reading the pages of *ONE* as well as the local newspapers, Durant would have recognized that homosexuals were becoming a more publicly persecuted minority. Especially in Florida, homosexuals (even those merely suspected of homosexuality) in the education system were more vulnerable to termination, arrest, and social shame. Though the U.S. Supreme Court ruled that *ONE* could be sent through the postal service, the magazine routinely carried stories from around the country about the lives ruined by overzealous postal inspectors. Durant would have been privy to this information, and when the FLIC began its operations against homosexuals in the education system, he would have certainly seen the risks he took by maintaining a subscription to the magazine.

Durant never renewed his subscription after it lapsed in 1960. He went on to become a well-loved and respected teacher in the Bay County school system, which he retired from in the 1970s. After leaving education, Durant continued to be actively involved in his church, and he died in the late 1980s. The very fact that he continued his teaching career in such a hostile environment indicates that Durant practiced self-silencing around his sexuality and likely avoided outness for the remainder of his life. Though it was difficult to know how he conceived of his own sexuality, his subscription to *ONE* magazine and the types of books he ordered point to at least a tentative acknowledgment of a homosexual identity.

Durant's story shows the ways that the punitive discourse of sexuality could silence queer people far beyond those immediately involved in particular arrests and cleanup operations. Though some could use negative information, such as newspaper reports of raids or arrests, as a guidebook to map and then enact their queer desires, others such as Durant heeded the warning and retreated to the closet. Though the FLIC did not publicly ruin his life, it is certain that living in fear of the committee had a profound impact on him.

Unlike Durant, Tom Baker could not be silent. The publication of his name in the newspaper meant that he had no choice but to face the consequences of outing. He poignantly described the fallout:

> I went to school and could tell as soon as I got there that word was spreading like wildfire. No one would talk to me. I could hear whispers in the background. Some of them not whispers and were meant to hurt as much as possible. I only lasted till lunch. By then I had been told I [was] off the baseball team, out of the Civics Club and out of the Glee Club. . . . I went across the street to the smoking area that I was usually in the middle of. But that day everyone moved away from me and left me alone. . . . So I quit school. I had worked in the past part time with a bricklayer as a laborer. I went to see him about going to work full-time, but he ordered me out of his yard and told [me] to never return. The same thing happened at a first cousin's house, and most everywhere I went . . . my entire world was gone, with nothing to replace it.[76]

As with the other Bay High School senior arrested in the public restroom, the court sentenced Baker to supervision by the sheriff. Baker was given permission to leave Panama City and, according to him, Sheriff Abbott was glad to see him go. He left the city to work on a ranch owned by his aunt and uncle in central Florida for roughly one year before returning to Panama City in 1963. The U.S. Army drafted Baker in 1965, and he served as a military police officer in Vietnam for two years, where he ran a brothel for Army personnel. After leaving the army, Baker led a nomadic life. He spent some time in Panama City over the years and was a bartender at the Fiesta Room. He owned a bowling alley, worked at a service station, drove a taxi, and imported flowers from South America. Periodically he set out on the road, hitchhiking across the country several times. Baker lived an out lifestyle and, in the classic identity-politics formulation, he self-identifies as gay and neatly articulates a distinction between those who live openly and those who live in closets.

Durant, on the other hand, chose the closet. It is unclear from the sources available whether he ever publicly acknowledged his sexuality. However, it would seem that he did not. As for the other men arrested, all but three had left the area in 1963. The 1963 city directory lists only one of those remaining as employed while the others were unemployed. The public shaming of the men involved had a profound effect, causing most of them to leave the area after paying their fines and serving their sentences. For many, the city was decidedly unqueer for several years.

The staff of the *News-Herald* won a Pulitzer Prize for their coverage of the events of May 1961 through May 1962, and Newcome, Callaway, and Brown enjoyed long careers bringing news to the residents of Bay County. Sheriff Doc Daffin was reelected in May 1962 and went on to serve in that role until his death in 1971. Charley Abbott continued his involvement with law enforcement in Bay County and the state of Florida through his participation in the standardization of training for sheriff's deputies.

Was this operation a success? That depends on whom you ask. The population of Bay County and its beaches continued to grow over the years. More new amusements, restaurants, condominium units, and motels crowded the beaches every year. Though paper and timber are still big business and the military continues to provide support to the area, tourists' dollars remain the sole source of income for many. From that standpoint, it worked; the goal of growing Bay County's tourism industry by policing the county's reputation was accomplished. However, for the men involved and even for those not involved, such as Durant, their answer is very different.

3

CRUISING AND BOUNDARY CROSSING

The term "cruising" carries a number of associations. It can mean to travel without necessarily having a purpose or to be on the lookout for something. It can mean a journey with stops at various points, as in a sea cruise. It can mean to proceed smoothly. For American men seeking sex with men, "cruising" has a decidedly sexual meaning. Cruising for a sexual partner can take place just about anywhere given the right conditions. On Florida's Panhandle, postwar expansion of economic opportunity, increased automobile ownership, and economic migration opened up greater possibilities for men who sought sex with other men. The ability to hit the road either locally or perhaps to the beach allowed men to escape both familial pressures and sometimes police persecution.[1] Beyond the watchful eyes of neighbor and community, men found greater sexual freedom.

Greater mobility changed the practice of cruising by collapsing, or at least mitigating, the physical distances between rural and urban environments. In addition to providing a means of conveyance that took men to cruising destinations, the automobile was also a semiprivate space where sexual acts could take place. This ability to travel, sometimes moving across boundaries of race and class, characterizes cruising on the Panhandle at mid-century. Access to cars, buses, and boats, coupled with the ever-expanding and improving transportation infrastructure, greatly expanded sexual possibilities.

Cars and Possibilities

Thinking about the car, the people using it, and the spaces the automobile occupies opens analytical possibilities when considering queer uses of space in the South after the Second World War. Historian John Howard writes, "there functioned a sense of space markedly at variance from that of dense, congested landscapes of the East Coast, for example, and these instances of coming together, often one-on-one, regularly involved automobiles."[2] Unlike more pedestrian-friendly urban areas, on the Florida Panhandle owning or accessing a car became a near requirement for many. Exploring what happened within the space of the automobile, around the automobile, or with the assistance of the automobile de-centers the urban cruising ground by opening up a wider network of paved highways and rural dirt roads.

The automobile complicates the gaps between contested public and private spaces. A car's interior can be private in the sense that it is one's space, separated from the outside world. However, except for when the car is inside the garage at one's home, it sits in public spaces where it and the occupants inside are visible. This complication has been the cause of much debate and legal wrangling since people realized that one could have sex in cars. Where does the public stop and the private begin? This question of boundary, of course, pivots on multiple axes and is specific to the race, perceived class, or gender of the occupants and the location of the car, especially in the Jim Crow South.

The regulation of sexual activity in cars in public spaces helped to define the automobile as a public space in some cases. The contest around sex in cars hinges on questions of visibility. The windows of an automobile make the occupants, and therefore some acts, visible to the outside world. Unlike the home, which though not necessarily inviolable for queer people is a space outside of the public gaze, and the public toilet, where walls and doors preclude at least a visual of what action takes place, an automobile's windows allow for a view of the action. Even when a car is parked on a dark country road, the windows create the possibility of visibility.

Unlike early cars, which as scholar David L. Lewis notes were little improvement over horse-drawn carriages, with the occupants riding high, later designs placed the occupants at lower elevations, partly hidden by doors and side panels.[3] This decreased visibility allowed for more privacy. As design progressed, the seats became longer and more comfortable, often taking on a sofa-like quality. These design changes facilitated sexual acts in cars by giving couples more space in which to maneuver.[4] As design progressed, the automobile could mitigate the weather's pernicious influence. More than simply granting the ability to traverse greater distances to find privacy, the automobile, with its protective shell of metal and glass, as well as air-conditioning and heating systems, created an ideal climate.[5]

With wide, roomy interiors and spaces that resembled the family parlor, certain cars seemed designed to be spaces for sexual activity. Station wagons were especially helpful for men out cruising. One Tallahassee resident said of his tryst, "His was the station-wagon—pretty well set up for the act in the way of blankets and stuff."[6] Tom Baker echoed that sentiment: "[I] had a station wagon. . . . Big station wagon. Put the back seat down and make a bed out of it. I always loved station wagons to go out cruising."[7] Station wagons could easily facilitate sexual activity with their front bench-style seats and rear reclining seats that could fold forward to create a large, flat, back area. Once folded away, the rear area of the car was roomy enough for two adults to get horizontal when desire struck.

Access to a car and the ability to drive altered the practice of street cruising, marking a clear distinction between car cruising and pedestrian street cruising.[8] Tom Baker relied heavily on his automobile for most of his life for the kinds of cruising it facilitated:

> Street cruising, looking for walkers, or hitchhikers, you know, other people who looked interesting. I've always had an ability to spot gay people. How people's looking. It's got that look; they got that look. Even if you're meeting someone in a car . . . and you're stuck in slow-moving traffic. There's somebody in the car over here, and you make eye contact. I've not been known to go in front of somebody, cut them off to go behind somebody, wanted to follow, see where they're going. Once they realize you're following them they will lead you. Usually, when that contact comes, it's between both people. It ain't just a one-way thing; it's between both people. I've always had a God-given ability to recognize real fast and move on it.[9]

Baker possessed a finely tuned—almost extrasensory—ability to recognize the signs of desire in other men. Though never one for flashing headlights or other more blatant behavior, Baker's cruising was heavily dependent on his automobile. He routinely cruised the streets of Tallahassee, Pensacola, and Panama City. In fact, Baker was in his words "almost always cruising."

More than simply a conveyance to a cruising ground, cars were useful along the Gulf Coast because they allowed men to take their partners to more secluded locales. Men could make contact at a variety of locations and go elsewhere to engage in sexual acts, especially if the original location was subject to interruption. If one man had access to a car, he was able to take sexual partners to more private locations, beyond the city limits. Several men describe bus stations as "sort of like a pick-up place. They pick them up and take them to an empty lot or their apartments or someplace like that."[10] Men who lacked a private home could consummate relationships away from prying eyes in a car on a dark country road, such as near Lake Jackson outside of Tallahassee. The physical confines of public restrooms combined with the high traffic meant that sexual activity often had to be fast since it could be easily interrupted.[11] However, taking a pickup to a more isolated location greatly diminished the threat of interruption as well as opening up space for maneuverability.

Bill Jenkins and Carl Wilson exemplify the ways an automobile could benefit men seeking sex.[12] Jenkins's first homosexual experience was in 1960; the majority of such experiences involved cars. On one occasion, a man took Jenkins from Tallahassee's Greyhound bus station out to Lake Jackson, where they had sex on the shore. For another encounter, he was taken by car from a bar to the same lake, which according to local legend was a popular cruising spot. Wilson claimed to dislike sex in the bus station and, like Jenkins, he was always reliant on others with cars to take action elsewhere. He stated, "I moved to [Tallahassee] and continued my practices at the bus station and around the city, being picked up by people and taken out in the woods, being made and making, mutual."[13] Wilson had long engaged in homosex and, when he moved to the area, cruised at the bus station. Both Jenkins's and Wilson's unwillingness to participate in sex in public restrooms, coupled with their lack of a car, limited the kinds and numbers of men with whom they could connect.

In the semi-anonymous car-cruising culture, the car sometimes served to identify a man. In the first several pages of Bill Jenkins's interrogation after police arrested him in Tallahassee, the investigators examined the contents of his wallet. They produced a card in which he had written "Plymouth, 1950."[14] Jenkins had made a notation of a favorable encounter, a note to jog his memory. Other testimonies of men who engaged in car cruising remembered men by their cars. When prompted for names, they were at a loss. When told of the car the man drove, their memory improved. In the semi-anonymous car-cruising culture, a man's car served to identify him.

More than a conveyance between meeting and orgasm, or space in which to have sexual acts, the kind of car that a man drove could be the deciding factor in a cruising encounter. Wayne Thompson of Dothan, Alabama, stated, "if [he] had of been driving a '55 or '56 Chevrolet, I wouldn't have done anything with him because I've had those guys approach me before and that was the only reason . . . about cars like that. That was the only reason."[15] Thompson became involved with Matt King, a helicopter pilot stationed at nearby Fort Rucker, Alabama, who drove a 1963 Ford Galaxie X-L convertible. When the interaction occurred in December 1962, the pilot's Galaxie was a brand-new car, and it was the automobile that first prompted conversation between the pair. Their relationship revolved completely around the car and illustrates the opportunities afforded by postwar mobility.

Thompson and King had a short but intense relationship. Thompson recalled, "I pulled up to the drive-in to get a barbecue and a Pepsi, and he pulled up fairly close to me, 10 or 15 yards away. And I was looking at his car—it was a pretty car—and I noticed him [*sic*] kept looking at me. I saw him slide across and roll the window down."[16] When King rolled the window down, he began a conversation under the pretext of directions for the quickest route to the beaches of Panama City. It is probable that King already knew the way to Panama City Beach. The beaches of Bay County were the favorite vacation spot of personnel at Fort Rucker due to a decade of advertising and promotion. King was attracted to Thompson, and when he noticed that the car caught Thompson's attention, he likely hoped that it would catch his affections as well. King's use of directions as a pretext for striking up a conversation was a common tactic with cruising men, according to scholars.[17]

Soon, the conversation turned back to the car, and within minutes the young man was behind the wheel of King's Galaxie:

> I asked him did his car have four-speed transmission in it 'cause I was getting one, a Chevrolet, and he said 'yes,' and then said "Why don't you come over?" So I got in not the driver's seat, the other seat. And so the boy was bringing my barbecue, and he had ordered a cup of coffee. And I set there and eat it, and we talked a while, probably about his car, I don't remember exactly what it was. So he asked me did I want to drive it and I remember that I told him no, that I didn't, that I'd rather not 'cause he didn't even know me and nothing like

> that. But he kinda' kept insisting, and natural I did. He was extremely nervous, and I had been out with a girl, and I had my shirt off, you know, and I had just put my sweater back on. It was unbuttoned and I had the sleeves pushed up on it.[18]

The pair drove State Highway 231 in the direction of Panama City, turned right onto State Highway 109, then looped back to Highway 231 to drive back to Dobbs Drive-in, a total of twenty-five to thirty miles, according to Thompson.

Though initially feigning ignorance, in Thompson's retelling it was not long before he realized what was expected in the encounter. "The first thing I knew that something was happening was he—I don't remember what he—just reached over there and run his hand through my hair or just made out like he did accidentally—that was what he did that was when I knew something was coming off."[19] The pair did not drive straight back to the drive-in. Instead, Thompson stopped the car, and the pair continued their conversation and progressed quickly to masturbation.

Parts of Thompson's recollections paint him as a shy and unassuming teenager seduced by an older man with a flashy car; other parts reveal that Thompson was fully complicit in the affair. In his own words: "I knew something was coming off." The investigators asked Thompson many times if King had "gone down on him," to which he repeatedly answered that he had not. "I mentioned it, but he said he didn't do that; said that this was the first time."[20] Perhaps it was King's first time, though the rapidity with which he escalated the encounter hints at a longer history of such activity.

This was certainly not Thompson's first time. Men had approached him before this encounter, and he was aware of what homosexuals were supposed to want. "I remember telling him that I had been with other guys before, but it was always for money or something else. I told him that if he wanted to go with me again he could but I wasn't doing nothing and it would cost him."[21] Later in the interview, he claims that he only heard of this practice from another friend who seduced Navy men in San Diego during the early 1950s. King refused the youth's demands for money and was upset that their relationship had taken that turn.

By reading between the lines, one can see how Thompson's testimony indicates that the pair had a far more intimate relationship than simply sex, and King may have come around to the possibility of financial exchange. At one point, King offers to rent an apartment in Dothan and to secure a job for Thompson at a local bank. At the couple's next meeting, King made it clear that he had already arranged the job. It seems that King was, in fact, willing to pay for Thompson's company. He does not indicate that any strings were attached to the offer, but there was almost certainly an "understanding." The testimony also points to another possibility.

Even if it was just an oxytocin-fueled love-at-first-sight experience of two young men, this relationship meant more to King and Thompson than either admits. The willingness of King to secure a job and rent an apartment on behalf of this young man speaks to a level of affection, and possibly commitment, far deeper than Thompson lets on. The silences and obfuscations in recalling this relationship are likely the result of the circumstances in which Thompson found himself. Agents of the FLIC were interviewing him in his family home with his father in the next room. The youth was very likely nervous and sought to minimize his involvement in order to avoid further repercussions.

The relationship between Thompson and King highlights the variety of factors at play on the Panhandle. King is young and mobile, and the Cold War military-industrial complex provided his class position. Like so many young men displaced or shuffled about the country because of military service, he enjoyed access to money and ability to travel, which put him in a position to be at Dobbs Drive-in that night. Thompson is also young, mobile, and employed; he has some disposable income and an interest in cars like so many young people at mid-century. If one takes the testimony at face value, their entire relationship happened in a car just off of roads that were built to make travel to the beaches of Florida faster and easier. Like so many other men, they drove away from their home environs, away from potentially prying eyes. Further, the evidence of this relationship exists because of the FLIC, whose position in enforcing conformity in "The Sunshine State" has been well established.

The Tallahassee Bus Station

At mid-century, men and women passed through the Greyhound bus station in the center of Tallahassee with a destination in mind. Most were blissfully unaware of the multiple uses of the station or that, for some, the station's public restroom was their final destination. To someone who was not paying attention, the station was just a bus station. There was a ticket counter, a white lunch counter, and chairs conveniently located for white people to wait. Nothing appeared out of the ordinary. People came and went; they waited to board a bus to take them somewhere else. Alternatively, they waited patiently for family and friends to arrive on a bus to then take them elsewhere. Strangers passed each other in the hallway, stood beside each other at urinals, or ate beside other white people at the lunch counter. The Greyhound station in Tallahassee was not simply a bus station. To some it was a sexual playground full of endless possibilities because of the endless stream of visitors. It was a site overlaid with multiple meanings and many layers of interaction thanks to the increase in travel brought on by economic expansion.

While the automobile gained ground as the preferred mode of transportation in the 1950s and air travel was still primarily reserved for the wealthy and business travelers, the intercity bus remained a viable means of transportation for many. Consequently, bus stations were active sites of movement and circulation for both locals and transients. Bus companies located stations in downtown or other high-traffic areas, with the Greyhound station in Tallahassee no exception. The station still serves passengers (and likely cruising men) from its location at the intersection of Adams and West Tennessee streets on the northern edge of Tallahassee's central business and government districts. This area of Tallahassee is laid out in a grid with long, straight roads, and the area was very pedestrian friendly in the early 1960s. Four blocks to the south is the State Capitol Building. Until its demolition, the Floridan Hotel and its Cypress Lounge (Tallahassee's unofficial gay bar) sat just two blocks from the station.

Bus stations in the South of this era pose unique problems for historians of sexuality given the realities of Jim Crow segregation. Though the bus station was legally desegregated several times throughout the 1950s, the actual desegregation of such spaces was a slow and highly contested process.[22] Despite multiple rulings by the Federal Interstate Commerce Commission and the U.S. Supreme Court, bus stations, restaurants, and other public accommodations in much of the South remained segregated in practice. Further, cities such as Tallahassee were on alert because of the general tide of civil rights activism throughout the South generally, and Florida specifically.[23]

Lead FLIC investigator R. J. Strickland reported in a December 1961 memorandum that Officer Burl Peacock, of the Tallahassee Police Department, observed four African Americans "just sitting in the section for whites, although two asked for service at the food counter and were refused but left quietly, after being told to do so."[24] When this incident occurred on November 30, 1961, white sections of bus stations had been banned (again). It had been six months since the Freedom Rides that sought to test the integration of bus-station facilities in the South, and it was six years after the Tallahassee bus boycott that resulted in the desegregation of the city's municipal bus services. Just as in other parts of the Deep South, desegregation was not happening with all deliberate speed.

How then did the FLIC discover men utilizing this public restroom for sexual liaisons? Evidence from earlier operations by the FLIC, such as the one conducted in Panama City in September and October 1961, indicates that the committee was well aware that homosexuals used public restrooms as meeting points. However, given the committee's dual purpose of maintaining segregation and fighting Florida's homosexual menace, coupled with local interest in the maintenance of the sexual and racial status quo in "The Sunshine State," Officer Peacock likely had several jobs to do in the bus station. The Tallahassee Police Department and the FLIC conducted a series of raids and arrests in December 1961 and January 1962, certainly involving stakeouts of the restroom. It is plausible that Officer Peacock was watching the restroom and took it upon himself to intervene in the attempts to cross the color line.

The desegregation of bus terminals and facilities should have, in theory, created a multiracial cruising ground as men of all races could technically use the formerly whites-only restrooms at the Greyhound station. However, according to the records of arrests that occurred throughout December 1961 until the spring of 1962, the Tallahassee Police Department arrested only white men in the bus-station toilets, with no mention of any operations or surveillance of the African American facilities.

Of the seventy-eight arrest records that have survived in the files of the FLIC, only two listed racial designations other than "w" or "cauc," and those men were not arrested until 1964.[25] A thirty-year-old African American man, a local janitor who lived on Saxon Street, was arrested just before 10:00 p.m. on the night of March 13, 1964, by officers Hanes, Lambert, and Mills at the Greyhound station and charged with "soliciting for lewd & lascivious acts." The FLIC did not interview him, likely because at the time they were dealing with the fallout from the "purple pamphlet," and no further records have been found for this brush with the legal system.[26]

It is certain that African American men increasingly cruised formerly whites-only public toilet facilities as the walls of segregation broke down in Tallahassee. However, the creation of an interracial cruising ground was a slow process. Given the amount of surveillance placed on African Americans in sites where segregation was contested, such as bus stations, it is reasonable to assume that, if African American men cruised the white public restroom after the autumn of 1961, they would have appeared in the arrest records in much higher numbers. This lack of evidence, while not necessarily conclusive, does speak to the ways that physically integrating certain spaces was a much slower task than legally integrating them.

Official records of African American men cruising in "colored facilities" have not been uncovered in this area, but of course this absence of evidence should not be read as evidence of absence. Though the experiences of queer African Americans in the South at this time were largely, though not completely, distinct from their white counterparts, as scholar E. Patrick Johnson has shown, it is reasonable to assume that black men cruised the spaces available to them in this region of Florida.[27] What does it mean that there were no law-enforcement operations to arrest black men cruising in "their" toilet facilities?

The FLIC was not unconcerned with African American queer people. In fact, the committee conducted an investigation at the historically black Florida Agricultural and Mechanical University (FAMU) in Tallahassee similar to those at the University of Florida in Gainesville and Florida State University in Tallahassee, both majority white.[28] Many believed that "this practice [homosexuality] is being condoned by the administration to the extent that they know what's going on but just failed to do anything about it."[29] One student described multiple incidents at FAMU that included propositions by administrators with threats of academic failure, as well as an incident when "three or four [male] band members raped another [male] student."[30] Others described relationships between gender-nonconforming women that were intense, passionate, and sometimes volatile.[31] Given the lack of African American men interviewed outside of FAMU, it seems the FLIC was not pursuing black men cruising in public in Tallahassee.

Because of their associations with travel, movement, and the anonymity of highly mobile populations, the bus station was an important node of circulation and sex(uality)-based network formation in this area. White men seeking sexual release near Tallahassee used this to their advantage. Some were simply passing through, and others visited the bus station specifically to locate sexual partners. Sources indicate that the bus station had been under surveillance by the FLIC for some time; however, it was not until January 1962 that the *Tallahassee Democrat,* the *Panama City News-Herald,* and the *Pensacola News-Journal* reported a major sting operation. According to news reports, "70 suspected homosexuals" were involved though only 47 went to trial.[32] Other similar operations around the country reveal that, when trying to incite moral panic, it was not uncommon for the distinction between those tried in the court of public opinion and those tried in a court of law to blur in order to increase the sense of order restored and justify continued vigilance.[33]

Over the remaining years of its existence, the FLIC continued its involvement with arrests at the bus station, but the intensity never matched December 1961 through February 1962. The records from this period indicate that white men from all socioeconomic levels used the bus station as a meeting point between locals and nonlocals. Roughly half of the men arrested listed Tallahassee as their home address, while the remaining records include nearly every southern state, with representation from both small towns and larger cities. Others listed home addresses in Michigan and as far away as Seattle, Washington.[34] The surviving records do not indicate definitively why many of them were in Tallahassee.[35] It is unlikely that many came solely for the purpose of engaging in sexual activity, though that was certainly the experience for some.

Tallahassee, as Florida's capital, brought some of the men arrested to the city because of state business. Tom Watson, the "County Agent for Calhoun County, GA," came to Tallahassee in an official capacity.[36] Much like Stanley Martin, the paper salesman from Alabama, Watson was drawn on official business. He took the opportunity away from his home environs to pursue sexual relations with men. Men came to the capital for various reasons and left with an arrest record and possibly ruined lives. The capital drew them in as much as the sex.

The Greyhound bus station, as a space for sexual release, brought together highly mobile white men. Strangely, at least in the surviving records of the FLIC, none came to the bus station to take a bus. One man stated that he "went to the bus station to ask about a time schedule and found out that they didn't have time—didn't have bus service. So then I had to go to the restroom. So I went in, and I sat down. And I was sitting there I saw a person through this slit in the wall."[37] Others were more direct and perhaps more honest in their reasons for being at the station. James Smith drove roughly two hours from Valdosta, Georgia, because he "had the urge I guess you would say to be done and I came to Tallahassee. . . . I come for the purpose of being given a blowjob."[38] For one man, the station was a site of convenience, though obfuscation must be taken into account; for the other, it was a destination in and of itself because of the sex available there.

John Miller and Robert Morse illustrate both the lack of understanding on the part of investigators and the safety strategies for men at this time. Miller was employed as a clothing salesperson with the George Mews Clothing Company in Atlanta and routinely traveled throughout the South. He knew how to cruise and, by his admission, had been cruising in Atlanta and other parts of the South for over fifteen years, averaging twelve liaisons per month.[39] Investigators told Miller, "It is rather hard for us to sit here and think that you are being truthful about this thing. A person that has had such [a] homosexual problem for the past fifteen years and have had on an average as many as twelve homosexual acts a month it is mostly impossible for you to not to know anyone by name and by being in your hometown, city, Atlanta it is hard to believe that you are being truthful."[40] While some of those arrested succumbed to the committee's abuse and named names, Miller refused to implicate others for fear of repercussions in their lives. The interrogators did not understand the anonymous nature of much public cruising. They asked Robert Morse, "Aren't you particular with whom you put your . . . ? Mr. Morse, in performing such acts, as you did tonight, you put your penis through that hole, you mentioned you never know who you have acts with. Why is it that you aren't more particular by putting your penis through a hole of that kind?"[41] Morse claimed ignorance because of the glory hole's anonymity. Miller's social circle was completely "on the up and up," and it is unlikely that Miller participated in information exchanges that might have jeopardized his outwardly heteronormative presentation.[42] Both of these men respected the anonymity of the encounter so that they could protect others. In turn, others could protect them.

Other men traveled great distances to make a homosexual connection at the bus station. Allen Pierson Jr. was one of the men arrested and tried in the downtown public-restroom cleanup operation in Panama City in October 1961. At the time, he was a sergeant in the U.S. Air Force and stationed at Tyndall Air Force Base. After his first arrest, the Air Force discharged him.[43] Soon after his discharge, he was arrested for cruising in Tallahassee's Greyhound station on December 10, 1961. He remained in jail until his trial in early January 1962.[44] There is no record in city directories that Pierson relocated to Tallahassee, and there is no record of what became of him after his trial.

On the afternoon of January 17, 1962, twenty-two-year-old James Smith left his home in Valdosta, Georgia (roughly eighty miles from Tallahassee), to begin a road trip that changed his life. Such trips were not uncommon for many, given Tallahassee's importance in the region. Driving was a part of Smith's life both personally and professionally. He worked for the Georgia Plate Glass Company, and his employment involved a significant amount of travel, sometimes as far as Miami.[45]

From the age of thirteen, Smith engaged in public sex with men in Valdosta. According to Smith, he met a man in the courthouse who gave him pornography and then fellated him. After this experience, Smith returned every other week to engage in acts with men.[46] As Smith became more mobile, his cruising expanded to the nearby cities of Jacksonville, Florida, as well as LaGrange and Columbus, Georgia. The entirety of his homosexual experiences occurred in public spaces, largely facilitated by the automobile in his adult years. He indicated that bus stations and courthouses were, for him, the most reliable places to find a sexual partner.

Though Smith never claimed a homosexual identity in his interview, his actions certainly qualify him as queer; he may not have been "like that," but he certainly "liked that." Once, on a family vacation to Jacksonville, a man at the pier picked up Smith. "I went up there, and I went in the bathroom to take a leak, and I came back, and I saw this guy while I was in there. He kept watching me, so I went back to the pier. He come up there and just talking and asked me if I would like to ride and see the sights and I told him yes. I figured what he was up for, naturally, I was prepared to please him and myself I guess you would say and we went off in his car and he parked somewhere."[47] Smith's next act occurred back in Valdosta, and he picked up a man as naturally as he had in Jacksonville. "He stopped and asked me about the town, I've forgotten what it was, and I was standing there talking to him . . . going to the show, and he asked me would I show him around and I said yes, and so we went in my car that night, and he naturally wanted to blow job, and I went out on this dirt road and let him give me the blow job that time."[48] Smith was well versed in the art of cruising and detecting men who searched for the same things he wanted. Unlike other ostensibly heterosexual males who traded sex for money or gifts, such as Wayne Thompson from Dothan, Smith never asked for money but very clearly enjoyed sexual relations with other men.

Smith claimed only one previous journey to Tallahassee and one other visit to the bus station. To pass the time while his sister visited their brother in the hospital, Smith decided to visit the bus-station restroom. He told investigators, "I was just around the bus station there, and I went in and I stayed in there for a while and didn't find anyone, so I got in my car and went back to the hospital."[49] A man on an undertaking such as Smith's, who was willing to drive two hours away from home for sexual release, was unlikely to waste time in locations where action was not guaranteed, despite his previous failure in Tallahassee's bus station.

Officer Burl Peacock arrested Smith at approximately 21:30 for "Disorderly Conduct by Soliciting for Lewd and Lascivious Acts."[50] Because Smith was not part of the initial wave of arrests, information regarding his trial did not appear in the newspapers. Smith never admitted to street cruising in Tallahassee, although this certainly was not outside of his skill set. According to Smith, his sexual activity in Tallahassee took place in restrooms, and his automobile was the conveyance to this particular cruising location.

Other men traveled by bus and used the station as their entry point to Tallahassee rather than their final destination, though their final destinations were certainly queer spaces. Two pilots stationed at Tyndall Air Force Base near Panama City, of whom Allen Pierson was likely one, routinely traveled to Tallahassee to attend "gay parties."[51] For these men and likely countless others, the bus allowed them to be part of larger queer networks and to maintain connections with other men throughout the state.

The bus station continued to be the focus of law-enforcement efforts to unqueer Tallahassee because in the minds of the police it remained "a popular hangout for homosexuals." In late 1965, the Tallahassee Police Department came under fire in the national press for employing college students from nearby universities as informants. Working in teams of two or three, young men hung out at the bus station and received ten dollars for each successful conviction of a "sex deviate." Officials claimed that the informants never approached or entrapped but, given police behavior in other sting operations, this is very likely a lie. The students were "more mature" seniors or graduate students, but several deans and even Governor Haydon Burns (who was also chairman of the cabinet board of education) all condemned the practice as dangerous.[52] They took the Tallahassee Police Department to task for not consulting with them prior to engaging students in this way.

Through their brief but tragic intersections with the legal system, these men provide glimpses into the centrality of movement in the postwar era. Cruising men knew that bus stations were likely to hold the promise of sexual activity. Miller, Morse, and Smith did not take buses or have plans to take a bus, nor did they simply happen upon sexual activity. The sexual activity was their destination, and the bus station was the place most likely to offer it. These men—like men and women across the country—were able to travel farther from their home locales *because* of the greater mobility afforded in postwar America. The roads that were steadily improving to keep pace with the demands of increased automobile traffic meant that these men could travel farther and faster than in previous years. Their experiences situate the bus station as a critical node in the queer geography of Tallahassee and the wider Panhandle.

Rosalee Isn't Here

Although there is no evidence of interracial homosex in public cruising spaces of Tallahassee, two instances in Pensacola show the ways that interracial homosex complicated boundaries of race and class in this segregated city. As John Howard writes in *Men Like That*, "Parallel black and white queer realms cautiously intermingled after the early sixties . . . whereas before, same-sex interracial intercourse usually involved advances by white men of privilege on their black class subordinates."[53] As the walls of segregation crumbled, black men and white men began coming together with more equal access to spaces—for instance, the restroom in Tallahassee's bus station. While some white men continued to sexualize and demand access to black class subordinates, black men could turn certain situations to their advantage. The experiences of black men complicate narratives of acceptance and homophobia.

In Pensacola, there existed a deeply rooted and entrenched culture of racial segregation that disadvantaged and endangered blacks in the name of white supremacy. Black pastor H. K. Matthews said that he has "often described Pensacola as one of the most racist cities in the world, and I think that was a pretty accurate description during that particular era."[54] Matthews's biographer, Dr. Lusharon Wiley, writes about the extreme ways in which Pensacola was racially divided, citing its proximity to Alabama (geographically and culturally) as a contributing factor in Pensacola's severe racial division. Pensacola sits at the western edge of Florida. Though this entire region is more culturally aligned with its Deep South neighbors than the majority of the state, Pensacola is especially close geographically to the two key battleground states in the fight to overturn racial segregation: Alabama and Mississippi. Both states were the focus of civil rights activities and the sites of horrific confrontations and retributions by those opposed to racial integration.

The walls of segregation were high and well defended, yet several interracial incidents confound expectations. As James Sears quotes Daniel Garrett in *Growing Up Gay in the South*, "The White community has made blacks into strangers: creative, exotic, passionate, violent; and the black community has made black gay men into strangers: emasculated, sensitive, weak."[55] White sexualization and fetishization of black bodies is not new.[56] How then did this work with homosexual desire for black bodies in an extremely segregated society? The stories of two African American locals, David Williams and James Bell, are illuminating in multiple ways. One was part of a group of gender nonconformists, and both men sodomized white men who paid them for it.

David Williams was a native of Pensacola, though he relocated to Miami in the years 1955–61 when he ran away from a male lover.[57] Upon returning to Pensacola, running away from another male lover while that man was at work, he worked as a fry cook at Family Grill. He never married and lived alone in the house owned by his parents before their deaths. Williams had several homosexual, or more broadly queer, friends, some of whom dressed in drag. When asked later about a particular man wearing a wig and a dress in photographs of a Halloween party, Williams deflected by citing rumor as the source of his knowledge about his friend's sexual choices.[58]

Others referred to these men as a group of sisters, with one man saying that one of the men "try to acts like a lady, and she, she's got long hair."[59] This particular party is interesting because the photographs show all of the men are naked and sitting on each other's laps except the man in the dress. If not homosexual, the photographs are certainly homoerotic. The photographs did not survive (or are not part of the available archive), but the descriptions lead one to believe the group of friends was comfortable enough with the attendees to be naked. Williams makes a significant slip when discussing the party's host.[60] He referred to him as "she," a common appellation within gay male circles. Williams quickly deflected by citing Halloween as the reason for the costume, but it is much more likely that "she" was an affectionate nickname, which again speaks to the closeness of the group.

David Williams was sitting in a room at the county solicitor's office with John H. Sullivan and R. J. Strickland, both investigators with the FLIC and both white men. According to scholar Lusharon Wiley, Pensacola's African American population was accustomed to maltreatment and violence at the hands of law enforcement. Certainly, Williams went into this interrogation cognizant of the potential for violence at the hands of white investigators. The obfuscation might not simply have been for the protection of friends, but might also have been an attempt to protect himself. It is likely that Williams was frightened of white retribution for his racial and sexual transgressions. Though the transcripts do not indicate any retribution, it was not uncommon for investigators to stop recording for the purpose of influencing a recalcitrant witness.[61] How much more so could investigators, already accustomed to extralegal interrogation techniques, use violence to enact retribution on "race mixers" such as Williams?

Another African American man identified this group of friends as "sisters," which speaks to a broader knowledge of their sexual and gender nonconformity within Pensacola's African American community. James Bell, an African American automobile mechanic, stated, "All of them around there—all of them sisters, I think, and all of them good friends, and all that junk. He used to wear them dresses and things—wigs on their heads."[62] It is unclear just how many of "them" were part of this group, but they were known in the African American community of Pensacola. More research is needed to determine the larger community's acceptance of these "sisters" in this instance. However, scholars have documented the place and time specificity of acceptance of gender variance in African American communities. For example, historian George Chauncey uncovered a high degree of acceptance of gender subversion in Harlem while scholar James Sears's narrators reported that southern African American communities were far less tolerant of gender-subversive behavior.[63]

Beyond simply being part of a group of gender nonconformists in Pensacola's African American community, Williams understood that his desirability had value and that value could be translated into financial gain, especially from certain white men.[64] His testimony about an encounter with a white man raises several intriguing questions.

Q: Have you ever had an act with a white man, David?
A: It was shortly after I came back from Miami one night. A fellow came by looking for Rosalee. Rosalee was working so he asked me to go off with him and I did. Somewhere out on 12th Avenue. . . . We went into a driveway, he tried, he asked me to go in the house but I wouldn't go in the house, so we pull in the garage.
Q: And you poked him?
A: Yes.
Q: And he didn't want to poke you?
A: No, that was all he wanted.
Q: Did he give you any money?
A: $3.00.[65]

The white man with whom Williams had an encounter was initially looking for someone named Rosalee, but Williams was able to step in and fulfill the man's desires and was paid for it. However, how does a man who is ostensibly looking for a female decide he wants to be penetrated by a man?

On the surface, it seems a strange twist for a man to suddenly desire to be penetrated instead of to penetrate. The investigators did not comment on the white man's switch. It was not uncommon for gay men to adopt a traditionally feminine name in some cases after their coming out to mark their gay, or later trans, personas.[66] "Rosalee" was more likely an adopted female name for a male friend of Williams or even for Williams himself. Williams and his friends were known in certain circles as sex workers—possibly in the same way that some white youth were part of a larger network of youth who traded sex for money or favors. Williams's experiences also hint at the possible existence of sex tourism, given that the white man came looking for Rosalee; he was on a mission of some sort.

While David Williams was part of a social holding based on sexual identity, other African Americans in Pensacola simply needed to supplement their income and disavowed any association with homosexuality. James Bell paints a picture of the process from meeting to proposition to payment:

> One night, I was up on the corner of Railroad and Thelma, and he passed by there and I was standing out there with some more people. And I spoke to him and he spoke to me. And then he started looking at me and asked me did I want to go home and wash dishes, and I went there, and he asked me what my name and all that, so I told him. He asked me did I want to spend the night with him and I told him no, I couldn't spend the night with him, I had to be back home by 10:00 or 10:30. And so he asked me did I want to stay there a little while, about two or three hours or something like that. And I told him I didn't mind, so he sent and got some beer and we sit down and drunk some beer and we—later he asked me did I want to lay on the bed. I told him that—I asked him how much money did he have. He told me four dollars, so he gave me the four dollars.[67]

Bell was picked up, ostensibly for performing manual labor, though washing dishes at someone's home reads more like a specious pretext for sex than a genuine need. He went on to state that the man who propositioned him routinely paid other young men in James's circle of acquaintances to wash dishes, signifying a prior knowledge on Bell's part as to the nature of the offer.

Other African Americans speak to the broader circulation of information among young men in regards to trading sex for money. According to one young man, "I was just going to school there and most of the boys would be out talking and say that [name redacted] invites them down to his house for parties at night. And I heard some boys say that they was gonna go on down and make some change."[68] Unlike Williams, who seemed part of a larger queer circle that identified as such, Bell seemed only interested in financial gain. Much like hustlers in other areas of the country, Bell viewed Williams and his friends as more homosexual because of their added gender transgression. The sisters were stuck between white fetishizing and black exclusion. Bell operated within a different system of classification than the investigators, and many other officials, who viewed any homosexual acts as indicative of a homosexual identity regardless of the sexual position or gender presentation. Yet, that simple classification was anything but.[69]

As historian John Howard shows in *Men Like That,* white men's transgression of the color line in the South and unfettered access to black bodies (particularly female bodies) was not necessarily a taboo, provided the white men maintain the "superior" or penetrative status.[70] However, a man penetrated by another man was more than some could handle, and a white man penetrated by a black man was too transgressive for most to handle.[71] These power-differentiated relationships might simply be another example of white men fetishizing and then seeking unlimited access to black bodies. I read into them the potential for black agency in this racially stratified society. E. Patrick Johnson shows in *Sweet Tea* that in southern society, which actively disadvantaged African Americans, many who sold sex sought out a white clientele because of white access to money and avoided black men because of their limited access.[72]

The act of a white man seeking out a black man to penetrate him, the ultimate racial and sexual taboo in a segregated society, coupled with Williams's acceptance of money before the act, could put some power in Williams's hands rather in than the other man's. Bell's and Williams's status and sex had value to certain white men, and they were able to parlay that value into financial gain. In this small way, they were able to exert a measure of control over a man who, while maybe not directly his oppressor, was part of the larger system of white oppression of black individuals.

While nothing in Bell's language indicates a consciousness of this role reversal or any retributive attitude, I assert that the possibility of that kind of consciousness existed in this and likely countless other encounters. Reading these opportunities into this particular act thereby opens a space for historians to think about the ways that men could transgress racial and sexual boundaries in a manner that was mutually beneficial.

It is uncertain at this point where African American men cruised. Just as in Tallahassee, white and African American men were unlikely to cruise many of the same spaces in the 1950s and early 1960s, except for public streets. As E. Patrick Johnson's narrators explain regarding New Orleans, "You could come over here and scrub the floor and clean the toilet and things like that, but you couldn't say I'm going to hang out in a bar and buy me a drink or something like that. You couldn't do that. But you could have in your own areas on the other side of the tracks."[73] This attitude certainly existed in Pensacola, given the city's culture of racial segregation. At mid-century, African Americans were excluded from many queer, white spaces unless they were engaged in service occupations. This changed as the region transitioned to a liberation economy. Though law and tradition excluded black people from white spaces, those same white people often had access to black spaces.

Down at the Waterfront

Bus stations, public restrooms, and other places could provide spaces for connection, and the automobile provided flexibility. What about on the water, the spaces adjacent to the Gulf, and the mythical effects of salty air? Water and the business of the military affected cruising and mobility for men in Pensacola, where movement by cars, feet, and boats played a major role. Unlike in landlocked Tallahassee or Dothan, men searching for homosex in Pensacola had the added benefit of the water and a variety of water-based activities.

In August 1962, Marvin Harrison was fifteen years old and in the eighth grade at Blount Junior High School. After school, he sold peanuts on the streets of downtown Pensacola. This occupation placed him in a unique position to observe the behavior of a vast number of people in public areas and positioned him at the center of Pensacola's most active cruising ground. Many men I spoke with in the context of this project echoed the notion that willing men—some free and some for a price—packed the downtown area.

More than simply selling peanuts and observing others, Harrison became involved in the practice of selling sex. A variety of authors document youth trading sex for money or gifts across the country, and Pensacola was no exception. The practice was common knowledge in places with concentrations of men who sought sex with men. According to Harrison, there was a network of young men in Pensacola who sold sex to older men.

> Q: You and———have discussed this thing quite often, haven't you?
> A: Well, he said that a friend of his whose name is———who lives at———. . . . Well, he told my brother that this guy—he drives a white '59 Chevrolet Impala with black streaks on the side, and he's queer. And he pays three bucks.[74]

Other men paid only $1.50. Harrison's brother initially gave him the information about the man, and that information was passed along from another youth. He later describes his brother-in-law's participation in trading sex for money before he was married. "He just told me that he used to go out with them and get money from them. He told me a couple of times that they didn't want to pay him and he had to get a little rough, and stuff like that."[75] Harrison makes clear that there is a network of young men circulating information relating to how much certain men are willing to pay. Though the young men do not know the names of the men, the description of the automobile is enough to give Harrison an idea of whom to look for.

Other young men in Pensacola echo Marvin Harrison and illuminate a clear network of young men trading sex for money. Andrew Holden and another friend had sex with at least three men in 1962.[76] On one occasion, the young men were in the car together and a man fellated them both. At other times the pair were met outside of the local Morrison's Cafeteria. Holden arranged regular dates with at least two men, and he was always paid $3.00 and sometimes packs of cigarettes in addition. A different young man claimed that paperboys in the city knew and traded information about homosexual residents on certain routes and how they could make extra money.[77] It is impossible to determine with any certainty if any of these young men ran in the same circles or just how extensive the network was in Pensacola. However, the men's testimony speaks to larger networks along which information was shared.

These young men illustrate some of the ways that sexual information circulates through rumor and innuendo as well as the shifting boundaries of identity. All of them shared information among their friends about either making extra money or simply the pleasure to be had. The paperboy was curious and "just wanted to see what it was like" while Andrew Holden enjoyed watching his friends receive oral sex from the men that propositioned them, in addition to the cigarettes and money. These young men never claimed a homosexual identity; they were in it for the money and the pleasure. All of the young men were adamant that they only ever received oral sex, thereby marking them in their minds as not homosexual. Men having sex with men has occurred since the beginning of our species. It is the identity descriptors and religious proscriptions of certain behaviors that are temporally specific. These young men were able to separate their acts from identities or even the need to identify as anything. To put it another way, it is one thing to let someone give you a blowjob; it is an entirely different thing to *be* gay.[78]

Incidents such as this happened around the country and went a long way toward cementing the narrative of gay men as sexual predators preying on the young. That narrative was one of the primary motivators behind the FLIC, the FBI, and later Anita Bryant's "Save the Children" campaign. To be clear, sexual abuse of minor children is a genuine, traumatic thing, and the actions of all parties were illegal and culturally shunned. Ages of consent vary wildly across the Western world, especially for heterosexual pairings, and sexual activity with postpubescent youths (boys and girls) is well documented throughout history. The evidence in these instances does not indicate abuse as it is often articulated as power over another. At least in the surviving records, many of these young men approached the older men after hearing they could make money. These young men kept going back, sometimes weekly, for money, for cigarettes, or simply for pleasure. These young men possessed more agency in these interactions than young people are typically given credit for.

The municipal pier, where Palafox ended at Pensacola–Escambia Bay, and which was the location of the Municipal Auditorium, was a popular cruising ground throughout the year. According to Marvin Harrison, "The first guy that approached me was the guy down to [*sic*] the Municipal Pier. He was the first one that approached me with this stuff."[79] Andrew Holden echoed Marvin's assessment of the area's popularity with cruisers, stating, "he picked me up at the auditorium, municipal auditorium. . . . He just told me he wanted to go for a ride and he asked me if I wanted to get together and I knew what he meant, so he took me out there to the Scenic Highway."[80] A man who regularly fished at the pier also picked up Marvin. However, only once did Marvin ever see him with any fish.

Located at the end of a major thoroughfare in downtown, in an area mixed with industrial shipping and retail business, the pier was a popular spot for fishing, picnics, sunbathing, and of course, cruising. This spot in the 1950s and 1960s was, in fact, ideal for cruising. People flowed through it constantly, which meant that men loitering or watching the crowds on warm summer nights (or days) would not necessarily draw attention. Other residents remember that the area was "crawling with" available soldiers and sailors.[81] This area combined the best of pedestrian cruising with the best of automobile cruising. One could drive a car the length of Palafox and circle the auditorium or walk the downtown streets.[82]

As was not the case in landlocked cities, men seeking sex with other men in Pensacola could use their boats, the consistently pleasant weather, and the lure of the beach to their advantage. A local man approached Mark White under just such a pretext.[83] White never admitted to homosexual behavior himself, yet his recollections disclose a great deal about men cruising Pensacola's streets and waterways. White remembered, "Well I was just walking down the street, he walked beside me and started talking to me, things, asked me if I worked downtown, said he saw me downtown often, nothing out of the ordinary."[84]

The next day, White happened to be eating lunch at a downtown Walgreens, and Andrew Fischer was there at the lunch counter. "He seemed like a real nice fellow, very good personality, real friendly and everything."[85] White started to notice the man downtown frequently. Over the next several days, this man sought out White and repeatedly invited him to his house at Oriole Beach, west of Central Pensacola, for skiing and swimming. Finally, White accepted the invitation and, by that weekend, he and another friend were at Fischer's beach house for a day of drinking and boating. Here, the weather and the water played key roles in Fischer's approach. The extended summer season with warm temperatures and sunshine allowed him to use his boat as an enticement for White, and likely other men.

The man was persistent in his approaches. He made several sexual advances throughout the day that the two men spent together. First, in the boat, "he looked back to see if Bill [White's friend] was looking, he didn't, and then he reached over and grabbed me."[86] Second, after the skiing ended and the two were alone in the house, Fischer blurted out, "I'd suck your dick for you."[87] Finally, when he was driving White back to Pensacola, "he reached across the car like he did on the boat and grabbed me by the penis."[88] The persistence with which this man pursued White is astonishing if the young man had forcefully rebuffed his advances. Again, it is likely that White masked the truth of his complicity in the encounter to minimize culpability, given that the police were interviewing him. A conversation that began as nothing, just a stranger being polite, or neighborly as one might say in the South, initiated a relationship between the two men. It is likely that Fischer noticed something in the young man's behavior that led him to believe that sexual relations were possible between them.

In Pensacola, the physical location of military bases also created cruising grounds where none had existed before. Unlike the streets of downtown, lonely stretches of U.S. Highway 98 or State Road 29 turned into active and fertile spaces to cruise. According to one gay magazine, "Drive west out of Pensacola on US 98 or State Road 29 and you will likely find a drunken sailor trying to find his way back to base. Help him out, won't you, especially if he has peeled off his shirt."[89] Though written in the 1990s, this cruising guide echoes what Allan Bérubé shows in *Coming Out Under Fire,* namely that picking up hitchhikers near military installations could be both dangerous and rewarding in the quest for sexual fulfillment. Bérubé writes, "Routes between military bases and the cities became cruising areas where civilian men with cars picked up men in uniform. Many gay male soldiers and military employees welcomed these erotically charged roadside offers."[90] The routes from Pensacola became just such spaces. Here again, the automobile facilitated a new kind of cruising on Florida's Panhandle.

As the walls of segregation crumbled, and people tried desperately to hold onto their segregated, straight, Christian, and conformist way of life, the FLIC set about purging homosexuals from "The Sunshine State." The men in this chapter appear in the historical record because of the FLIC and larger efforts to unqueer the Florida Panhandle. What their interrogations show are some of the inventive ways that men sought each other out. Driving around on the roads built and improved as part of welcoming visitors to "The Sunshine State," men found sexual partners. They turned their cars into queer spaces, and they queered public restrooms. They found each other in downtowns. Young men shared information about how to procure sexual partners and supplement their income. A group of young men in Pensacola played with gender and notions of community. Despite efforts to erase and unqueer the Panhandle, these men chart a queer geography and remind us that we can find connection in all sorts of places.

4

DRINKIN' AND CARRYIN' ON IN SEARCH OF COMMUNITY

Outside of the search for anonymous sex, men found each other and formed friendships in the very spaces that benefited from expanding economies. Further, many women enjoyed increased opportunities because of federally funded military installations and greater employment opportunities in the private sector in North Florida. Before market forces created gay and lesbian community institutions, what scholar Jeffrey Escoffier calls the "liberation economy," some gay, lesbian, and otherwise queer people used their race and class privileges to find others like themselves in the spaces around them.[1]

Bars, house parties, and friendship networks reveal the ways that postwar mobility shaped queer socializing through complex negotiations of desire and access. In Tallahassee, the Cypress Lounge at the Floridan Hotel became an unofficial gay bar, and some remember it as the after-hours home of Florida's power brokers. In Pensacola, Trader Jon's and the Hi-Ho Five O'Clock Club were queered by sexually and gender-nonconforming individuals. These spaces represent a transition from closeted economies to more open, identity-based, gay and lesbian spaces because they fostered social networks beyond the sex act.

The Cypress Lounge

The Cypress Lounge in the Floridan Hotel was located at the intersection of Monroe and Call Streets, just around the corner from the Greyhound bus station in Tallahassee. The Floridan Hotel opened in May 1927. Its Cypress Lounge served residents and visitors to downtown Tallahassee until its closure in 1978. The entire building was demolished in 1985.[2] Like many hotel restaurants and lounges across the country connected to lodging and major thoroughfares, the Cypress Lounge became a nexus of exchange between locals and visitors.

According to Lynn M. Homan, "Many politicians discussed prospective legislation over cocktails in the hotel's Cypress Lounge."[3] It was not uncommon for the real machinations of government to take place with drinks in hand after the legislative workday ended. Sitting around tables or standing at the bar, Florida's influence peddlers made decisions and contacts. For them, the Cypress Lounge was a space beyond the official halls of government where politicians and other VIPs could conduct business in a more relaxed atmosphere. Like many such spaces, the Cypress Lounge was multilayered, with various worlds coexisting and intermingling around the bar. While legislators made decisions and discussed the governance of Florida, queer men appropriated the Cypress Lounge to make connections—erotic, platonic, and romantic. While queer people were always conscious of the various ways in which they were forced to navigate those worlds, it is doubtful that all legislators were fully aware of the queer happenings around them.

Pickups could happen anyplace where men gathered. Anyone attuned to the signs of cruising would be able to navigate and find other queer people among the presumably heterosexual crowd. The available evidence indicates that the Cypress Lounge was more than just a place of chance encounters or a statistical anomaly. Rather, the lounge was a destination of choice for some of Tallahassee's gay or otherwise queer men. In addition to being an unofficial extension of the Florida legislature, the Cypress Lounge was also Tallahassee's unofficial gay bar.

The reputation of the Cypress Lounge and its designation as Tallahassee's gay bar spread far beyond the environs of the city. In July 1960, Gordon E. Wilkinson of Buffalo, New York, wrote a letter to ONE, Inc., in which he enclosed a list dated 1957 of purportedly homosexual-tolerant bars across America: "I am not sure of the origin of this list and am sure there are many changes since it was made up."[4] The list of bars covers five pages arranged alphabetically by city with several additions penciled into the margins. The list includes a number of hotel bars across the country as well as bus-station restaurants and lounges. Wilkinson listed twenty bars in South Florida, most of which were clustered around Miami and Ft. Lauderdale, evidence of increasing homosexual visibility. Men and women who relied on Wilkinson's list would likely find many of the bars shuttered or fundamentally changed, given Miami's 1954 moral panic.[5] Jacksonville and Jacksonville Beach were represented by three bars, and the listing for Daytona Beach consists of only two bars. The only listing for the Panhandle is the Cypress Lounge, lending it a semiofficial status in the gay press.[6]

By 1966 the Cypress Lounge was no longer the only "officially recognized" place to pick up men in a social setting on the Panhandle. According to *The Address Book*, compiled by Bob Damron, Le Roc (another hotel lounge just two blocks from the Cypress) was also viable as a site of connection. The 1966 guide also lists Trader Jon's and the Fiesta at the San Carlos Hotel in Pensacola.[7] The inclusion of the lounge in both Wilkinson's list and later in Damron's *Address Book* designates it as a bar where gay and otherwise queer men were likely to find others like themselves. Beyond simply happening upon places where one might meet other men, gay men made the Cypress Lounge a destination because of these lists. The inclusion of it on these two lists, with an ostensibly national circulation, meant that gay men and likely lesbians could more easily navigate their way to a queer space when they found themselves in North Florida. These lists are early forms of the advertising-driven travel guides that evolved later with the growing gay and lesbian print media.

There are limitations to the availability of information about the Cypress Lounge. Homophile and sometimes nudist and fitness magazines carried advertisements for bar guides such as Wilkinson's list. Thus distribution was limited to those willing to purchase those magazines who were also literate and who had the means and inclination to travel. To this segment of the population, the bar became a visible space. If one simply happened upon the bar, however, it likely would not have appeared to be a bar that allowed homosexuals.

The Cypress Lounge, and indeed many other bars on Wilkinson's list or in Damron's *Address Book*, did not conform to post-Stonewall notions of what constituted a "gay bar." The term did not have the same meaning in 1960 as it would later in the decade. While certainly some bars on the list—especially those in the larger cities of San Francisco, New York, Los Angeles, or Miami—were exclusively gay or lesbian bars with recognizable signifiers and an "out" clientele, the majority probably did not fit that description. Instead, spaces such as the Cypress Lounge should be viewed as relatively safe for gay men and lesbians to congregate. Though comparatively safe there, many gays and lesbians socialized in secret or at least in less overt ways much of the time. Also, depending on the mood of the time or even the mood of the owner or bar staff, known homosexuals (even the non-overtly so) could be subject to harassment or rejection from an establishment.[8]

As gay and lesbian visibility increased across the United States, so too did the number of establishments which catered to those wishing to socialize with others who shared particular senses of identity. Queer capital and access to power led to an economy characterized as a "liberation economy" in places with gay and lesbian critical mass. Thanks to legal challenges and activism such as New York's "sip ins" and Stonewall riots, San Francisco's Compton's Café Riot, and the variety of other demonstrations throughout the 1960s, gay men and lesbians increasingly earned the right to socialize openly. As bars that catered explicitly to gays and lesbians proliferated, a list such as Wilkinson's with "safe" bars became less of a necessity. This was a slightly slower process in the Panhandle, given the region's cultural affinity with Deep South religiosity and general southern disdain for spectacle.

The Cypress Lounge was not simply a place to procure a sexual partner for the evening. Connections made there turned into friendships and even served to connect homosexual men to sex(uality)-based networks on the Panhandle and with larger identity-based movements. Information shared and friendships initiated over drinks acted as "a vital form of community initiation, imitation, and belonging," to use historian John Howard's phrasing.[9] Unlike outdoor cruising spaces based around quick and anonymous sexual acts, the atmosphere of the Cypress Lounge was not likely to be solely populated by men searching only for anonymous sexual release. Unlike the semi-anonymous glory holes in the public toilet, visibility was key in a public space. Cruising and ascertaining desire in a space such as the Cypress Lounge involved successfully interpreting glances and correctly picking up dropped hairpins. This involved seeing and being seen, in addition to a queer listening.

Michael Patterson, who managed the Howard Johnson's restaurant in Tallahassee, was arrested on December 7, 1961, outside the Greyhound bus station for disorderly conduct after he picked up a man for "immoral purposes."[10] Patterson was a regular at the bus station as well as the Cypress Lounge, both of which he visited "two or three times a week, or more."[11] Patterson was part of a group of men who made rounds between the lounge and the station in their search for sex and community. When police arrested Patterson, he was in possession of several copies of *ONE* and the *Mattachine Review*, both homophile magazines written and published outside the South. According to Patterson, a man he met at the Cypress Lounge gave him the publications. It is unclear whether this man was a friend or merely a stranger who recognized their mutual interest. Such connections allowed men to move beyond anonymous sex to become part of communities. Further, they connected men to a growing political consciousness over the course of the 1960s as national movements, inspired by the civil rights movement's victories, began to coalesce around discourses of access and the rights of citizens.

At least five others subscribed to *ONE* according to the subscription records of ONE, Inc.[12] Gay men were not the only people in possession of these magazines. Law enforcement used seized copies of a variety of political publications, usually mixed in with pedophilic, sadomasochistic, or other types of pornography to shock and warn the public about the ways homosexuals were "recruiting." A campy letter written to ONE, Inc., told of an exhibit at the county fair in Tallahassee sponsored by law enforcement "with lots of info on the nasty homos and what our good police are doing to combat this evil."[13]

Though not necessarily restricted by gender, often race and class limited access to spaces such as the Cypress Lounge. Unlike public restrooms, which were legally segregated by race and not class, restaurants and bars were private businesses where bartenders and managers served as gatekeepers to control access to these spaces. In the South of this era, the Cypress Lounge would have likely been segregated. White skin, certain modes of dress and decorum, the outward signs of social respectability, guaranteed access to the lounge. As one man interviewed by the FLIC recalled, "There is somebody by the name of [*redacted*] who hangs around The Cypress Lounge and is a real neat dresser, and he always wears coats and ties and vests, things of this nature. I am reasonably certain that he is a homosexual."[14] The freedom to stay in the Cypress was predicated on access to money, which made it distinct from the classless spaces of public toilets. Given that much of the clientele was white and involved in government, it is likely that anyone poorly dressed would have seemed anomalous in the lounge.

Because the lounge was connected to the Floridan Hotel, it was a site that benefited from mobility. Specifically, it was attached to a certain kind of postwar mobility, one that was a result of the economic development of the region. Though not a beach destination, Tallahassee as the seat of government profited from the influx of tourists and their money. Around the bar and across the tables, tourists mingled with locals. The Cypress's importance among government staff and their fawning courtiers, in addition to its location in the central business and government district, meant that the Floridan Hotel was a prime location for those coming to the city on business.

Anecdotal evidence of tourists sharing their beds with locals at the Floridan Hotel is, at this point, hard to obtain. However, using Norman Hayner's "moral holiday" thesis opens up analytical possibilities for the Cypress Lounge and the Floridan Hotel. How many men on vacation or business in Tallahassee stayed at the Floridan and cruised the hotel's bar? Or, how many men after they had just enough liquid courage could be talked into homosexual shenanigans? The Cypress Lounge had a reputation for success, given its inclusion in two bar guides a decade apart. It is reasonable to assume that tourists on a moral holiday, far from their home environs, would find connection around the bar.

Though the Cypress Lounge was likely the only cruising and socializing spot for a few queer Tallahassee residents, other men made a circuit between the bus station, the courthouse, and the lounge. Some spoke of men they saw in all three locations. Charles Taylor recalled, "there is a man who owns a men's shop in Thomasville, GA who I see over here quite often in Cypress Lounge and at the bus station."[15] The driving and socializing habits of Taylor and others point to the lounge as part of a regional queer geography. Carl Wilson, one of the men arrested at the bus station, regularly made contact with other men at the lounge in addition to the station. He admits to visiting the Cypress Lounge twice per week and picking up at least five men there.[16] Others saw gay and queer men only at the Cypress Lounge despite their regular patronage of other bars around town.[17] Some men made full use of the queer geography of Tallahassee.

At mid-century, men and women in Tallahassee were forming friendships and relationships based on shared identities. Though many men continued to cruise the public spaces in the area, the Cypress Lounge was a place of connection that allowed people to move beyond sex. Searching for connection meant different things to different people. For some, it could be their way into larger sex(uality)-based networks of friends and companions, opening another world of socializing.

Gay Parties

Removed from the public sphere of bars and bus stations, private homes came to be an important part of the queer geography of the Panhandle, bringing together friends and acquaintances from far-flung places. For gay men and lesbians, and even those who did not necessarily articulate those identities, the house-party scenes were especially significant in the growth of sex(uality)-based networks and later visible social institutions. I use the term "gay parties" regardless of gender mix or sexual preference at each party because this was the term employed by the people who experienced them.

The private home was the bedrock of postwar consumption and the "American dream." However, home ownership also highlights the disparity between the rhetoric and the reality of America at mid-century, since it was bound up with issues of race, class, and gender.[18] In theory, home ownership was open to all. The reality, however, was that African Americans and single women were especially discriminated against. Even African Americans with means often found it difficult or impossible to buy homes in certain areas because of segregationist lending practices.[19] Restrictive covenants, redlining, and gender norms kept others off of the property ladder.

Unlike sharing an apartment or dormitory with potentially hostile people, the private home greatly opened up sexual and social possibilities. If one met a potential partner at the Cypress Lounge or the bus station, they could be brought back to an ostensibly private space where activities could take place in secret. Also, if one had a network of queer friends, one could invite them over to socialize in a relaxed atmosphere. However, these private parties were never completely safe from police harassment. If a party became too public or too boisterous, police had an arsenal of public-order statutes at their disposal to shut down gay parties and then publicly shame the attendees.[20]

Parties and other gatherings held in private homes are a well-documented phenomenon in LGBTQ history, and these generally small gatherings were essential to queer socializing.[21] Along with cruising, and in some areas bars, they provided a way to bring people together around sometimes-shared senses of identity or sexual desire. House parties were an essential part of the sex(uality)-based networks and cultural formations in North Florida as people traveled great distances to attend gay parties, in the process creating networks that spanned the South and the state.

Mike Nelson, of Tallahassee, made all of his homosexual friends through the house-party scene. He was lucky in that his housemate was the instigator for the parties in the apartment they shared. Though Nelson later relocated because the parties became too raucous, they represented a significant space through which to develop close, queer contacts for him. "Well the atmosphere is supposedly cozy and all that bit—lights turned down low and everything—there's a hi-fi going and about three-fourths of the party was sitting around in conversation and naturally in conversation with all of one kind, the conversation was usually homosexual."[22] Nelson described a scene in which the guests were comfortable with each other. At a time when gay men and lesbians across the state were hounded, harassed, and arrested, they had to be constantly on guard. How freeing it is to be in a space with others like you and finally drop the masks, pull out all the hairpins, and let one's hair down.

Since securing an invitation to a gay party usually occurred through friends or friends of friends, it lent an added layer of security. A small and intimate gathering such as the one Nelson described would have a more tightly controlled list than would a larger party. Nelson later stated that when too many unfamiliar faces showed up at a party it "would break up a party pretty fast because it was getting infamous."[23] Hands in the wrong place or lips on the wrong gender were incredibly risky if plainclothes police officers were in the crowd. Depending on the location, some parties drew large crowds before they were broken up. Nelson recalled a party that was constituted mostly by students that "was really pretty garish."[24] When people who simply hear through the grapevine that a party was happening dropped in, the chance for undercover police officers increased. Breaking up a party in this way, the party's guests could feel more secure in their conversations and affections, as Nelson indicated. In addition to local students, "Usually to a large extent, they would be constituted by out-of-town people."[25] It is hard to determine just what he meant by "large extent" given that his discussion of the parties indicates that they were equally divided between locals and visitors. Others such as Charles Taylor recalled,

"There were two people from Panama City present" at the parties he attended around Tallahassee.[26]

Men from as far away as Panama City attended the parties held by Mike Nelson and his housemate. Two men stationed at Tyndall Air Force Base traveled by bus from Panama City to Tallahassee to attend the gay parties, which brought them through the very bus station under surveillance by the FLIC and the Tallahassee Police Department. According to Nelson, one of the men was romantically involved with his housemate. Without cars, these men used the bus to maintain and strengthen the sex(uality)-based networks that spanned the Panhandle. As the ability to own homes, attend university, and travel expanded in this period, these two men could make friends in ways that were unimaginable a generation before.

The mixing that occurred because of the gay parties was between the local and the nonlocal. Through the gay parties, people forged friendships and made connections that spanned the South. In an era when people were more mobile than ever before thanks to better roads and greater numbers of individuals who owned cars, the mixing of so many people from different locales is an example of the mobility afforded by the postwar economic boom. The connections allowed by mobility and travel meant that sex(uality)-based networks could spread across the South as never before.

The location of parties could provide a level of security for the participants. In a situation that was already fraught with danger—both legal and personal—a party held in a house a great distance from town provided safety. John Anderson attended a party at a house "out Tennessee Street, way out. I had to walk home one night, and it was terrible."[27] Only men were present at this party, and the attendees felt secure enough in their space to engage in same-sex dancing, a practice outlawed in most places at the time. Anderson stated that there were at least thirty men at the party. The physical distance from the road, from town, and from neighbors meant that this party and others like it were less likely to be raided.

Others around Tallahassee found it helpful to own a second property that could serve as a weekend getaway or place to host gay and lesbian gatherings. According to Dorothy Peters, several individuals routinely used her home on Lake Talquin, west of Tallahassee, for weekend get-togethers. Sometimes she gave permission for these gatherings, and at other times they occurred without her knowledge. Peters also rented the cabin for longer stays to friends and other people she knew and trusted. According to her, two men who rented another property from her took the cottage for the summer. These "boys," likely a couple and part of the social network of Tallahassee, reported to Peters that women sometimes brought dates and others to the property in an attempt to organize parties.[28]

From the available source material, it seems that a mixture of men and women attended a majority of the parties. This may simply be a function of the available records, and it is hard to generalize about gender segregation at "gay parties." In a place where there were no visible social institutions, gay men and lesbians often socialized together. The same holds true for segregation along racial lines as evidence indicates that at least some of the gay parties thrown in Tallahassee were racially mixed.[29] Though it is difficult to ascertain just how far integration went, the FLIC was keenly interested in attendance at gay parties by African Americans, asking multiple times about the amount of "race mixing" at each mention of a gay party. Given the frequent elision by the FLIC of "race mixers," "communist," and "homosexual," the line of questioning is unsurprising.

How did people secure invitations to a gay party in a seemingly closed system such as Tallahassee? While no direct, anecdotal evidence has surfaced for this area, other historians have documented how people became part of queer networks. John Howard names outdoor cruising grounds as a necessary form of community initiation. It is easy to theorize about how one became socialized into sex(uality)-based networks. It is productive to think of the house-party scene as an extension of the queer networks of 1950s and 1960s Tallahassee. Perhaps a chance meeting in the bus-station toilet or the Cypress Lounge led to a friendship and introduced one to a gay world beyond the act of cruising for sex. Perhaps young men and women drawn away from home to the universities began experimenting. People were on the move and came into contact with others like never before.

In Tallahassee and likely other locations, there is an indirect link between cruising for sex and gay parties. However, not everyone who cruised for sex became part of the gay scene. Most of the men interviewed by the FLIC confessed no knowledge of the gay parties or even of a queer network outside of the public toilets. This is consistent with Laud Humphreys's work on the divide between those who became part of gay networks and those who simply enjoyed homosexual activity.[30] As the 1960s progressed, other spaces along the Panhandle helped foster networks of gay friends and furthered the development of an LGBTQ community in the region.

The Navy and Pensacola's Nightlife

Not long after the first airplanes saw combat in World War I, Pensacola became central to the process of training those destined to fly for the U.S. Navy. According to local boosters, the Navy chose Pensacola as the site of the nation's first Naval Air Training School because it was found to have "the most good flying weather after a careful, nation-wide survey."[31] In 1939, the War Department further expanded the training facilities by purchasing the property that became Saufley Field, the primary training ground for Naval Air pilots in the United States.[32] By the 1950s, the entire Naval Air Training Command was consolidated in the Pensacola area. The countless numbers of men and women the military brought through Pensacola over the decades have left an indelible mark on the city and helped create a transient culture of movement and flow. In addition to the Naval Air Training operations in Pensacola, Eglin Air Force Base, located just across Escambia Bay, provided a steady stream of people, including gay men and lesbians, to the area. Though mostly men, the Women in the Air Force (WAF)[33] Squadron located at Eglin brought women together who would later settle in the area. This has led to a long tradition of both respect for and dependence on the military for the bodies and dollars it adds to the area.

Entertainment venues and social spaces for the military men and women stationed in Pensacola have long been a source of worry for the city's concerned citizens. According to scholar Kendra Kennedy, the 1940s was a pivotal time in the history of Pensacola's waterfront district. She writes, "The entrance of the United States into World War II brought more officers and flight trainees to the Naval Air Station and thus more military individuals who spent their leave in Pensacola's dance hall and billiard parlors."[34] To protect service-personnel commanding officers tasked Pensacola officials with cleaning up the available nightlife in the downtown area. Experience showed that the regulation of vice, debauchery, and entertainment was essential to maintaining military vitality.[35] Shortly after Pearl Harbor, local commanders threatened to place the downtown area out of bounds for military personnel if the saloons and "jook joints" were not cleaned up. Rather than risk the loss of such a significant contribution to local coffers, and to do their part for the war effort, city officials enforced midnight closing times for places that served alcohol and further ordered that such businesses close on Sunday during the war.[36] Some did; others did not. The "jook joints" that operated outside the newly sanitized space of downtown fared better than the bars and saloons that remained.

Though the number of service personnel declined from the wartime level, Pensacola remained an important hub for the training of the Navy's pilots after demobilization. Many of Pensacola's sailors and new residents sought entertainment in marginalized spaces. The most culturally, and often geographically, marginalized—yet also most fun—spaces were the "jook joints" in African American neighborhoods.[37] According to a letter written to Judge Ernest Mason in 1949, "in the lower part of the city, there are a number of houses of ill fame. They are operated by negroes."[38] The letter is from the local district attorney's office, and the attorney in question is looking to clean up the city's African American districts and further rigidly enforce the color line. "Buddy," the letter's author, seems unaware (or unconcerned) that the "houses of ill fame" were only recently removed from the downtown area, just outside his office, in an attempt to make it safe for soldiers stationed in Pensacola during World War II. Buddy believed that the sailors would return to downtown, where it was more respectable and "safer" if the African American establishments in other parts of the city were closed and therefore no longer a temptation.

Buddy was enraged because these bars "for fifty or seventy-five years . . . have catered to fisherman and are now actually catering to young sailors and young soldiers. I cannot understand how these young white people would associate with such filthy people."[39] Buddy was less concerned about the fisherman—perhaps they were too far beyond the moral pale already—but appalled at the thought of young soldiers and sailors at risk of the moral corruption that, in his mind, must surely follow "race mixing." The letter goes on to explain his intended cleanup of such places and asks for Judge Mason's help in sentencing the offenders. Note that it is not the young white people he wishes to arrest, but rather the operators of the establishments. Buddy relieves white clientele of responsibility while at the same time punishing black business owners.

The U.S. military and the industries that surrounded Pensacola shaped the nightlife in other ways. One woman and the network of female friends she met through a job at the local Chemstrand plant regularly queered the Hi-Ho Five O'clock Club. The group of friends stood out from the other patrons because of their sexuality and their gender presentation. The "12 of these girls that went together," six of whom lived together, were something of a fixture at the Hi-Ho and made little attempt to hide their desires or identities.[40] According to the club's singer, the group wore male attire and had short, traditionally masculine haircuts, which placed them in the butch/femme dynamic so prevalent in lesbian culture at the time. At least one of the women was not shy in her advances or making her desires known. The singer recalled that the leader of the group "would just lean on the bar and look at me and then when I came down from the bandstand, she would say 'I could just eat you up.'"[41]

It is unclear just how long the Hi-Ho Club was a little queer, but the singer's testimony speaks to a longer tradition at the club. According to her, longtime patrons took it upon themselves to warn new servicemen about the group: "One of the guys [who] had tried something before would say 'Oh, don't fool around with them lesies' or whatever you call them."[42] The cluster of friends was regular enough at the bar that they amassed a collection of rejected male suitors. This statement speaks to something of a toleration of the group of obvious lesbians. It is unclear if the relationship with management was tense or tolerant. As with other bars, it is likely that lesbian patrons were tolerated to a certain point as long as they spent money and did not bring unwanted attention to the bar, and, of course, their status depended on the mood of the owner. After all, as one gay man later described many business owners' attitudes: "It's money, honey."[43]

The Hi-Ho appears to have been the primary site for lesbians to socialize in Pensacola until the Aquarian opened in the early 1970s. The club was a major locale until the conversion to the liberation economy of bars and clubs that catered to an out clientele. This particular group of lesbian friends patronized it regularly enough to develop a reputation. The group was open and obvious enough that nearly everyone knew what they were and what they were about. Men interviewed by the FLIC never mentioned bars such as Trader Jon's, but the few women who were interrogated by the FLIC in Pensacola mentioned the Hi-Ho Club, indicating its significance in the city's queer geography.

Bars have long been considered social centers in the communities they serve, and there is a symbiotic relationship between the bar and the community. As the composition of a given locale changes, so too does the neighborhood bar. However, few bars in our nation's history have enjoyed the international reputation of Trader Jon's in Pensacola. What began as a quiet bar on Palafox in the heart of downtown grew quickly to be the bar of choice for naval aviators, their admirers, and a variety of others. The eclectic nature of the bar and the freedom within its space also meant that it was more than just a military bar or a quasi-museum space.

Martin Weismann, who earned the nickname "Trader Jon" in childhood because of his uncanny ability to trade nearly anything and make money, trained in the U.S. Army until an injury led to a medical discharge.[44] He always wanted to fly, and this discharge took away that dream, though he maintained a profound respect for service personnel. After the army, Trader Jon moved around for a time, eventually settling in Key West, where he opened a bar with his wife and befriended locals, including Ernest Hemingway. By the early 1950s, Trader Jon "wanted something bigger. I knew the Gulf Coast was going to grow and the Keys were becoming a little tiresome."[45] He and his wife settled in Pensacola after a brief stop in New Orleans. He opened his bar at 511 Palafox in a building formerly occupied by a shoe-repair shop, "near the wharf where the gunboats once docked and ladies of the night used to roam."[46]

Palafox was Pensacola's main street, and it connected the waterfront with the remainder of the city. Though the shoreline itself was still largely industrial, as one moved inland the area transitioned to a more traditional American downtown with a mix of shops, restaurants, and bars as well as government and office buildings.[47] Also, the civic center was located on the waterfront at the southernmost end of Palafox. Trader Jon's was in the middle of Pensacola's queer geography with the marina just down the street where Marvin Harrison sold peanuts and men regularly cruised.

The bar was an instant hit with locals and service personnel. Fred Brown, a reporter for the *Pensacola News-Journal,* writes that "almost immediately, men of the navy showed up to while away the empty hours and to ease the pain of training, drawn by Trader's unique brand of hospitality."[48] Trader Jon's hospitality is partly how he built up such a collection of memorabilia. If sailors or aviators did not have enough money, they might trade pictures to settle their tab.[49] Trader Jon's became internationally famous for the pictures that crowded its walls, as illustrated by a group of visiting nuclear scientists. According to Trader, "This was their first trip to America, but they knew of Trader Jon's, knew that they had to bring a picture. . . . These are the greatest men in the world. Nobody in the world has all these pictures."[50] Trader amassed both a reputation as a collector and an impressive collection of autographed photographs of the famous and not so famous.

The imposing entrance on Palafox greeted sailors, pilots, and others and welcomed them into a magical world of possibility. Brown calls Trader Jon's a "bawdy international depot, the Montmartre of the Gulf Coast, more institution than watering hole, the low den of high chic."[51] Numerous sources repeat that Trader Jon's attracted a diverse cast of characters over the years of its existence. "War heroes, astronauts, entertainers including John Wayne, Elizabeth Taylor and Bob Hope, and royalty" (Britain's Princes Charles and Andrew) have stepped through Trader's door.[52] Without the many characters continually inscribing meaning onto the space when they crossed the threshold, it would have been just one of the many bars that came and went.[53] The bar's eclectic nature also speaks to larger freedoms enjoyed in beach towns along the "Redneck Riviera."

In addition to the wealthy and famous, military personnel made it their second home. Troy Moon remembers the bar as "a place where thousands of sailors have drunk away their homesick blues, where thousands of young lovers have spied their soul-mates from across a hazy bar, where as many hearts as beer bottles have been broken, where old friends toasted one another before shipping off to a new port."[54] The vast array of bodies, mostly U.S. Navy, which crossed the threshold of Trader Jon's speaks to the kinds of mobility that the military's training schedule brought to Pensacola and the general importance of military spending to the area. Over the years, thousands of men and women trained in Pensacola and made Trader Jon's their local spot, and when they left they took their memories with them, creating an international community of devotees. The bar was even immortalized as "TJ's" in the 1982 film *An Officer and a Gentleman*.[55] The experience of Trader Jon's united these men and women, many of whom returned for one last round when the bar announced its closing in 1998.

The bar was an eccentric and eclectic space, which according to reports matched the character of its owner. Matt Hilburn, a reporter and former patron, remembers, "to a newcomer, the first view of the Pensacola, Fla., bar could be overwhelming. Dark and overrun with memorabilia, it had concrete floors, high ceilings draped with flags, a heavy wooden bar surrounded by stools, and walls covered with every possible type of aviation paraphernalia, from photos to plaques to flight suits and helmets. Hundreds of model aircraft dangled from the ceiling, giving it the quality of a crowded, eccentric and informal museum."[56] Trader Jon's was an institution. Its quirky decor and even quirkier owner gave the bar a feeling of freedom and possibility. In this space, sailors, soldiers, strippers, princes, drag queens, and queers rubbed shoulders in an atmosphere of permissiveness.

Trader Jon's deserved its reputation for permissiveness, and the bar was, at least in the 1960s, the site of raucous sensuality. In the *Pensacola News-Journal* on September 7, 1969, John Waite profiled five women who danced at Trader Jon's. According to the article, "thousands of men, and women as well, turn out weekly to watch Trader Jon's girls."[57] The article is surprisingly uncritical of the women who danced at Trader Jon's. Waite delves into their private lives and even their views on marriage and spirituality, seeking to dissuade the public from viewing these women as sex objects or sex workers in favor of a view of women who simply liked to dance and earn money. Instead of moralizing about "fallen women" or the fallen nature of the establishment itself, he makes the point on several occasions that these women had lives and families and were, more importantly, sexually chaste, despite their chosen profession. According to Waite, for these women, it was about the money, power, and fame rather than sex. The entire article normalizes and glorifies Trader Jon's and the activities that went on there. However, complete nudity was not allowed. Trader Jon hung a sign in the women's dressing room to remind them to keep their dancing under control: "If you show your tooter you're fired."[58]

Waite's article served as a means to assure the public that Trader Jon's was not like the other strip clubs along Palafox. Trader Jon was always sensitive to the mood of his community. As the winds blew in a more conservative direction—sweeping away a variety of imagined threats to the area's family-friendly image—Trader Jon was in support of the ordinance to ban topless dancing in Pensacola. When he appeared at the city council meeting where the anti-topless ordinance was debated, there was concern about how he would react. Never wanting to distance himself from the community he served, Trader came out in favor of the ordinance and admitted that he had considered ending the practice of exotic dancing for some time.[59]

Ever eager to try new things, in the middle of the 1980s Trader Jon's even had female impersonators. Trader's welcomed a review show because of the Broadway show *La Cage Aux Folles*'s popularity. The timing of this addition to the lineup is telling. Pensacola took a decidedly anti-queer turn in the early 1970s. By the 1980s there was a swing in the opposite direction, though this should not be read as acceptance of gay and lesbian sexualities within the city. Female impersonation has long been an intermediate activity. It could be a little queer but, depending on who was doing the cross-dressing, it was not necessarily "gay."[60]

This highly charged mix of sometimes-veiled sex, sensuality, alcohol, and testosterone created a unique space for queer men, and likely a number of lesbians. Despite the overwhelming majority of presumably heterosexually identified military men, women, and their admirers who made up the clientele of Trader Jon's, certain gay men knew the bar as *the* place to pick up sailors and other "rough trade." This reputation spread throughout the Panhandle, the South, and the United States. In addition to word-of-mouth advertising, Trader Jon's appeared in the 1966 issue of the *Address Book*, compiled by Bob Damron. Though Damron's circulation was limited to men with a certain level of outness and the means and ability to travel, the appearance of Trader Jon's on the list gives it a certain status as a queer destination. As gay and lesbian travel guides increased in frequency and coverage area, they gave queer tourists a map to vacation destinations.

Tom Baker, from Panama City, drove to Pensacola just to cruise and connect at Trader Jon's. "I'd heard about Trader Jon's and went there purposely. . . . It was crazy; I loved it down there. I'd go there just for the entertainment. It was entertaining to go there. You know, lot of sailors."[61] Baker picked up two sailors during his times at Trader Jon's. Though he initiated contact at the bar, they did not have sex at the bar. According to Baker, sex at Trader Jon's was not usually possible because of the restroom's lack of cleanliness and the frequency of interruption. On one occasion, Baker accompanied a sailor to his hotel room and on another Baker performed oral sex on a sailor in an alley near Trader Jon's.

The bar did not formally advertise itself as a free and open space (word of mouth took care of that), yet that is exactly what it was. Tom Baker remembered "an atmosphere that everything was ok. Everybody seemed to get along."[62] Baker remembers seeing an openly affectionate male couple on one occasion, though he could not be sure of the date. That affection seemed not to draw a passing glance from other patrons. According to Baker, there was a gay side and a straight side; it was not official but just seemed to develop that way. He never saw any violence motivated by the sexuality of particular patrons. How did a bar in the early 1970s, with a clientele overwhelmingly drawn from the ranks of the U.S. military, allow open displays of male-male affection? It shows the malleability of concepts such as our postmodern "homophobia" as well as possibilities for queer affection in some cases and within certain boundaries. The actions of these two men occurred at a unique moment in Pensacola's history.

Outside of the walls of Trader Jon's, gays and lesbians were becoming bolder in their assertions in Pensacola. Inside, Trader Jon's was a microcosm of changes happening along the "Redneck Riviera." At the dawn of the 1970s, municipalities all along the Gulf Coast were in the process of redefining their target audiences. Struggles over a singular message threatened to rip apart the community several times over the years. Some called this a fractured identity that was sure to repulse tourists, and others called it multifaceted. Trader Jon's had a little bit of everything, and it had something for just about everyone. It resists simple classification as a military bar or a straight bar. Rather, it is queer in the broadest sense of the word, and it represented the best of what the area could be.

Bob Shaw, a reporter for the *Miami Herald,* wrote an article in 1975 about the gay social organization in Pensacola that called itself the Emma Jones Society until its demise in 1974. In the article, he states that Trader Jon's was not just a place to pick up sailors; it was clandestinely becoming a gay meeting place, though outness was discouraged. One man told Shaw, "You'd go out, have drinks, nod and they'd talk about work. And, every so often, scream 'Yeaah!' at the stripper taking her clothes off."[63] This seems to contradict Baker's assertion that the bar's atmosphere sometimes tolerated same-sex intimacy. However, it is another example of the quiet accommodation of the queer that was ever shifting along the Gulf Coast. The winds of change sometimes blew in a conservative direction and foreclosed queer expressions while at other times such expressions flourished.

The bar's owner created and fostered the general atmosphere of openness. He further elaborated and enforced it every time he escorted an unruly customer out of the building. Fred Brown recalls an incident in which Trader Jon removed two rough-looking merchant marines that were staring at a regular patron and friend of Trader's. After physically removing the two men, he went to the patron and said, "Don't worry about it, Bill. They are just ignorant."[64] Jon did not tolerate disturbance, and he accepted almost everyone. He did not turn anyone away as long as they did not cause trouble.

It is unsurprising that the "official" histories do not mention anything queer about the bar. After all, how many such histories of other places remain silent or actively disavow anything queer? The prevalence of gay cruising, the reputation as a cruising destination, and Bob Shaw's assertion that the founders of the Emma Jones Society regularly gathered around tables at Trader Jon's make it a very queer space. Much like the Cypress Lounge in Tallahassee, Trader Jon's was layered with multiple meanings and multiple worlds coexisting within its walls, complicating the historical understandings of this part of Florida. In a time when police raided other bars across the state that even tolerated homosexuals, Trader Jon's was mostly safe, though it lost its liquor license at least once for serving alcohol to minors. When other bars were swept away in moral crusades against vice or general heterosexual debauchery, Trader Jon's was not.

Is it possible that Trader Jon's was allowed such open license for debauchery because it was not located in a poor area and was run by a white man? Though bars such as Trader's are often located in geographically or culturally marginalized places, the whiteness and masculinity of Trader Jon's gave it a level of protection for all sorts of debauchery. Also, its location right in the heart of downtown, where "young white people" would not have to associate with "such filthy people," to return to Buddy's phrasing, meant that individuals in a "safe" or officially sanctioned space were given great liberty.[65] So long as debauchery and sexuality were segregated and policed, they could be sanctioned—to a point.

Trader Jon's was a site layered with differing meanings. For the sailors who remember it fondly as their favorite watering hole, it was an integral part of their life in Pensacola, and when it closed, sailors and aviators across the United States mourned its passing. For many of Pensacola's gay men, it was also an integral part of their life in Pensacola. For them, Trader Jon's was a prominent spot in Pensacola's queer geography. It was a space where sex was readily available and the roots of a larger community began to take hold. Trader Jon's had a reputation for queer shenanigans that make it essential to North Florida's queer past.

• • •

Florida at mid-century represented in miniature many of the changes happening nationally. Men and women across the country were articulating and coalescing around gay and lesbian identities in ever-increasing numbers. As leisure spending became a pillar of postwar capitalism, more and more people flocked to the Gulf Coast for vacations, employment, and retirement. They caused fundamental changes in the landscape. They Cypress Lounge, the gay parties, Trader Jon's, and the Hi-Ho Club were sites of connection for a variety of communities. Across the bars, men and women with homosexual desires found each other. Many men moved beyond the furtive world of public cruising to form deeper and longer-lasting connections. Thanks to increases in mobility and the wider availability of queer print media, many also started to consider their place in "The Sunshine State" and think about ways to resist the unqueering that they saw all around them.

5

EMMA JONES

Queering the Fourth of July

Pensacola is not a resort city. A Naval Base is located there. No gay bars and no overt behavior is allowed. With discretion, one may enjoy the fruits of one's labor.

J.R., 1963

Increasingly after mid-century gay men and lesbians reached out to one another across the country, forming networks, communities, and alliances. Economic expansion and ideas about the free market had a profound impact on what magazines and books were able to print as well as distribute. This meant that queer folks in far-flung places could gain access to information about homosexuality, civil rights activity, and identity-based discourses. The desire to keep abreast of the latest news and other homosexual happenings, coupled with a campy sensibility and a love of fun, helped launch the Emma Jones Society in the late 1950s. By 1965, members started what became by 1973 one of the largest gay social gatherings in the country on the beaches of Pensacola.

The National Gay and Lesbian Press

ONE, Inc., began in Los Angeles in 1952 and published its first magazine in January 1953.[1] Many homophile individuals across the country were divided by various kinds of distance. In his book *Contacts Desired,* historian Martin Meeker writes: "The leaders of the movement decided the most important contribution they could make to improving the situation of gay men and lesbians in the United States was to build new communication

Figure 6. Invitation to the 1970 Emma Jones Society Party. The images used in this and other years' invitations display the campy sensibility of Ray and Henry Hillyer when it came to Emma Jones. In author's collection.

networks as well as reinforce the more precarious and small-scale networks that already existed."[2] Across the United States, though based in California, the Mattachine Society, Daughters of Bilitis, and ONE, Inc., attempted to bridge the gaps between homosexuals through the publication of newsletters and magazines as well as sponsoring meetings. *ONE*, the *Mattachine Review*, and the *Ladder* all sought to raise awareness among homosexual people of the existence of others like them, but also to bring them into a more national imagined community and civil rights–based discourse.[3]

Much of the ink in *ONE* was devoted to arts and literature as well as the struggles of gay men and lesbians around the country (and sometimes the world) who dealt with discrimination and harassment. In addition to stories of police entrapment and fears over job loss or the consequences of familial revelations, *ONE* routinely carried letters from men and women who dealt with postal inspectors who overzealously pursued their role as moral guardians.[4] For instance, after a rather lengthy treatise on the causes of local trouble, one man from Tampa wrote, "Therefore, I argue that it must rather be the local postal authorities; having especially noted your return address, who helped and abetted the local gendarme."[5] Though writing his letter in 1962, four years after *ONE* was ruled legal, this man makes clear that postal inspectors were alerting local authorities as to who was receiving mail from which place.

Since the establishment of the Comstock Law in 1873, the U.S. Post Office wielded great authority in the battle against "obscene" material.[6] Postal authorities seized early issues of *ONE* and inaugurated a fierce four-year legal battle in 1954. Helped along by the precedent set by the 1957 *Roth* decision, which ruled that sex did not automatically equate to obscenity, the U.S. Supreme Court ruled in 1958's *ONE v. Olesen* that homosexuality was not automatically obscene. This ruling was one of the most important LGBTQ rights decisions because it protected the nascent gay and lesbian press and rights movement at a time when federal, state, and local governments around the country were engaged in witch hunts of homosexuals. Though the magazine was not on its face obscene and was therefore legal to send, this did not stop postal inspectors from collaborating with local authorities, including the Federal Bureau of Investigation and even the FLIC in Florida, in their searches for homosexuals. Postal employees and other federal agents continued harassment of homosexual-themed publications well into the 1960s.[7]

The policing of morality by postal inspectors was a national issue that caused anxiety among subscribers as well as potential subscribers to publications such as *ONE*. In his exhaustive study of letters written to ONE, Inc., scholar Craig Loftin calculated that 5 percent of the 812 letters for his survey dealt exclusively with harassment by postal inspectors while many others touched on it.[8] A man from Washington, D.C., wrote: "Mailing lists of 'male' magazines, pen pal clubs, etc., are at the instance of P.O. Inspectors, being subpoenaed by either local authorities or Federal D.A.'s. This is done as quietly as possible—no news items if possible. Most of the seizures are entirely illegal and, if the courts reject the case and the lists are ordered returned, microfilms are made for the P.O. Dept. secretly. From then on comes the chain reaction."[9] Though the seizures were illegal and unlikely to stand up in court, the damage was already done in many cases. A person was forever marked in the minds of investigators and the court of public opinion. The ONE letter writer then spent several pages detailing conversations and interrogations between suspects and authorities in a typical case of postal entrapment. He made clear that many people across the United States did not know their rights and were scared to publicly challenge the Post Office for fear that a challenge automatically equated to guilt.

Postal inspectors in Pensacola were no different from those in other parts of Florida and the nation. According to scholar John Loughery in *The Other Side of Silence,* locals knew that area inspectors had a habit of opening plain brown packages addressed to unmarried men. He writes, "Between the intelligence officers at the nearby military base and the local police, the existence of a list of the names and addresses of gay men in Pensacola was an open secret."[10] Military police also regularly used photographs of enlisted men entering the homes of known homosexuals as blackmail.[11] Charges of obscenity could ruin a person's livelihood, and in the 1950s and 1960s "homosexual" was almost always conflated with "obscene," even after the Supreme Court's 1958 ruling.[12]

In addition to reporting harassment and explaining legal issues, many wrote letters to ONE, Inc., that expressed the desire to connect beyond the practice of cruising for sex, especially in rural and nonmetropolitan areas. One man from Mobile, Alabama, just around the bend from Pensacola, shared his frustration at the dearth of nonsexual meeting places for gay men when he wrote to *ONE,* "Now here is the joker! Where would I find a young man like this—in a gay bar, a bus station toilet, or at the Y[MCA] perhaps?"[13] By attempting to connect with other homosexuals through the pages of *ONE* magazine, this man tried to move beyond the traditional locales of gay sexual contacts. Unlike men who sought connection at the Cypress Lounge, gay parties, and the bus station, this man wanted something different. He imagined the world without the stigma attached to his sexuality. Connection to a national "imagined community" could end the isolation and desolation felt by so many homosexuals who knew that there must be more to their lives as gay men than a quick encounter in a public restroom.[14]

The man's previous experiences with gay bars caused his disillusion. He wrote, "One does not have to be a bar flirting, limp-wristed fairie [*sic*] to qualify as a desperately lonely homophile."[15] Though men at mid-century often found their initiation into broader queer networks, friendships, and romantic relationships through cruising public spaces and ostensibly straight bars, not everyone was able, or willing, to make use of those.[16] Even once they had made their entrance, the feeling of loneliness and isolation could still be profound, prompting many to seek companionship in the imagined community of homophiles accessed through publications such as *ONE*.

Though area newsstands did not stock homosexual publications, some Pensacola homosexuals were aware of national homophile organizations and the discourse surrounding their plight. In May 1954, a Pensacola doctor sent a request to the Mattachine Society after reading an article about Mattachine in an unnamed magazine.[17] He wished to become a member of a society trying to bring about "reasonable laws protecting the abused and misunderstood homoerotics."[18] Soon, an organization for those "homoerotics" would exist in Pensacola. Drawn by the white sands of Pensacola Beach and the "naval meat rack," the area was increasingly popular with gays and lesbians from around the South and became a hub of queer activity and organizing after mid-century.[19]

The Not So Discreet Lovers of Emma Jones

Pensacola was a city of seeming contradictions in the 1960s, like "a suddenly gangly teenager somewhat puzzled about what to do with its growth"—it was a Navy town, it was a farming town, and Baptists ran it.[20] It was the contradictions that first drew Bob Shaw, then a reporter for the *Miami Herald,* to the story of Emma Jones. Shaw was the state reporter for the *Herald* and was routinely on the lookout for interesting stories. His editor at the time was also keenly interested in "good stories." According to Shaw, his editor was as interested in the Emma Jones Society as he was a story about car insurance. Shaw remembered reports of men arrested in Pensacola's Wayside Park coming across the wire in May 1974. Then, he was anonymously sent a clipping from a New Orleans–based magazine about the Emma Jones Society parties. He began to wonder how the two coexisted in the same city. Here was a town that arrested and publicly shamed gay men, yet there existed this rather open, rather public party for homosexuals. Shaw pitched the story to his editor and set out to pound the pavement in Pensacola. After contacting several friends at the *Pensacola News-Journal*, he was put in touch with a freelance reporter who happened to be gay. It was through this connection that Shaw was able to travel deep into the inner workings of the Emma Jones Society.[21] He produced a six-page story for the *Herald*'s Sunday magazine, *Tropic.*[22] Shaw's story was the first mainstream story about the group and, until LGBTQ scholars started digging, it was largely unknown outside the area.

In 1957, under the watchful eyes of Charley Johns, his committee, and the other players in the complex web of surveillant authorities tasked with enforcing moral and racial compliance to mid-century norms in "The Sunshine State," a star was "born" in Pensacola. The name was Emma Jones. She was born out of a desire to connect with other homophiles and become part of national homophile movements and discourses circulating in publications such as *ONE*, the *Ladder,* and *Drum*. Her birth was cloaked in the secrecy, intrigue, and the subterfuge employed by so many queer men and women in the 1950s. She was the brainchild of Ray and Henry Hillyer, adopted brothers and lifelong lovers whose network of friends covered the South and whose beach parties became the stuff of legend.

Beyond Emma Jones, Ray and Henry's story also exemplifies the intersections of military presence with growing tourist capital. Growing up in Texas, the pair settled in Pensacola after Ray's time at Eglin Air Force Base. Though unofficially adopted by the Hillyer family, Henry did not officially share the surname until the early 1960s. This made renting an apartment for the pair difficult until they were able to convince the landlord that they were adopted brothers.[23]

Figure 7. Artist's representation of "Miss Emma." She looks as sassy and campy as one would imagine her to be. This image was included in the registration forms for 1972 and 1973. It was also likely used on other "promotional material" for other years as well. From Hillyer scrapbook, in author's collection.

The climate of fear and paranoia over "the homosexual menace" or "sexual psychopaths" in the 1950s was a response to ever-increasing homosexual openness and visibility around the United States.[24] Wishing to gain access to homophile publications and therefore be part of national discourses surrounding homosexuality, the Hillyers decided to start a book club.

Given the reality of their place and time, they realized that subterfuge was necessary. To protect their identities and guard their safety, they partnered with a female friend who opened a post-office box under the name "Emma Jones." They assumed that postal inspectors would not suspect a woman of receiving obscene material.[25] They thought long and hard about the name of their "society" and eventually settled on "Emma Jones" because it was the most nondescript and boring name they could think of.[26] According to one of the founders, "Emma because it was such an awful name; 'Jones' because it was so common."[27]

The four men at the heart of the fledgling society subscribed to homophile activist publications such as *ONE*, the *Mattachine Review*, and "stag films," according to one source.[28] These magazines kept readers informed of national and international developments in the homophile movement. For many, these publications were a vital link with other homophiles and sexual nonconformists around the country. It was not uncommon for reading groups and other private forums for discussion and information sharing to spring up around people who subscribed. Carson Weaver of Durham, North Carolina, wrote in a letter to ONE, Inc., in October of 1961, "I eagerly look forward to each issue of the magazine because when you live in such a dry, forsaken area as I do you become very appreciative of any and all news from other areas. My friends, most of whom are afraid to subscribe to the magazine, come over every month for a time of reading and discussion. We are heavily dependent upon the information and entertainment offered."[29] Not everyone could or would take the risk of having their own subscription to the magazines. For these people, meeting at the homes of friends to share the publications was preferable. Dick McConchie of Corpus Christi, Texas, wrote that he preferred reading at the homes of friends to "being gleefully shoved into a paddy wagon" for ordering the magazines for himself.[30] These publications were a lifeline to the wider homosexual world for many. The growth of queer print media allowed gay men and lesbians to feel part of the larger imagined community, which contributed to later political movements.[31]

The Emma Jones Society parties were definitively part of a local initiative to aid "misunderstood homoerotics," to return to the aforementioned doctor's phrase, though not through legal challenges. It was not an activist homophile organization in the tradition of ONE, Inc., the Mattachine Society, or the Daughters of Bilitis. Members never staged any marches or demonstrations and were primarily a social club. Yet, "like a pagan goddess, originally created to ward off fear of the night Emma Jones became a symbol of openness, identity, and community for gay people all over the South." It was this openness, identity, and community building that made Emma's parties so important and so essential to the development of Pensacola as a gay and lesbian capital.[32]

The social opportunities for gay men, lesbians, and the otherwise queer in Pensacola were sometimes segregated, generally limited, and often secretive in the two decades after the Second World War. Some men met in Wayside Park, nicknamed "Gayside" park. Others met at Trader Jon's, and others met at private house parties, yet still others made sexual contacts on the streets of downtown, where men were freely available.[33] Though each area attracted a distinct following with its own cast of characters, some individuals regularly crossed the imagined boundaries. Men like Ray and Henry Hillyer, whose networks touched each of those worlds, could see that members of the "community" of Pensacola were desperate for contact with each other.

Cruising for contacts that led to more than a sexual release in outdoor spaces is well known in the history of queer men. This practice was often a man's first or only entry into the larger gay world and led to the emergence of specifically gay bars.[34] Pensacola was no exception. "Gayside Park" was a small roadside park with a few picnic tables, a parking lot, and public restrooms. During the daylight hours, this space was filled with families and groups of people fishing and enjoying a variety of water-based activities. At night the occupants of the park changed drastically. Men came in small groups and entered the men's restroom, which conveniently faced away from the highway, to make pickups. The area under the pier and the bathroom's stalls became the sexual playground for many men over the years.[35] The sentiment is echoed in a 1975 analysis of the society's demise in an *Advocate* article, which named "Gayside Park" as the one area where otherwise unknowing Pensacola residents could not deny the existence of homosexuals because it was so blatantly obvious.[36]

For some men who were looking for sex with other men, this was their only outlet. Unable or unwilling to take their partners home, they had sex there on-site. In the days before gay bars, gay men and outwardly straight men would have populated places like "Gayside." Some went for adventure, some because it was their only outlet. For some who could not or would not risk the exposure of arrest—a few times every year law enforcement would "clean up" sites like "Gayside" well into the 1990s—private house parties were the only way they met others like themselves. As with gay parties, there was a social register maintained by a few couples in Pensacola, including the Hillyers. According to friends of the Hillyers, they were social butterflies and loved a party, so they were at the center of a number of friendship groups. There were many elaborate affairs, including one formal New Year's Eve party that was described simply as "really funny," though I suspect that "campy" might be a more apt description.[37] If one were lucky enough to secure an invitation to these soirees, one enjoyed some degree of safety since the guest lists were often strictly controlled.

For others, Trader Jon's was the preferred place to meet men. A small table "to the left of the door . . . well away from the tourists and businessmen staring at the bumps and grinds onstage" became a gay space, perhaps even where the Hillyers first dreamed up the Emma Jones Society beach parties.[38] According to some, Trader Jon's was the "site of the first openly public gatherings of Pensacola gays."[39] A very eclectic space with a rather eccentric owner, Trader Jon's was the perfect place to launch Pensacola's "gay community."

The distinct areas of community needed a way to come together. "It was a community longing for contact with each other and the outside world."[40] Other scholars have found a similar trend across the country in the middle of the twentieth century. Ray and Henry Hillyer were sociable men; they noticed a need for togetherness and provided a space for it. Ray, Henry, and two to three other men had pooled their money to open the Emma Jones post office box in the mid-1950s.[41] Over the first decade of the society's existence, they became increasingly aware of the need for community from the pages of the magazines and their own observations.

In June 1963, *ONE* published yet another report on the status of the FLIC investigations in Florida. Though some were beginning to criticize the committee, it still struck fear in the hearts of gays and lesbians across the country. That article ended with the admonition: "Our suggestion where to vacation: ANYWHERE BUT FLORIDA. A gay person that'd spend a dime in that state should have his or her head examined."[42] Legislative committees, various law-enforcement agencies, and others were making the situation very difficult for gays, lesbians, and the otherwise queer in

Florida. According to the national gay and lesbian press, the unqueering of "The Sunshine State" was working.

Seemingly in preparation for the July 1965 demise of the FLIC, the members of Emma Jones were ready for an even larger public presence. As a challenge to *ONE*'s assertion, and thanks to the need for community fostered by Trader Jon's, "Gayside Park," the private house parties, and Emma's secret meetings, coupled with shifting attitudes in the 1960s, the founders decided to have a beach party. According to a longtime friend, they wanted a fun way to bring their distant friends together.[43] They did not intend to make a fuss; "we meant it to be innocent. We didn't mean to offend anyone. She wasn't created to sit in or raise rabble. She was here for love, fun, and patriotism."[44]

They were aware of the national homophile discussions of rights; they were conscious of the political activities of activists, but according to author John Loughery, "many gay men in the mid and late 1960s were reevaluating the strategy of the homophile movement in the light of its unwillingness to establish at least some connections between the pleasures of the homosexual life and the need for action."[45] Gay men and lesbians across the country made attempts at social activities that were both fun and political such as the Reading Picnic in Pennsylvania.[46] The Emma Jones Society was part of this reevaluation. As greater numbers of queer people from around the South descended on Pensacola Beach for Independence Day festivities and activist discourses across the country shifted to calls for equal rights of citizenship for gays and lesbians, the parties became increasingly political. But they never lost their campy sensibility.

The Fourth of July is one of the most famous and widely celebrated national holidays in the United States. It marks a celebration of American independence from Great Britain, and towns and cities across the country celebrate the occasion with displays of fireworks preceded by parades and carnivalesque street fairs. It is a day for families and friends to come together and celebrate American-ness and "freedom" (a term that is race, class, and gender specific), especially in the postwar era of ostentatious patriotic displays. Backyard barbecues, beach parties (where possible), and a spirit of togetherness often abound on that day.

Holding a beach party on the Fourth of July was an ideal choice for the friends of Emma Jones. It was already a day when large groups of people from around the South traveled to the Panhandle's beaches. One more group of men and women on the beach was not out of the ordinary, and the numbers of people out enjoying the day's festivities provided a layer of camouflage for the group, provided they maintain a certain level of "respectability." The founders always invited an equal number of men and women just in case anyone happened upon the party. As the years wore on, the party moved farther and farther down the beach, away from the more populated areas. Nothing would look out of the ordinary because the celebrants could quickly pair off. However, one important feature of Emma Jones parties that might have drawn attention was the racially diverse crowd on a Deep South beach in 1965.

From the outset, the party was campy. Longtime friend Tommie Shields remembers that they just wanted to bring friends together and the politics came later. However, according to the founders (likely Henry), several years after the society's demise, "the real theme was patriotic. . . . We're Americans. This is our Fourth, too. . . . Thank God we're in America where we can be independent enough to be gay."[47] What began as fun became fun plus political. Emma's parties fit with the traditional Independence Day celebrations, though with a campy queer twist. Even the food was traditional. According to Bob Shaw, "it was an Independence Day celebration, complete with hot dogs, potato salad and the full red, white, and blue treatment." Wrapped in the trappings of Independence Day, the only difference was the sexual identities of the partygoers.

Across the United States after the middle of the 1950s, gay men, lesbians, and the otherwise queer claimed their rights of citizenship—their American-ness. Through so many protests, letters, and riots, queer folks worked out and asserted their identities. In Philadelphia, the birthplace of the United States, gay men and lesbians staged what became the "Annual Reminder" in 1964. Barbra Gittings, a Philadelphia-based activist, stated, "We are here today to remind the American public that in its homosexual citizens, it has one large minority who are still not benefitting from the high ideals proclaimed for all on July 4, 1776."[48] This protest/demonstration served to link the plight of homosexuals in a very visceral way with the minority-rights discourses that had been employed by so many other marginalized groups in the United States throughout the twentieth century.

The Annual Reminder was not the only way activists sought to claim access to the rights guaranteed in America's founding documents. Historian

Marc Stein also documents the nationally coordinated demonstrations on Armed Forces Day in 1966. Thousands of leaflets were distributed that claimed the right to serve in the military as one of the rights of citizenship: "we don't dodge the draft; the draft dodges us."[49] These demonstrations, as well as the Annual Reminder, were written up in the LGBTQ press, which Emma Jones's founders and members were reading. Across the country, gay men and lesbians claimed their rights of citizenship by enacting patriotic rituals, a strategy deployed successfully by the civil rights movement.

The founders of the Emma Jones Society were part of the national claiming of rights for LGBTQ Americans, though not in the way one would expect. Indeed, activism on the Fourth of July was common in Florida through the late 1950s and into the early 1960s as civil rights organizations waded in to challenge segregated beaches.[50] On the beaches of Pensacola, Emma Jones's devotees were both gay/lesbian *and* American at the same time. Through the decision to hold the parties on the Fourth of July and to include all of the usual trappings of that celebration combined with the theme of the drag show, everything screamed patriotism. The decisions of the founders and those attending the parties showed patriotism and their place in America.

The fact that Emma Jones's events were parties instead of marches should not lessen the impact on raising the consciousness of attendees. As John Loughery and others argue, "community building could not be ignored while the political strategizing was under way."[51] Just as changing laws was necessary, so too was "the establishment of an attractive social atmosphere and constructive outlets for members and friends."[52] Partying does not always lead to thoughts about further political action, but sometimes it does. Loughery writes concerning San Francisco's Society for Individual Rights, "the task of enabling gay men and lesbians to feel more at ease with themselves—ultimately a political objective—was set in motion by the dances and other activities sponsored by the community center. The concrete benefits of that change were not immediately apparent, but they were none the less real." Though the results would be years in the making, the Hillyers and their Emma Jones parties were an essential component of making "The USA's Gay Riviera." On the beaches and at the drag shows, networks of friends and lovers were cemented, and they kept coming back year after year. They claimed their place on the sand and then invited more friends.

The founders sent out twenty-five invitations made by hand from "campy rearrangements of old magazine cut-outs" for the first gathering in 1966.[53] Nearly a hundred people showed up on the Pensacola beach. The party began at dusk with banners flying and bonfires blazing. Someone read a letter from "Miss Emma" that apologized for her absence but urged the attendees to have fun without her.[54] The next year, the invitations were more professional and featured Uncle Sam in heels, pearls, and earrings pouting, "We want you" on the cover and "In Pensacola for the Fourth of July" on the inside.[55] In 1968, 250 guests showed up for the party. In 1970 the invitation featured American icons: George Washington, wearing a pinky ring, in a warm embrace with Abraham Lincoln. The interior read:

It's the Age of Aquarius,
And to all those adventurous,
We shall meet again at last
On the sands for a blast.

George and Abe liked this time,
For it gave them reason and Rhyme.
You will need a car or a gondola;
So let's get together in Pensacola.

Attendance for that year had increased to six hundred. Though numbers are unreliable for the later years, reports indicate that in 1971 the attendance was such that the food service for the beach events alone took up six cabanas.[56] According to the *Advocate*, there were two thousand hot dogs cooked that year, and the convention attendance at the San Carlos Hotel was nearly the same.[57]

The first parties were discreet in that they were miles from the "family section," though they were never actually hidden. As can be seen from the photos, there were full-dress stage-set productions with banners, cabanas, and torches. The sand dunes concealed the beach from the road, but attendees were never in doubt about the party's location. According to Bob Shaw, an "enormous red hot dog bun—with a blue wiener sticking out" marked the site for the first year's party.[58] Another year guests found the location by looking for a pink truck parked beside the road.

By 1971 the parties had grown so large that the event morphed from simply a beach party into a full-scale convention in downtown Pensacola.

Figure 8. Setting up for the Emma Jones beach party. The image is likely from 1969, given its placement in the Hillyer scrapbook. In author's collection.

Some remember that the beach parties ended because "a combined force of military and local police came sniffing around," thereby causing the founders and others to "freak out."[59] Also, holding an event in a private space for which attendees purchased tickets meant they could be freer since the open beach made it difficult to monitor for trouble. Emma Jones was not about flaunting, and the semiprivate, or at least more tightly controlled, space of a hotel ballroom allowed for the practice of selected visibility.

After a trial run on New Year's Eve, the organizers booked the San Carlos Hotel and several other downtown hotels to capacity on July 4, 1971. That year marked the birth of the Red, Hot, and Blue Revue.[60] The San Carlos Hotel was, by this time, "a fading dowager" and welcomed the convention since the gay crowd tended to drink more and tip more than the family crowd, according to locals.[61] Benton Abbey of *Figaro,* a New Orleans–based newspaper, described the San Carlos as "every bit as obsolescent and faded Floridiana as it sounds" in his report of the weekend.[62] The Hillyers urged their friends and other attendees to stay at the San Carlos, and the income

Figure 9. Atlanta resident and drag personality Billy Jones was a frequent guest at the Emma Jones beach parties. His collection at the Atlanta History Center contains several images of him on the beach with friends. Here he is part of the annual show that became the Red, Hot, and Blue Review when the convention moved indoors. From Hillyer scrapbook, in author's collection.

for the weekend was estimated at $17,000 ($106,000 adjusted for inflation). The hotel was routinely listed in gay guidebooks as the place to stay, and the hotel's bar was the place to drink and cruise, so it seemed a natural choice. The hotel staff was certainly not unaccustomed to an "eclectic" clientele.

The weekend included a "Welcome Aboard Party" on Friday night at the Top of the Town Bar at the San Carlos, which as the name implies was on top of the hotel and overlooked the city. Saturday was a beach day with the action returning to the San Carlos in the evening where the Mr. US Gay Contest, full of "groovy boys on parade," was held. Saturday night and Sunday night were both given over to dancing at the Top of the Town as well as "Emma's July 4th Gayla" that included drag shows with annually changing themes.[63]

A notable feature of the Emma Jones parties and conventions was their interracial composition. Contemporary newspapers failed to comment on this, implying that by the middle of the 1970s it was de rigueur. However, an unidentified man quoted in Loughery's *Other Side of Silence* reminds readers, "In the south twenty-five years ago it did mean something."[64] In the *Advocate,* Bill Rushton called one of the drag performances "a minority-consciousness *tour de force*; a black drag affecting a New York Jewish accent, tap dancing and pretending to be an Indian."[65] In the Deep South, of which Pensacola is part, the early 1970s were not known for racial tolerance. Segregation was legally over, and the civil rights movement of the previous decades had gone a long way toward ending racial prejudice. The multiracial composition of Emma Jones's parties is another example of the ways that "she" challenged prevailing norms—queering the "Redneck Riviera."

The drag show was, of course, campy, a little risqué, and a lot outrageous every year. The indoor space of the San Carlos allowed for greater set design and range of performances than did the beach. The show for the first year was titled "Emma Jones' Tribute to the Golden West." It included renditions of *Oklahoma* and a Wild West rendition of *Swan Lake.* "The hunters were played by cowboys in flesh-colored tights and ankle-length, leather-fringed vests, hunters who chased ducks with shotguns instead of swans with arrows—ever so roughly following the original choreography."[66] In addition, "Miss Emma," played by a fifty-two-year-old woman wearing a blue dress, white fringe, mesh red stockings, blue boots, and a crown, mimed the words to "Indian Love Call" from atop a model Mt. Rushmore while a man in a gold-lamé Native American costume mimed the male part.[67]

The show for 1972 featured "Emma Jones' Salute to Broadway" in addition to a parody of World War II based around the theme song "Over There." It featured "sailors, and sailorettes [*sic*], and Marlene Dietrich and all."[68] By 1973 the show had expanded to three performances and included

Figure 10. Miss Emma and her love interest acting out "Indian Love Call" as part of the Red, Hot, and Blue Review. From Hillyer scrapbook, in author's collection.

a salute to Mardi Gras, with a full-scale parade. "Emma Jones Proudly Presents the United States of America" was the highlight of this season. It was an original drag opera sourced from *1776* and Stan Freberg's recording of *America*. Rushton called it "as political and biting as anything by Brecht and Weil." Unwilling to confine their political commentary to the status of gay and lesbian rights in the United States, the show included segments about the most recent political action at Wounded Knee, which began in February of that year and led to Marlon Brando's famous Academy Awards action.[69] The performance of "Indian Love Call" was part of the "Tribute to Wounded Knee."[70] This kind of intersectional activism is telling in this period and fits with the larger themes of citizenship, patriotism, and American-ness.

Shaw described the finale of each year's show: "A man dressed as the statue of liberty, his face and wig silvered and carrying a lighted torch, was pulled into the ballroom by four others dressed as sailors. As the statue began a slow pantomime to a Mary Martin recording of "America the Beautiful," cast members would come forward with flowers, kissing each bud as they handed it to the statue. Finally, the music switched to "God Bless

Figure 11. Bill Rushton describes this part of the 1973 Emma Jones show in his article for the *Advocate*: "The signing of the Declaration of Independence featured all the actors with their hair tied up in bows, dripping with lace and cruising the drawing room as if it were a bar." From Hillyer scrapbook, in author's collection.

Figure 12. This image from the 1973 Emma Jones review was described as "a composite minority-consciousness *tour de force*" in Rushton's January 15, 1975, *Advocate* article "Killing of Emma—III." It shows the interracial and multi-gendered composition of the cast, which was one of Emma Jones's progressive features. From Hillyer scrapbook, in author's collection.

Figure 13. Mardi Gras processional during the 1973 Emma Jones show. Ray and Henry Hillyer were involved in costume and other design work for parade "krewes" from Mobile and New Orleans. The indoor space of the San Carlos Hotel allowed for more complex performances, such as this indoor parade, than did the beach location. From Hillyer scrapbook, in author's collection.

America," and the statue, one at a time, kissed the flowers and threw them into the audience."[71] The emotional finale drew tears from many, and cheers from all in attendance. This show capped off the weekend and made it the premier event of the year. How better to end a weekend of Fourth of July celebrations that were explicitly designed to make patriotic assertions of rights, than with a drag queen and "God Bless America"?

Despite the emotional finale each year, the *Pensacola Journal* gave a rather neutral review of the show and the festivities. Despite the show's gay, lesbian, and queer attendance, the paper treated the gathering like any other convention, even saying that "delegations from as far away as California" were in attendance.[72] The placement of this article is telling. One could easily assume that the normally conservative paper had taken a step forward with the publication of a review of the Emma Jones Society parties. It even named the event as homosexual. However, the article appeared directly beneath a story titled "He Looks Back at His Liberation," which details the experiences of William Aaron, who had recently written

Figure 14. The finale of each year's Emma Jones Society convention featured the Statue of Liberty wheeled around the room, handing out roses. According to observers, it drew tears from many and a standing ovation from all. From Hillyer scrapbook, in author's collection.

a book titled *Straight: A Heterosexual Talks about His Homosexual Past*. The article reads like a book review and details the ways in which Aaron "overcame" his homosexuality. Though the piece lacks the violence normally associated with ex-gay therapy, the placement of these two articles was an attempt to assure readers that the paper was not condoning the homosexual shenanigans of the Emma Jones Society.

The Emma Jones parties garnered national attention in the gay press. The *Advocate* published stories about the weekend's festivities in their August issues of 1972 and 1973. According to the 1972 article, nearly three thousand gays from eight states were in attendance.[73] The different audiences meant that the *Advocate* story's author highlighted the campy displays on the "wide marble staircase, which was used by many convention participants to display a wild assortment of costumes seldom seen in this conservative city."[74] According to the author, there were so many gay men in the Hotel San Carlos that it came to be known as the "San Carlos 'Y'" for the weekend, a reference to the reputation for openness and free availability of sexual activity associated with the all-male environments of YMCA clubs across the United States. Attendance was down slightly in 1973, according to *Advocate*, which gives a figure of two thousand attendees for that year. Despite the fire that destroyed the Upstairs Lounge in New Orleans just the week before, the attendees were still "a happy, boisterous herd."[75] The drag show for the evening included a Mardi Gras theme, made all the more poignant because of the Upstairs "holocaust."[76]

At this time, the *Advocate* was still a weekly paper, though one with a national circulation. Over the following years, the publication became a magazine and was "desleazified" with most of the staff fired by self-described "practicing capitalist" David Goldstein.[77] By the 1990s the magazine was fully glossy and devoted to the "gay lifestyle."[78] As the magazine's new owners and editor sought to appeal to the more "upwardly mobile" gay man, coverage such as the 1975 articles by activist Rushton would be ever less likely. In the heady world of post-Stonewall political activism, at the very beginning of pink capitalism, coverage of Emma Jones's gatherings and the subsequent multi-issue coverage of "her" death was a big deal. The coverage devoted to the Emma Jones Society lends credence to Rushton's assertions that this was one of the largest gay-organized events in the country. Not until the early 1990s would Pensacola again make such a splash in the gay and lesbian press.

Toward a Liberation Economy

The party could not go on forever. The Emma Jones Society was very much a product of the times, and "her" discretion did not fit with the increasing commercialization and flaunting of gay identity that was sweeping the nation. Emma Jones's parties had inspired more than one gay bar in Pensacola, an example of the liberation economy. According to Burke Williams, who opened the Quiet Village, Pensacola's first gay bar, Emma Jones was the reason he came out: "Emma Jones brought me out of my closet.

There was a lot of gay activity here, but it was all on the streets. I brought it inside."[79] Williams refers to the extensive cruising and lack of dedicated gay spaces in Pensacola. There were beach gatherings and private house parties, but in keeping with post-Stonewall liberation and outness, Pensacola's sizeable gay and lesbian community lacked a dedicated space.

Scholar Jeffrey Escoffier calls this a "liberation economy," whereby gay men and lesbians' social institutions expanded beyond tolerant bars and mail-order businesses (closet economy) to bars and institutions that were "out" thanks to increased queer capital and purchasing power and decreasing official harassment in cities across the country.[80] The openness and visibility of gay men and lesbians was increasing year after year, and Pensacola was no different except in size. With the opening of a gay bar, and then another gay bar, and the attempt to open a massage parlor, gay men and lesbians were becoming more and more visible—or, in the words of Pensacola's mayor, "uppity."[81] White racists most often deployed this particularly charged term against black people who challenged segregation or otherwise upset race relations. Its use by a southern, moral entrepreneur in this time and place, to describe people starting to enjoy a place at the table, is telling. At a time when conservatives across the country were gearing up for a culture war, this dog-whistle phrase had the potential to unleash the full force of the coming "moral majority."

Bill Rushton called the Emma Jones parties "the largest gay-organized social gathering in the United States" in his *Advocate* article, though the claim is difficult to substantiate given the proliferation of "Christopher Street Day" or gay-pride celebrations happening in the early 1970s.[82] Soon after Williams opened the Quiet Village, Robert "Robbie" Llewellyn arrived from Atlanta to open the Yum Yum Tree. His bar sponsored and hosted commercial beach parties on Fourth of July weekends. Though they were not officially part of Emma Jones's celebrations, they contributed heavily to Jones's discontinuation because of increased publicity. Llewellyn also began advertising the "Mr. Gay USA Pageant" on radio stations across the Southeast. As other private and commercial events began "to cluster around the nonprofit, non-commercial skirts of Emma Jones," quiet accommodation of the gay and lesbian communities was pushed to breaking point.[83]

Across Florida, gay and lesbian visibility was on the rise. Just a decade after the demise of the Florida Legislative Investigation Committee, in cities as diverse as Miami, Tampa, Gainesville, and Tallahassee, gay men and lesbians made themselves known and pushed for equality in myriad ways. The South's first chapter of the Gay Liberation Front (GLF) was established in Tallahassee on the campus of Florida State University in 1970, to be followed by the People's Coalition for Gay Rights in 1974.[84] Students on other campuses also sought inclusion while gay and lesbian residents of Miami sought the legal protections that would result in the 1977 Anita Bryant "Save Our Children" campaign. Across the country, the sentiment that fed into the Bryant campaign helped cement individuals' identities into opposing imagined communities with gays and lesbians on one side and their opponents, conservative Christians, on the other. Nixon's "silent majority"—a reductive misnomer—was on the march against a variety of social issues, including abortion and women's rights. By the 1980s, policing various sexual bounds was firmly part of "family values" and would continue to spell trouble for LGBTQ Americans.

On the local level, the increased visibility did not sit well with Pensacola's elite and powerful, especially the recently chosen mayor, Barney B. Burks, who had only just appointed an inner-city task force to revitalize downtown and enhance the city's tourist appeal.[85] Beginning in May 1974, police began cracking down on the most visible sites of queer socialization in Pensacola. Mayor Burks claimed the city was "fast becoming a city with an immoral reputation." Police Sergeant Jack Odom echoed this sentiment when he told reporters, "Pensacola is fastly [*sic*] becoming known throughout the Southeastern section of the United States as being 'the gay city.'"[86] In their minds this held the potential to shatter the area's family-friendly reputation and drive away tourists. Pensacola was on the verge of moral panic.

In the first ten days of May 1974, police targeted Wayside Park and the Hotel San Carlos for raids that netted a total of seventeen men. The men were arrested and charged with vague "lewd and lascivious" acts as well as "soliciting for immoral purposes." Most of the men pled innocent with only four pleading guilty and accepting their fate to avoid a public trial.[87] After the arrests in May, the regional advertisements, and a local disc jockey's announcement that Pensacola was becoming a "gay capital," authorities turned their attention to Emma Jones's conventions. The police began the bulk of what was to be a major operation when they "learned that 3,000 people were expected to arrive here for an annual gay convention where 'Mr. Gay America' was to be named."[88] Sergeant Odom went on to say that the investigations would continue until the city was a "safe place for citizens to live in," a sentiment echoed by Mayor Burks.[89] The "stay in your place" rhetoric that came to dominate national conversations about gay and lesbian rights was strong in Pensacola.

Gay men were well established and enmeshed in Pensacola's business community. They largely controlled the economic activity of historic preservation at the start of the 1970s in areas such as North Hill. According to Bill Rushton, "House after house is occupied by middle-aged gay lovers from an established upper-middle income level of the Pensacola creative, professional, and business leadership."[90] There were significant business relationships between city leaders such as Pat Dodson, chairman of the inner-city task force and owner of a substantial portion of the downtown area to be "redeveloped" (gentrified), and the banks that financed the growth of the city's gay establishments. For instance, the bank where Dodson served on the board issued the mortgage for Robbie Llewellyn's Yum Yum Tree.[91] One of the sticking points for the mayor and the task force was Llewellyn's plan to open a massage parlor on the edge of the historic district. These historic districts were to be a vital part of Pensacola's continued evolution as a tourist destination. With four hundred years of history—and much like New Orleans, Mobile, and Charleston—Pensacola had a great deal of historical architecture to attract visitors. A gay massage parlor was not part of the vision and, though not the final straw, was certainly a contributing factor in the unqueering of Pensacola.

The deep ties, both personal and financial, between city leaders and gay-community leaders and the relative freedom given to gay and lesbian establishments until the early 1970s speak to the ways that policing the bounds of sexuality, specifically cracking down on visible sites of queer socialization, was about public image and heavily depended on who was in power. Quiet accommodation of the queer could occur until it threatened "The Sunshine State" and the money that was possible. As one anonymous cashier told Benton Abbey, "It's money, honey," when he asked for her thoughts on friends of Emma Jones taking over the city. That was true, to a point. Shaw found when he spoke to locals that "a number of residents, by no means all of them gay, believe that Caldwell's ambitions and Burks' political economics were the principal motives behind what happened."[92] Moral entrepreneurialism goes a long way in an election. This should be seen as part of the larger unqueering of the region and the country. The backlash against Pensacola's gay and lesbian happenings was part and parcel of larger trends and conservative discourses.

The *Advocate* reported, "During the summer of 1974 when all the police trouble and publicity began, delicate Miss Emma Jones suffered a terrible and ultimately irreversible seizure. . . . 'Emma Jones died in the streets of Pensacola on July 4, 1974.' She was 17."[93] Emma Jones's "death" reveals larger issues within the LGBTQ zeitgeist. While some activists were urging gay men and lesbians to come out and become part of organizations such as the Gay Liberation Front, other often older gays and lesbians were unwilling to make a stir. Having spent so long in their closets unable or reluctant to come out, they looked askance at the new openness. Even Emma's founders remained anonymous in the *Herald* and *Advocate* articles for fear of reprisals, and their friends remember that their sexuality was a closely guarded open secret in Pensacola until later in life.

The Hillyers and the other organizers had already canceled the official celebrations for fear of "bad vibrations," but nearly two thousand people showed up anyway. According to locals, "drag queens were cruising from downtown to the Yum Yum Tree on the beach . . . right through the heart of everything. . . . they had the top down and were making quite a spectacle."[94] On July 6 and 7, 1974, police raided the Yum Yum Tree, the Red Garter, and several other bars and arrested more than thirty people.

According to Pat Jennings in *Womanews,* "It started out like any other 4th of July. We were in Florida to have a good time." After dinner, the lesbian friend group decided to attend the Miss Universe drag-queen contests at the Red Garter. Just after the first contestant's talent portion, two young men approached their table and announced the group was under arrest. Jennings did not believe the young men until they produced badges. The six friends were loaded into a paddy wagon and taken to Escambia County Jail, where officers charged them with "lewd and lascivious acts," a charge which Jennings had to spell for the arresting officer. According to Jennings, the women suffered homophobic abuse at the jail. When one woman asked about the charges, officers placed her in solitary confinement—actually "a large chicken coop with a chair." Asked why she "didn't just get a man?" by the arresting officer, Jennings's reply of "For what?" was answered by "for a little sex? What else?" Jennings responded that she "would rather have someone competent." Her charges were amended to include disorderly conduct for this insult to the officer's manhood.[95]

After booking, the women spent the night in "the tank," so called because it is the large cell for multiple people, also referred to as the "drunk tank," where inebriated arrestees sober up. "Once there we flushed the toilet repeatedly and sang 'We shall overcome' with the 22 gay men who were arrested the same night and were in the tank next to ours."[96] The choice of song was not accidental. It harkens back to other southern jails filled with people arrested during the civil rights movement just a decade before and is an explicit appeal to the ideals of that movement. The common refrain would have undoubtedly been familiar to the arresting officers and certainly contributed to the "uppity" label applied by city leaders.

This moment of solidarity is telling. There was a growing divide between gay men and lesbians, and in many parts of the country they socialized separately. One of the consequences of the liberation economy was the further division of the community into separate worlds. Though the response to the AIDS crisis went a long way toward bridging the gap, solidarity across identities was not a given. The Emma Jones parties and conventions were gender integrated as well as racially integrated, and the drag shows made explicit comment on current events, such as the occupation of Wounded Knee. The solidarity fostered by the events surrounding Emma Jones, as well as the display of queer power, make the society incredibly important in the LGBTQ history of the United States.

In response to the arrests and overall harassment of gay and lesbian establishments and events, locals came together to form the Southeast Activists Alliance (SAA). Bob Ragin (owner of the Red Garter), Burke Williams, and Robbie Llewellyn were all elected cochairs of the alliance. The group of activists—some local, others not—assisted with legal defense, coordinated bail, and worked with city officials.[97] There is no record of the SAA as the 1970s wore on, and it is likely that the group fell apart when legal troubles and infighting ran Llewellyn out of town. Some reports indicate that the alliance never paid the attorney's fees for the women arrested, so it may have simply fallen apart because it was so hastily put together and lacked organization.[98] However, it is clear that the networks established by Emma's parties, and the visibility she fostered, laid the groundwork for the alliance.

Authorities accomplished their mission of driving out the LGBTQ community in Pensacola. "The gay community went underground, and gays were afraid to come to Pensacola for several years." When asked if the crackdown on gays and lesbians worked, one of the women arrested at the Red Garter told reporter M.G., "I don't know, but we're never going back to find out."[99] At least for some, the unqueering had the desired effect. The Emma Jones Society was never about flaunting, but that is just what her weekend had turned into. The discreet celebrations of Emma Jones gave way to the commercialized flaunting of sexuality that ultimately led to her death. The situation was apparently so dire that, when Rushton interviewed the founders for his 1975 articles, he reported that "fearing subpoenas or firebombs, Emma's friends have packed their library of old invitations and letters, their mailing lists, and other items off to safe refuge in another state."[100]

Emma's parties had a profound impact on queer people in the South. As John Loughery writes: "Innumerable friendships had been made, an example of gay economic clout was established, and an exuberant gay presence had asserted itself on the Florida Panhandle that, whatever the setbacks ahead, would never disappear entirely."[101] In addition to the ephemeral notion of "pride" or "consciousness," there were more concrete results from the Emma Jones Society gatherings. Beyond politics, there were cultural implications for Emma Jones's time in Pensacola. Drag queens, actors, and technicians rehearsed for three to four months for the one show. Many of them went on to stage other shows for the larger public. Some went on to travel the South training other professionals and recruiting new talent to Pensacola. Financially, the worth is incalculable, "but four bars, a magazine, an entertainment production company, a bath house, an increased volume of commercial transactions between gay business people, and a gathering sense of gay pride can be cited on the surface."[102]

The human connection is the organization's most significant contribution because ultimately that is what Emma Jones was about. She was "you, me, and every other faggot in here," all sharing the weekend as gays and lesbians.[103] She was men, women, and all of the colors of the rainbow. Ray, Henry, the other founders, everyone who attended the parties, and everyone who worked so hard to put on the events brought people together. The Hillyers went on to personal success as both were involved with the Little Theatre and designed floats and costumes for the Festival of Five Flags. Ray worked for the St. Regis Paper Company and Henry for Gayfers Department Store. Henry became increasingly politically active as the years wore on and became involved in organizations such as Appetite for Life, which provides meals and nutrition for those living with HIV/AIDS and other disabilities. They felt a deep love for and sense of commitment to LGBTQ people in the region. Their stately home in the quiet neighborhood was always open, some even joking that it became a "home for wayward boys" when homophobic families threw them out of their homes. Both men died within a year of each other, Ray in 2010 and Henry in 2011.[104]

For at least one man and his family, Emma Jones made the world a better place:

> The old man, perhaps the oldest Gay to attend the convention, was ever so carefully escorted to his front row seat each year before the performance would be permitted to begin. "He enjoyed it more than anyone else and looked forward to the Fourth of July like no other time of the year—even Christmas." The old man died this past year also, and his niece, aware of what Emma Jones' Convention had meant to her childless uncle's twilight years, set pen to a letter thanking Emma's friends for extending and embroidering the last days of his life. He was from a generation of gay men who had lost forever the years of freedom younger Gays now fight for, but he had not been sitting out on the front row merely as a spectator. He had felt keenly his sense of participation in the emerging currents of change, she said, and he was full of hope. His niece was grateful; he had spoken of Emma Jones once again shortly before he died, and she said she thought that was something about which his other survivors ought to know.[105]

Emma Jones brought people together, giving them a sense of community and empowerment at a time when the larger public was mobilized against them. For at least one weekend out of the year, men and women could be together and they could be gay. They deployed their bodies in the emerging currents of change to say, "We are here."

6

FROM REDNECK TO GAY RIVIERA

There's a lot to see and do all along the Gay Gulf Coast, and there's not a better time to do it than summer when the area swarms with attractive guys, both locals and visitors. If you get a chance, you should join them.

—RICHARD KAVANAUGH, 1977

In 1965, around the same time that Ray and Henry started hosting beach parties, a few gay men in Panama City came together and opened a bar called the Fiesta Room Lounge.[1] It was in a small and unassuming space with a darkened glass door that opened onto Harrison Avenue, Panama City's main street at the time. Until it closed in 2014, it was located just two blocks from the site of the infamous downtown public restroom. It was not a strictly liberation-economy gay bar—owned by and operated for a predominantly gay clientele—when it first opened. Rather, according to Tom Baker, its customer base at first consisted of a few gay men huddled nervously in a corner. The bar therefore straddles the closet and liberation economies. After an altercation in 1968 between "queens hitting with everything they could find" and the fishermen who patronized the Bayshore Bar across the patio, the bar became definitively gay in the sense that it was gay owned and operated and dedicated to giving gay men, lesbians, and their friends a place to socialize freely.[2]

Throughout the years of its existence, the bar has served a diverse clientele. As with most towns that had only one gay bar, the crowd was multiracial and multi-gendered. As time progressed and more and more tourists ventured to the Gulf Coast, the Fiesta Room Lounge became an attraction for gay tourists when their vacations took them to the Gulf Coast. The proliferation of LGBTQ print media in the 1970s opened spaces in which the region's bars and other offerings could advertise. This, in turn, meant that gay and lesbian southerners, who were already present among the ranks of the automobile tourists streaming onto the beaches every summer, could find a place to socialize *as* gay men and lesbians. Over the remainder of the twentieth century, these gay and lesbians tourists and locals crafted a "Gay Gulf Coast" that became "The USA's Gay Riviera" thanks to LGBTQ market forces.

The Gay Gulf Coast

The Fiesta compound was made up of two brick buildings, both built early in the twentieth century. The structures shared a patio that faced Harrison Avenue and were connected in the rear by storerooms and offices. Before 1975 the two bars operated separately with one side called the Fiesta Room Lounge (mostly gay) and the other called the Bayshore Bar (definitively heteronormative). As business at the Bayshore declined, due in part to the decline of commercial fishing from Panama City's marina, the owners renovated and made both sides part of the same complex. The building formerly occupied by the Bayshore Bar became La Royale Lounge and Package Store. A renovation of the patio that connects the two spaces made both bars part of the same gay complex by 1977. Over the years, locals and visitors began to refer to the entire complex simply as the Fiesta, even though each bar had its own sign and different opening hours.

The relationship between the Fiesta and the larger community of Bay County over the last fifty years has been, at times, fraught with conflict. The bar's owners grew tired of replacing the front windows, which were smashed by bricks or shot out, so they simply covered the spaces with painted wood.[3] In one instance, the owners supplied police with the license-plate number of a truck whose occupants shot out the windows. When the officers later tracked down the vehicle, the drivers admitted to shooting the window. The police sent them on their way. That is but one of many incidents demonstrating the lack of police protection for the Fiesta Room Lounge.[4]

Just as the Emma Jones Society began to host parties on the beaches of Pensacola, the opening of the Fiesta represented a shift in the ways that gay men and lesbians could socialize on the Panhandle. In addition

Figure 15. The Fiesta Room Lounge, *left,* and La Royale Lounge and Package Store, *right,* as they appeared in the middle of the 1970s. The patio between the two buildings allowed customers to go from one to the other, making it one big gay-and-lesbian bar. Both closed in 2014 after the death of owner Bubba Gilbert. "La Royale Lounge and Package on Harrison Ave. in Panama City," 1970s, color slide. Courtesy of Florida Memory, State Archives of Florida.

to private house parties, or reliance on the possibility of meeting other queer folks in a "straight" bar such as Trader Jon's or the Cypress Lounge, the Fiesta Room gave those with some degree of outness a place to socialize *as* out gay men and lesbians, though initially within certain limits.[5] In this space, men and women did not have to rely on backward glances or the dropping of hairpins to determine another's sexuality. It did not preclude the other forms of sex(uality)-based networking along the Panhandle. Rather, it opened an entirely new way to socialize commensurate with national trends in identity politics in conjunction with other forms of queer socialization.

Every year, more and more tourists and migrants journeyed to the Gulf Coast for their holidays, drawn by the promises of "The Sunshine State" and the affordability of a beach vacation. As with every wave of tourists, some of these visitors were gay, lesbian, or otherwise queer. The Fiesta's renovations and expansions coincided with the increasing numbers of gay and lesbian visitors and locals. At certain times the owners wondered if they would be able to fill the newly enlarged space. If you build it, they will come. And come they did. Just as the "Redneck Riviera" transitioned into the "Gulf Coast" or the "Emerald Coast," over the course of the 1970s, it was also becoming the "Gay Gulf Coast."

Initially, only rumors and innuendos guided homosexually inclined people to the inconspicuous door at the end of Harrison Avenue. However, by the middle 1970s, certain southern gay publications took notice of the bar and other gay and lesbian happenings on the Gulf Coast. Because *ONE*, the *Ladder*, and the *Mattachine Review* opened the door to gay and lesbian publications through various legal challenges against censorship, other publications aimed at gay men and lesbians increased in number throughout the 1960s and 1970s, a trend that continues today, though online resources have replaced many print publications. In addition to the national LGBTQ press, local magazines appeared in cities across the United States. These magazines were locally or regionally based and funded by advertisements. They kept residents and visitors apprised of their respective local scenes. In addition to local information, magazines often featured stories that dealt with travel and highlighted nearby areas. These travel features were distinct from previous list publications in that they focused on visible social institutions rather than "relatively safe" bars.

Some of the area's clandestine queer offerings were well known by the middle of the 1960s thanks in part to Bob Damron, Gordon Wilkinson, and publications such as *ONE*. They publicized certain places along the Gulf Coast, should one happen to find oneself there; however, it was not until southern gay and lesbian publications and presses proliferated that the discourse changed to one of LGBTQ tourist destination—the "Gay Gulf Coast." The reputation as a gay and lesbian destination presaged discussions of the "pink dollar" later in the century and was helped along by Emma Jones and her network of gays and lesbians across the South and the country. While publications based in the South showcased the area's activities beyond cruising and bars, they constructed an image of the "Gay Gulf Coast" as a tourist destination in the minds of landlocked southern gays, especially in cities like Atlanta and Birmingham.[6]

For a time in the early 1970s, Tallahassee shared the LGBTQ spotlight with Pensacola. According to historian Rictor Norton, who did his doctoral work at Florida State University, the Cypress Lounge became progressively "out" during his time in Tallahassee. He left in 1974, but Norton remembers the Cypress Lounge as a "long-established typical 'hotel bar' used by local men, mainly married men, to pick up trade." By the time he left Tallahassee, it "had go-go boys dancing there on weekends."[7] This represents a remarkable shift from just a decade before. What was once a clandestine spot where power brokers rubbed elbows with queer men had become a very gay bar.

As the 1960s drew to a close, gays and lesbians were becoming increasingly politicized across the country, including the Panhandle. In December 1970, *David* magazine, based in Atlanta, listed the Tallahassee chapter of the Gay Liberation Front (GLF) as "Red Boar Tavern, Floridan Hotel." The Red Boar Tavern became Tallahassee's next unofficial gay bar after the Cypress Lounge. Norton remembers that the Cypress faded over the years and the young student crowd tended to patronize the Red Boar. Norton recalls that it was an easy place; the students felt comfortable dancing together, and the owner made it available for nonprofit groups.

The Red Boar Tavern was an ideal place for Rictor Norton and Judy Fee to hold meetings of Tallahassee's GLF chapter since they were not allowed on campus. According to Norton, the tavern was not at the Floridan, and it is likely that the Atlanta-based magazine was merely mistaken. Hiram Ruiz, Judy Fee, Rictor Norton, and a man called "Malcolm" were the driving force behind the GLF on the campus of Florida State University.[8] Though other GLF chapters desired to radically transform society, Norton calls their chapter "assimilationist" in that they mainly promoted "equality and fairness and the idea that society need not fear the homosexual."[9] However, according to interviews conducted by historian Jessica Clawson, Ruiz remembers the organization very differently.[10] Ruiz spearheaded the first chapter of the GLF in the South, at Florida State University, after attending a GLF meeting in Los Angeles. The FSU student senate recognized the group on May 5, 1970, but the university refused to allow the use of its facilities.[11]

In addition, Norton was instrumental in organizing and teaching two courses in the student-controlled "free university" system. One was simply called "Homosexuality" and dealt with social and political issues of concern to homosexually identified students. The other was called "The

Homosexual Literary Tradition" and dealt with homosexuals throughout literature. This latter course caught the attention of the National Council of Teachers of English, who asked Norton to guest-edit an entire issue, published in 1974, devoted to homosexual literature and teaching.[12]

According to Clawson, the GLF faced an almost immediate backlash from the university and the surrounding community after placing an advertisement for GLF meetings. The university went so far as to threaten the student paper, the *Flambeau,* with closure for the ads. Because of their solidarity with other marginalized student groups such as the Tallahassee Women's Liberation and the Malcolm X United Liberation Front, local chapters of those groups came out in support. At the same time, national expressions of solidarity and actual instances of solidarity were more complex than those in Tallahassee.[13] Though the GLF folded soon after its beginnings, all was not lost. FSU hesitantly approved the People's Coalition for Gay Rights (PCGR) in 1974.

Tallahassee has boasted a number of gay bars, and even a "secret lesbian bar described with the alias 'Whispers'" over the years. The owners of Whispers would not give their names or the location of the bar to the *Flambeau* reporter, and they charged a cover to protect it as a safe space for local lesbian or queer women.[14] None of the bars remained open long-term. Some blame high overhead while others blame the transient population exacerbated by the ever-shifting student populations of Florida State University and Florida A&M University. City of Night, Club Park Avenue, Billy's Bar, and Brothers have been the most memorable, according to several longtime residents.[15] Though Tallahassee continues to be the state capital and is home to universities, museums, and other cultural institutions, it is increasingly distant from the tourism and tourists of the rest of the Panhandle and receded from the "Gay Gulf Coast" over the last quarter of the twentieth century.

In 1976 a new magazine that catered to gay men and lesbians appeared on the scene in Atlanta as the liberation economy began giving way to the "territorial economy" of gay neighborhoods.[16] *Cruise: The Entertainment Guide to Gay Atlanta* promised to "provide an up-to-date guide to all of those bars, restaurants, lounges, discos, baths, cinemas, bookstores and other places of entertainment that welcome the gay crowd."[17] In recognition of the explosive growth in the number of businesses and events that catered to lesbians and gay men in the city, the publishers put out a weekly social calendar in addition to the monthly magazine. Because of the expanded networks, the publishers realized the need for a publication that covered LGBTQ happenings throughout the South. At certain times the guide to gay Atlanta became *Cruise: The Guide to Gay Entertainment in the South.*

In 1977, the year Anita Bryant urged Americans to "save our children," reporter Richard Kavanaugh and photographer Bob Swinden set out on a tour of the Gay Gulf Coast. The grand gay tour took Kavanaugh and Swinden from Tallahassee to New Orleans with stops in Panama City, Pensacola, and Biloxi, Mississippi. Kavanaugh was impressed with the Gay Gulf Coast. He wrote, "The area between Tallahassee, Florida on the east, and New Orleans on the west is always fun, but during the summer the beaches become the place to go for summer vacations, weekends or just a day off if you live close enough."[18] Just as non-gay southerners chose the Gulf Coast for its proximity and ease of travel, gay and lesbian southerners increasingly did also, illustrating the success of "The Sunshine State." The article's title proclaimed, "It's Hot! Hot! Hot! This Summer on the Gay Gulf Coast."

In 1977, Tallahassee boasted two gay bars: the Panhandle Mining Company and the Foxtrot. The Cypress Lounge did not make the list, a fact that is telling in the post-Stonewall era. Men still cruised at the Cypress Lounge and the Greyhound bus station. Because of the shift in focus to a liberation economy based on identity politics and outness as well as a decrease in municipal harassment of gay establishments, gay and lesbian places were safer. This should not obscure the myriad ways that queer men and women continued to find each other to form relationships and networks, though like the Fiesta Room it does illustrate the transition from closet to liberation economy in the Panhandle.

The Fiesta Room Lounge featured prominently in coverage of the "Gay Gulf Coast." In addition to the fun that one could have at the Fiesta at night, Panama City Beach offered lots of activities on or near the sand. One could rent boats, ski, play golf, swim, or simply soak up the sun on the sugar-white beach. At night the action moved inland to the Fiesta. It was around this time that the bar expanded and added a stage for dancing. Though mostly collegiate-aged men populated the bar, Kavanaugh makes the point that, "as in any town with only one gay bar, you'll find a few people of all types."[19]

By the middle of the 1970s, other bars dedicated to gays and lesbians had sprung up along the coast, with even Fort Walton having a bar called the Lobby that attracted a "mixed crowd" because of its location.[20] Pensacola was the most prominent of Florida's cities on the "Gay Gulf Coast," with four bars: the Red Garter, the Quiet Village, the Aquarian, and the Fiesta at the San Carlos Hotel. Though gay men remember the Fiesta as a very cruisy bar, it is not necessarily a "gay bar" in the same way that the other bars were. The Fiesta and the San Carlos Hotel, because of their association with the Fourth of July conventions thrown by the Emma Jones Society, certainly qualify for a mention in a gay guide. The Aquarian catered to a mostly female crowd, making it the only lesbian bar on the "Gay Gulf Coast" at the time. As in other cities across the country, as gay men and lesbians increased in number and visibility, the communities could support multiple bars and the groups drifted apart. If one judges "gay community" by the number of gay establishments, then it is clear that Pensacola was the gayest city along the "Gay Gulf Coast."

The military remained a contributing factor in the growth of Pensacola's gay and lesbian scenes. Both the Fiesta at the San Carlos Hotel and the Red Carpet (a "straight place") were popular with sailors and hustlers. It is likely that gay and lesbian sailors populated the other bars, including Trader Jon's; their presence only seemed worth mentioning concerning cruising at the Fiesta and the Red Carpet.[21] Kavanaugh, Rushton, and Shaw wrote their articles in the middle of the 1970s, and all three made explicit mention of the military's impact on local gay and lesbian life. The influx of gay and lesbian soldiers continues to this day.

As a result of the publicity and word-of-mouth advertising that endeared the Gulf Coast to southerners generally, a direct consequence of the policies and practices of selling "The Sunshine State," Panama City and the entire coastal area held a special place in the hearts of gay and lesbian southerners.[22] Robert Bosch, a gay resident of Atlanta, remembered: "all of gay Atlanta went to Panama City when they wanted to go to the beach."[23] Atlanta residents made up a significant percentage of the condo and vacation-home ownership in Panama City, and a great many Atlantans, both queer and not, made Panama City their vacation destination of choice. According to another gay Atlanta resident, local gays chose Panama City as a vacation spot over other coastal areas partly for the ease of travel, partly for the beautiful beaches, and of course partly for the gay nightlife.[24] The writer of the *Cruise* article, Richard Kavanaugh, believed that the sentiment was held throughout the South as well and that the area attracted folks from all over the region. He wrote, "guys and gals from Georgia and other southeastern states head for the Florida beaches."[25]

In the same way that print media and word-of-mouth advertising in conjunction with local business, municipal boosters, and the state government created and sold the Gulf Coast as a tourist destination, the gay media, along with gay and lesbian southerners and locals, created and sold the idea of the "Gay Gulf Coast." As gay men and lesbians around the country were participating in more visible identity-based social institutions, they sought to replicate these along the Gulf Coast. Though unlike the policies and practices of selling "The Sunshine State," which were built on exclusion, the "Gay Gulf Coast" was built on inclusion. As gay men and lesbians populated the beaches, bars, and nightclubs of America's major and minor cities, so too did these southern queer people create a destination that was much like the world they had back at home.

Though Emma Jones's parties were no more, beach parties and gay and lesbian events did not stop. Locals simply moved the party elsewhere because of the friendship networks established in years prior. Ft. Walton Beach became the host for Memorial Day festivities while gays and lesbians celebrated Labor Day on Pensacola Beach. The Fourth of July alternated between the two. Though the events did not attract the same numbers as in the early 1970s, men and women from the surrounding states came to the beach. The Coldwater Creek Cocktail Cruise held over Labor Day weekend became Pensacola's premier gay event. Another Pensacola couple, Tyler and Thornton, started the event to compete with Ray and Henry, and it included brunch and a canoe trip. Kurt Young remembers one particularly festive year when his partner made his entire costume from green lamé. The canoe trips and other parties kept gay men and lesbians coming to the region, where they quietly inhabited beaches with little fuss.

The Gulf Coast's gay reputation continued to grow over the last quarter of the twentieth century, and so too did the parties. From the first gatherings on the sand, the Memorial Day events grew. Like the Emma Jones parties, they spread into town. Stories conflict about how Memorial Day was chosen. According to reporter Jessica Forbes in her article "Queer and Here: The Long History of Gay Tourists on Pensacola Beach," some people think the party started when a couple invited friends from Atlanta for the weekend while others say it began when different locals invited friends from South Florida.[26] A friend of the Hillyers stated that it was they who brought the crowds back. Gay men and lesbians came for vacation just as did so many other families and friend groups. Bars began to capitalize, and then promoters from other cities such as New Orleans made the weekend into a circuit party. The undeveloped Gulf Islands National Seashore, Emma's old stomping grounds, was a perfect spot for gay men and lesbians to gather.

A Battleground in America's Culture Wars

A contentious relationship between gay and lesbian residents and tourists as well as the communities they inhabited or visited marked the remainder of the century. As the liberation economy opened spaces for social activities and gave clear indication of the economic impact of gay and lesbian tourists, the country was in the throes of a moral panic. Anita Bryant had convinced people to "save the children" in 1977, and Ronald Reagan was elected president in 1980. AIDS devastated gay communities across the country, and the "moral majority" sought to roll back protections for women and a variety of minorities.

In 1986, the building that housed La Royale's side of the Fiesta bar complex in Panama City was severely damaged by fire.[27] After fire crews extinguished the flames, architects and structural engineers surveyed the building and declared it structurally sound. However, city officials disagreed over the structure's soundness. Despite agreements to the contrary, the city pushed one of the walls over, away from the street, and destroyed virtually everything within the bar except the cash register. Upon witnessing the destruction, patrons of the bars gathered in the back parking lot to weep and mourn the loss of their community space.[28]

Locals remember this event as an attempt to erase the gay bar, and newspaper coverage indicates they may have been onto something. Despite extensive coverage in the local papers, there is not a single mention of the kind of bar it was. Reporters give the history of the building but never once mention it was a gay bar. Most everyone knew what the bar was, so it was perhaps not necessary. By focusing on the history of the building and its historical significance, then maybe the rhetoric of God's judgment by fire that was so likely to appear in the letters to the editor could be avoided.

Within days, local gay men and lesbians began coming together in a literal community-building exercise to salvage the bricks to rebuild La Royale. In a rare instance of cooperation, the bar was rebuilt with the help of local gays and lesbians, the Bay County Historical Society, and a variety of other community partners interested in saving the city's oldest brick building.[29] The Fiesta side of the complex reopened within weeks because it suffered only minor smoke damage. La Royale remained closed for nearly a year until bricks of a sufficient age could be found to replace those that were damaged. The new building lacked the original upper floor but was entirely made from reclaimed bricks.

Though the patrons changed over the fifty years of the bar's life, the decor changed very little since the fire. That is what gave the Fiesta Room and La Royale their charm. The bar in the Fiesta Room looked just as it did when Kavanaugh conducted his grand gay tour.[30] Over the years the owners enlarged the room to include a dance floor, which also doubled as a stage for the bar's drag performers.

In the early 1990s, the issue of LGBTQ visibility, spending power, and tourism's contributions to the region's economy came to the fore once again, this time in Pensacola. Again there was pushback from Pensacola city officials as queer folks got "uppity." Scholar Steven F. Philipp points out the increasing visibility brought about by nationally televised events such as the "1993 Gay and Lesbian March on Washington" and "1994 Gay Games and Stonewall International March on the United Nations."[31] This was also a peak moment in what came to be called the "culture wars"; as scholar Anthony J. Stanonis finds concerning other southern beach towns, "economics depended on fostering a religious aura," and moral entrepreneurs were ready to reap the benefits from publicly pushing back against LGBTQ events.[32]

The focus on Pensacola was especially acute in the early 1990s because of two murders. In 1991 Jack Braun was killed on the beach below "The Chimney," a beach-access spot on Escambia Bay that had long been a cruising ground for local men. Braun was not gay but liked to stop at the beach to unwind after work, according to friends and family. Three young men bludgeoned him and were apprehended later because one bragged to his girlfriend, "I got me a fag." The murder raised the specter of gay visibility in Pensacola. Some claimed that Pensacola had always been home to divergent lifestyles and "a live and let live beach and nautical community that rubbed elbows with the Deep South" while others claimed that gay men were "always targets of hatred and suspicion by teenagers, fundamentalist Christians, employers, and the police."[33] Bob E., chairman of the West Florida Gay Pride Committee, and Reverend Lee Carlton, pastor of the Holy Cross Metropolitan Community Church, both echoed the sentiment that there was a sizeable gay and lesbian population which was not extremely public.[34] Two years later, an antiabortion terrorist murdered Dr. David Gunn. These events propelled the city to national prominence as pundits, politicians, and others fretted over "clinic terrorism" on the one hand and a general liberal attack on conservative morality on the other.[35]

In 1993, *Out* magazine and various other gay and lesbian publications named Pensacola as one of America's top ten gay and lesbian beaches and called the city "gay-friendly." In February of that year, the *Pensacola News-Journal* reported on the growing violence against gay men and lesbians across the world in light of discussions to end the U.S. military's ban on openly gay service personnel. The men interviewed echoed the gay-friendly sentiment but did not want to be identified. They were afraid for the larger community of what might be unleashed in the coming months, given the military's importance to the region and the uptick in homophobic violence on American military bases internationally.[36] They saw the war and attack rhetoric of the "culture wars" growing more and more heated and leading to increased physical violence.

In May 1993, Steve Hatch opened a pride store in the downtown section called Just For Us. He was also instrumental in changing the regulations that prevented businesses from flying the rainbow flag. According to Hatch, the city classified the flag as a banner. Strict rules governed the display of banners in the historic district, though flags were allowed. Hatch spoke with manufacturers and even a federal office to officially classify the rainbow as a flag. Hatch's tenacity paved the way for other businesses to show their support for LGBTQ visitors by flying the official pride flag.[37]

In the run up to Memorial Day Weekend (May 29–31) that year, WEAR-TV, a local station, carried a story that explored the history of gay and lesbian tourists to the area, specifically as they related to the upcoming holiday weekend. It named Pensacola the "gay Riviera."[38] Moral entrepreneur and city councilman Doug Proffitt—a name that could not be more perfect for this story—wrote a letter on city stationery to the television station rebuking the assertions made. He added, "All God-loving people in the world are unfriendly to this very small group of people."[39] The councilman feared the city becoming another San Francisco, which in his mind was the "object of jokes around the world."[40] The mayor later appeared in national news outlets supporting the councilman's position.[41] "This community has been branded, what with the abortion demonstrations and this latest thing. We are not gay-friendly, or a gay haven or any other such term. We are tolerant, but we are a family-oriented city. We are not a sexually oriented community—no matter what kind."[42] The stage was set for a summer of controversy.

The *Pensacola News-Journal* weighed in with an editorial in its May 24, 1993, edition. "Proffitt, Mayor out of line," conveyed disappointment in the councilman and the mayor and expressed gratitude that enough people disagreed with their inappropriate remarks. The editors ask, "What's the problem? Gays in large numbers have been coming to Pensacola for years, and hardly anyone noticed." They go on to point out that the ones who have noticed were the many businesses who depend on the variety of conventions, gatherings, and holiday-weekend traffic for their livelihood. They closed the editorial by reiterating that gay and lesbian locals and tourists had coexisted for years without fuss, and "if that makes Pensacola 'gay-friendly,' so what? We like to consider Pensacola people friendly, period."[43] This response is markedly different from 1973 and speaks not simply to the recognition of buying power, but a more tolerant "live and let live" attitude adopted by many.

Local response was swift and polarized. Reading the letters to the editors through May, June, and July, one is struck—though not necessarily surprised given the town of 65,000 had 450 churches—by the amount of vitriol draped in the Bible. The linking of AIDS with being gay or lesbian was common, as was the injunction for Pensacola to repent. Many letters did both, as was the case with Janelle Popp: "Why don't more people realize that accepting this behavior encourages the spread of AIDS and ruined lives? May our country never become like Sodom, which God engulfed with destruction."[44] Many others simply expressed support for Proffitt's statement and were glad that he was taking a stand. One letter writer identified his religious affiliation "as somewhere between 'Bible thumpers' and the amoral," and echoed "silent majority" rhetoric in his support for Proffitt's stance and ability to speak out for what he called the majority's values.[45]

Andy Anderson, publisher of LGBTQ magazine *Christopher Street South*

Quarterly and president of Christopher Street South, Inc., weighed in on the controversy with her own letter to the editor published on Saturday during the Memorial Day festivities that year. She reiterates that the stretch of beach had been well known since the early 1970s, though I assert that the Emma Jones beach parties pull that date back to the middle of the 1960s. Anderson cites national marketing studies about the pink dollar and the variety of companies that were starting to court it. She ends her letter with the words: "Grow up! We won't go away."[46]

By the early 1990s, it was easier to make that statement. People were coming out across the country, and another march on Washington occurred in 1993. Absolut Vodka had been advertising specifically to the LGBTQ market for over a decade by then. A host of other companies were advertising to the gay and lesbian market. Many high-quality, glossy magazines devoted to gay and lesbian "lifestyles" were on the shelves. Some of these, such as *Advocate,* were focused nationally while others were more local, such as incarnations of *David* in most major American cities. National advertisers projected images of gay and lesbian consumers, and gave a grossly overstated sense of their importance. It seemed that "the gays" were indeed everywhere. Yet, according to a number of contemporary theorists, many of those consumers mistook representation for acceptance or as a sign of validation and legitimation and were surprised at the conservative backlash.[47]

Thanks to the Associated Press, newspapers across the country and even in Canada reported on the controversy in Pensacola throughout 1993 and 1994. The most in-depth coverage came in southern papers, the *Atlanta Journal-Constitution,* the *Sun-Sentinel* in Ft. Lauderdale, the *Orlando Sentinel,* and the *Palm Beach Post.*[48] LGBTQ-focused publications such as the *Stonewall News* also carried parts of the AP story.[49] Some wondered how the tourist industry would fare. Would the area suffer from the negative publicity? Others, such as Stephen Handelman of the *Toronto Star,* predicted that the "holy war" between Christian fundamentalist/reconstructionist terrorists and the civilized world would get much worse before it died down.[50] In 2017 it is hard not to see Handelman's statement as prescient, given the number of atrocities committed by white nationalists in this country.

Many authors asked why the gay and lesbian tourists were such a problem after gathering for decades without incident on Memorial Day, the

Fourth of July, and Labor Day. On the other side, the reconstructionists who sought a return to an imagined past of moral purity were joined in their espousing of conservative Christian morality by more moderate voices in the culture wars. Skirmishes flared throughout the 1990s. In 1992 Vice President Dan Quayle used an episode of the television show *Murphy Brown* to wade into the family-values conversation. President Clinton promised to end the ban on openly gay and lesbian service members, but by the time Clinton's idea became policy, the military could not ask, and service members could not tell. Nineteen ninety-three was also the year that the first combination therapies to treat AIDS were tested across the country. The twenty-four-hour news cycle meant that people were virtually surrounded by discourses of cultural change. The world they thought they knew was not the world the news media told them they lived in. Many conservative moralists were convinced that the End Times were upon them as society seemingly broke down around them.

On the local level, a number of Pensacola residents were experiencing a religious revival. The "March for Jesus" began in 1991 in Austin, Texas, and the first march in Pensacola was in 1992. It drew over two thousand locals to march through downtown with banners that indicated their support, love, obedience to, and desire for America's return to Jesus. Though attendance declined markedly for the 1993 march, likely due to rain, the movement and its message appeared in the newspaper, on local billboards, and on church marquees around the area.[51] In response to the murder of Dr. Gunn in March, the National Organization for Women (NOW) organized a march in Pensacola on May 9, 1993, to be titled "We won't back down—Stand up for Justice."[52] Given the daily messages that "American values" were under attack, it is unsurprising that the councilman and the mayor acted the way they did and that parts of the citizenry of Pensacola responded the way they did. As the rhetoric of war increased, so too did the violence.

Local gay men were nervous about the forces unleashed. They were right to be nervous. According to an article in the *News-Journal,* Memorial Day 1993 festivities started with roofing nails scattered about the parking area of "the gay beach." Though it was reported that only two tires lost air, the message was clear since the nails showed up across only the three miles of beach used by LGBTQ visitors. Park rangers refused to speculate on the target publicly, saying only "you read into that what you will." Atlanta resident and frequent Pensacola tourist Jim Little was less equivocal with the reporter: "I think [it] was definitely caused by that [Proffitt's] statement."[53] The mayor once again backed the councilman and expressed sympathy for the victims, unable—or, more likely, unwilling—to see a connection between the words of his friend and the action of others. No, the councilman probably never directed anyone to scatter nails, but saying that "all God-fearing people are unfriendly to this very small group of people,"[54] he might as well have.

Steve Hatch, owner of Just For Us, had what he believed to be the perfect response to Proffitt and his ilk. According to Hatch, he "ran down to the printer" and had the words "Welcome To Pensacola, the USA's Gay Riveria [*sic*]" printed on items as diverse as T-shirts, bumper stickers, and maps.[55] In the *Christopher Street South Quarterly* for February 1993, Andy Anderson wrote that Pensacola is "now known around the world. Thank you, Mr. Proffitt, we couldn't have done it without you."[56] Over the next several years, Pensacola became known as the very thing Proffitt feared: the Gay Riviera.

Despite the negative coverage in the press, or perhaps because of it, the Memorial Day events drew increased numbers of gay and lesbian tourists from all over the Southeast. According to Tanya Dewhurst and Hannah Thompson's story in *Our World*, the festivities grew in solidarity with locals.[57] Andy Anderson estimated that, for the 1993 weekend, attendance was 37,000. Local Liz Watkins remembered, "by 1994 we talked about crowds of 20 to 30 thousand."[58] Philipp's study on the weekend estimated that, in 1994, 27,000 gay men and lesbians visited the beach just on the Saturday of that Memorial Day weekend, making it one of the largest LGBTQ events in the South and the biggest tourism event in the region. The study showed that 89 percent of those surveyed were from the surrounding southern states.

Just how much money did LGBTQ tourists bring to the area's economy? Christopher Street South, the local gay and lesbian organization, estimated that LGBTQ travelers and locals paid $25 million into the region's economy every year. Philipp's study and subsequent article estimated that, over Memorial Day Weekend of 1994, LGBTQ tourists spent $18.7 million dollars. In 1993, the Associated Press carried stories of "gay money" circulating in Pensacola. An unnamed bar—likely the Office—and more than a few locals started stamping their money with "Gay Money." Andy Anderson in the February 1994 issue of *Christopher Street South Quarterly* urged readers who wanted to pay by check or credit card to indicate that they were gay travelers and carry on the tradition. According to Anderson, this would provide visible proof that gay and lesbian tourists had an enormous impact on the economy.

Steve Hatch sold those "gay money" stamps at his pride store. According to Hatch, FBI agents visited him in connection with an investigation of the stamped money, but as he pointed out to the officers, it was not illegal to sell the stamps, and he had never personally stamped any money. The investigation was dropped.[59] The stamped money provided a visual cue to the amount of LGBTQ money circulating through the economy. The legacy of the action lives on. The annual LGBTQ film festival held in October is named "Stamped" in honor of the act, linking visibility with representation on film.[60]

The act of marking "gay money" with stamps purchased at a pride store in the downtown historic district illustrates the fundamental shifts in the larger queer political economy of the Panhandle. The commercialized flaunting of gay capital contributed to Emma Jones's murder in the 1970s, when larger political forces could not be mobilized. In the 1990s a few "near-sighted newly elected officials and their inability to have insight into the future without instilling hate and bigotry" still debated over which was more important, "the religious right or cold cash in the merchant's pockets."[61] The winner was very different from 1974. Gays and lesbians in Pensacola leveraged their market share to demand a seat at the table.

Capitalism needs markets, and consumption is an essential right of citizenship in capitalist countries. American "freedom" is the freedom to consume, and minority-rights movements often make explicit appeals to this freedom. Access to money is access to power in our system, and Americans used spending power long before the term "boycott" entered the lexicon. Increasingly over the final decades of twentieth century, LGBTQ Americans asserted their rights to citizenship, and they flexed their financial muscles. This newfound power relied partly on a number of studies that cited the gay and lesbian market as a vast storehouse of disposable income. The myth of gay affluence, though problematic in its erasure of economically marginalized queers, provided a boost in the political power of gays and lesbians. In addition, national identity-based rights organizations such as the Human Rights Campaign (HRC) and the Gay and

Lesbian Alliance Against Defamation (GLAAD) urged gays and lesbians to spend wisely. The respectable gay tourists awash in pink dollars used their buying power or their potential buying power to ask for a seat at the table. The politics of respectability and gentrified thinking, which sought to distance the sex from the sexuality, especially during the AIDS crisis, was embodied by the marketing concept of "lifestyles."

The coming-out events and the visibility of respectable gays and lesbians that were "just like everyone else" disrupted previous webs of facticity about gays and lesbians. The "common sense" knowledge of homosexuals as deviants, perverts, and child molesters began to give way to a less devious and pathological set of imaginaries. Gay men and lesbians came out and routinely adopted conformity in exchange for participation in the privileges of class and sex.[62] This confluence of forces at the end of the twentieth century allowed gays and lesbians in Pensacola to marshal a public response to the conservative Christian right. They possessed the critical mass of bodies and dollars, and they deployed them. Thanks to Steve Hatch, those bodies could be decked out with rainbow merchandise and carrying maps/guides that were emblazoned with "Welcome to Pensacola: The USA's Gay Riveria." It was all the more funny because Hatch's misspelling stuck and became something of a campy joke.

Though publications and other media across the country practiced a respectability politics that sought to publicly distance gay life from gay sex, the sleaze was never very far from the party. In 1994 an author who pseudonymously called himself Randy Mann wrote an article for *Steam* entitled "Pensacola, Florida and nearby Gulp [*sic*] Coast Playgrounds."[63] The article covered the coastal cities from Panama City to Mobile, Alabama, and described the cruising and other sexually based opportunities for tourists and locals along the coast. *Steam* was published in San Francisco on a quarterly basis and distributed via mail order around the United States. Its tagline read: "A Quarterly Journal for Men," explicitly dedicated to "sex—all kinds of sex, but especially public, publicly disapproved, *exciting* sex."[64] The author claimed short-term residence in Panama City and, during that time, he developed a system to determine a man's availability for sexual activity: "if a young man is (1) hitchhiking at 3 a.m., (2) shirtless, and (3) barefoot, he generally is available." According to Mann, he "tested this theory diligently, and it is just plain weird how well it holds up."[65]

Further along from Panama City and Fort Walton, a desolate stretch of State Road 399 that runs along the beach is what Mann called "the least-known but probably most cum-drenched gay beach in the US."[66] He went on to write that "On the Gulf Side, you will meet guys from all over (but mostly from the surrounding states); on the dunes side, get ready to meet the dick of your dreams because it's probably in there somewhere."[67] Mann's inclusion of "mostly from surrounding states" shows that, just as in years before, southerners (and especially gay southerners) continued to populate the beaches of North Florida. His anecdotal evidence, based on personal experience, echoes the narratives of other sources.

Thanks to the Emma Jones Society and the beach parties held regularly in Pensacola, the holiday weekends of Memorial Day, the Fourth of July, and Labor Day were memorable experiences for many gay men and lesbians (though Mann only wrote about men). According to Mann, "you will find thousands upon thousands of guys out there during the day—but make absolutely sure, even if you never cruise another scene in your LIFE to come back to this location at night. . . . by some strange quirk of nature, men and boys have found their way to this beach for those nocturnal sojourns year after year after year, without any interference from 'outside' sources."[68] It was not a quirk of nature; it was place claiming. For thirty years men and women had journeyed to that beach for Emma Jones and then to gather with friends. Through so many photographs and word-of-mouth recollections passed along to friends, gay men and lesbians had inscribed this stretch of beach as a queer destination.

Looking beyond the search for sex, Mann affirms the appeal of Pensacola more broadly. He writes: "The Festival city of Pensacola, with 200,000 residents, has several positive things going for it: a very good bar scene, outstanding gay-owned and operated restaurants and business . . . a large Navy base, a large Air Force community, thousands of horny tourists, and a law enforcement attitude of 'hands off the gay tourists because they pump $$$ into the economy.' All of these factors combine to produce a unique and colorful time for the gay traveler in search of the perfect cock."[69] As Pensacola drew more and more tourists and residents, it drew ever-increasing numbers of gay men and lesbians. Pensacola had something for everyone. For those wishing to partake in the outness of a "gay community" of bars and restaurants, those were on offer. For those searching for different kinds of connections, Pensacola and the surrounding beaches provided those as well.

Our Pride Memorial Day festivities in 1994 produced less controversy in the press but more violence in the streets. Over the course of that weekend, someone threw eggs at cars near the beach and the Office bar's street party near downtown. Also, homophobes vandalized at least one car by slashing its convertible top and smashing its windows. The most frightening incidents occurred on the final night of the festivities. Someone fired a single shot into the window of the Pensacola Grand Hotel across the street from the Office, and someone called in a bomb threat to the bar. According to police reports, the unknown caller made the call from a local payphone and told the club: "you better close the Office gay bar in thirty minutes, or I will blow it sky high."[70] These incidents were a direct result of the escalating violence in the larger culture war.

The 1995 coverage of Our Pride's Memorial Day festivities in the *Pensacola News-Journal* was far more positive than in years previous. The front page of the Sunday edition proclaimed that "Pensacola's Shores Beckon Gays." According to reporter Winnie Hu, gay and lesbian tourists ventured to the beaches in "greater numbers than ever in the two years since some city officials pulled in the welcome mat." In interviews, Hu invited several individuals to speculate on the increase in numbers. Jim Goldman, president of the White Heat AIDS foundation, stated, "Word just got out two years ago (about) how many people are here, and once it got a reputation, then everybody wants to be here." Billy Kolber, the editor of a gay and lesbian travel newsletter in New York, told Hu that the controversy only stirred more interest in Pensacola.

In 1993 local bars threw the only dance and street parties. However, by 1995, club promoters from around the country rented spaces around the city for large circuit parties. Pensacola's parties had grown to the third largest event for White Party promoter Jeffrey Sanker, president of Los Angeles–based J. S. Enterprises. C&J Productions out of New Orleans and Steve Berman Productions out of Atlanta both rented spaces for parties that numbered in the thousands. Nineteen ninety-five was also the first year for a lesbian party, "Shore Leave," which filled the Bayfront Auditorium. Pensacola was on the "circuit" of gay nightlife by the middle of the 1990s, and party promoters wasted no time in capitalizing on the weekend.

Others reported drastic changes in Pensacola in the two years since Proffitt's letter. Hu's article occupies the entire second page of the paper. Trish Johnson, a first-time visitor and resident of Toccoa, Georgia, told

Hu, "I'm from a very conservative town. I feel at ease here, and I can be myself." Other attendees compared Pensacola with the beaches eastward along the coast in Panama City. Steve Bragg of Atlanta told Hu, "We always get to show off our gay paraphernalia. In Panama City, you get people calling you names."[71]

The height of the Memorial Day festivities was, according to some, from 2001 to 2004, before Hurricane Ivan devastated parts of downtown Pensacola. According to Ted McCrary, manager of Emerald City, competition with "Gay Days" at Walt Disney World in addition to the damage caused by Hurricane Ivan were the primary reasons that numbers dropped off after 2004: "People were starting to have to decide if they were going to one or the other."[72] Once again increased competition hurt the local tourist economy. However, this time it was gay men and lesbians choosing to go elsewhere; they became an ever-larger niche market rather than being forced out.

In the early days of North Florida's joining "The Sunshine State" and adopting its strategies, politicians, business owners, and local boosters fretted over reputation. In the 1990s they still worried over reputation although, by the final decade of the twentieth century, cooler heads prevailed. In a 1994 editorial, the *Pensacola News-Journal* asked: "At a time when there seem to be more questions than ever about our image to the nation and what it takes to attract tourists and new businesses, maybe the reality is more reflected by what's happening this weekend—our tourism facilities are maxed out."[73] The thing that everyone feared did not happen. It seemed that nothing could keep people away from the beach. Other editorials, letters to the editor, and articles about tourism challenged people to see the area's reputation as multifaceted as opposed to fractured. Unlike the prophets of doom from earlier decades, the loudest voices in the 1990s reminded people that Pensacola and the larger Gulf Coast had many things going for them and that negative publicity, such as that which surrounded gays and lesbians, or abortion, was unlikely to have much of an effect—a profound attitude shift from previous years and a direct result of increasing LGBTQ visibility.

EPILOGUE

We cannot simply say that this is a resort area and such things are bound to happen. . . . If we are to keep our beaches attractive for tourist families, we must discourage, through strict law enforcement and strong penalties, such disgraceful occurrences.

—EDITORIAL, *PANAMA CITY NEWS*, JULY 31, 1961

It got out of hand, and I believe it stopped some good people from coming here. I think it reached the point where we were killing ourselves. Our image was being hurt so badly.

—LIZETTE ALVAREZ, "SCALED BACK SPRING BREAK COSTS FLORIDA TOWN," *NEW YORK TIMES*, MARCH 22, 2016

Fifty-five years separate two opinions by a newspaper editor and a mayoral candidate in Bay County Florida. Yet both express the same fear: "bad tourists" with their "bad behavior" are bad for business because they will scare away "good tourists" with "good behavior" who are good for business. Growing up in Panama City in the 1980s and 1990s, I saw this conversation rehashed yearly in the halls of government and the pages of the local newspaper as tens of thousands of college students descended on the beaches for spring break. Every year the drunken antics of this creature—the spring breaker—caused momentary outrage. Every year some business owners and residents shook their heads at the thought of Panama City Beach's reputation and the countless families that were afraid to come to the area because of the spring breaker. For others, however, it was their Christmas season, that time when the account books go from red to black. To my young mind, it seemed as though construction continued unabated and traffic to the beach only ever got worse. If tourists were so scared to come to Panama City Beach because of the spring breaker, it sure did not seem like it. The crusades were never really about protecting tourism, though; they were about attracting and keeping the chimerical "right" tourist.

Though not the first time that young people on spring holidays were the focus of "wholesomeness" campaigns, the "spring breaker"—imagined as white, male, drunk, reckless, horny, and dangerous—was the bogeyman that scared local politicians into passing anti-alcohol ordinances in 2015. After two decades of college-aged spring breakers and their alcohol-fueled heterosexual antics shocking the sensibilities of upstanding locals—yet officially tolerated because of the revenue—spring break died. Hospitality workers took to the streets on Friday March 11, 2016, to protest the extreme loss of earning. The beaches were finally quiet enough to satisfy some, but they were certainly not profitable.[1] Maybe now the mythical moneyed clientele that has supposedly stayed away will come to the beach.

In 1961, 1974, and 1993 "the homosexual" and more broadly queer shenanigans were the bogeyman that would supposedly scare away tourists. The knowledge of homosexual activity was not new information in any of those instances, though the will to not know was strong. The suddenness with which homosexual behavior became a problem speaks to the ways that managing the perceptions of outsiders was the primary cause of moral panic. As the century ended, gay and lesbian visitors marshaled their market share to push back against moral panics. They may not have won, but when the other side wants to erase your existence, détente can feel like winning.

Just as the revelation of homosexual shenanigans did not kill the tourist industry in the 1960s, or the 1970s, or the 1990s, and the shenanigans of spring breakers did not kill tourism in the 2000s, the loss of spring-break season will not kill tourism in Panama City Beach. It will, however, produce a different landscape. Businesses that once depended on those intense ten weeks, with a fresh crop of youngsters every week, will shutter. Maybe this time the publicity around "cleaning up" the beach just might finally attract the "right" tourists—if anyone can figure out what that is. If the last seventy years are any indication, there is no right tourist. Everyone who wants to come to the beach will come to the beach, though fewer and fewer can afford to come to the beaches of the rebranded "Emerald Coast." Hurricanes and capitalism will continue to plow under the old and make room for the new.

Writing this in the summer of 2017, I am struck by how much the world has changed for gay and lesbian folks along the Gulf Coast. At the national level, equal marriage is now the law of the land. ABC Television broadcast the miniseries *When We Rise,* the problematic story of West Coast activism as told through Cleve Jones. Two new colors have been added to the Pride flag, and there are continued protests over the place of corporations and police forces in Pride parades. Some positive changes have been made, and yet there is still a very long way to go. As the old proverb says, we certainly live in interesting times.

This book has taken a journey through North Florida tourism in an effort to begin restoring gays and lesbians to the region's history. Despite the best efforts to unqueer the region and drive the LGBTQ folks away, we kept coming to the beach. In the 1990s there was even talk of opening a gay and lesbian destination resort on the Gulf Coast—something unimaginable just years before. When gay entrepreneur Steven Dunlap and a business partner were turned down for the financing for a gay business, they realized that others across the country also likely struggled to finance gay and lesbian businesses. Their solution was G&L Bank, headquartered in Pensacola and dedicated to gay and lesbian customers. On October 11, 1999, the bank opened, conducting its business primarily online. As of November 15 the bank had received four hateful emails and one ninety-minute protest by three picketers. According to Dunlap, "they got their five minutes in the news to push their message. We haven't seen them since."[2] Unfortunately the bank was short-lived and closed in 2002, along with so many other niche-market Internet banks.[3]

Activist organizations have come and gone, just as bars have. Pensacola continues to be the queer hub for the region even as LGBTQ folks assimilate into the wider culture. Gay Grassroots was founded in 2008 in response to Florida's marriage amendment and has hosted Pride festivals and a variety of other activist-training and community-building events. The organization and its cofounder Doug Landreth have been instrumental in getting youth involved by helping organize Gay-Straight Alliances (GSAs) at area high schools. They have also conducted training sessions for a variety of groups interested in promoting diversity and equality.[4]

Pink or rainbow capitalism is once again in the news. Increasing numbers of activists question what exactly is being done when a burrito chain sponsors a float in the Pride parade or a national department store sponsors a line of #takepride merchandise.[5] Queer people, especially those of color or nonbinary gender expressions, are most likely to be victimized. Are they helped in tangible ways by a Facebook profile filter? In the absence of federal nondiscrimination legislation, corporations have instituted nondiscrimination policies. Yet some of these same corporations' investment portfolios are appalling. Many are calling for a return to the spirit of protest that marked the first Pride celebrations. Others are offended that people would protest Pride and block the parade.[6] The coming years, as the left pitches further towards the left or atomizes over these and other questions, will likely produce further ruptures in LGBTQ+ identities.

I hope this little chip of a book has shown that there is plenty of room in "The Sunshine State." Whether on the sand or the back roads, queer folks have made this part of Florida their home. They've been an essential part of making North Florida the colorful tapestry that it is today. They lived, they laughed, they cried, and they loved. They queered the Redneck Riviera.

NOTES

Introduction

1. J.R., letter to *ONE* magazine, March 25, 1963, ONE Editorial Correspondence, 1956–1965, box 46, folder 29, ONE National Gay and Lesbian Archives, Los Angeles. The writer's name is illegible beyond the initials "J.R."

2. Stacy Braukman, *Communists and Perverts Under the Palms: The Johns Committee in Florida, 1956–1965* (Gainesville: University Press of Florida, 2012).

3. "Report on discussion at a meeting on problems of homosexuality in Florida," January 22, 1962, FLIC Records, ser. 1486, carton 1, folder 11, p. 9.

4. Harvey H. Jackson III, *The Rise and Decline of the Redneck Riviera: An Insider's History of the Florida-Alabama Coast* (Athens: University of Georgia Press, 2012), 2.

5. Norman S. Hayner, "Hotel Life and Personality," *American Journal of Sociology* 33, no. 5 (1928): 784–95.

6. Robert D. Shaw Jr., "The Discreet Lovers of Emma Jones," *Miami Herald, Tropic* supplement, March 16, 1975.

7. Jackson, *Rise and Decline of the Redneck Riviera,* 65.

8. "Redneck," *Oxford English Dictionary,* www.oed.com.proxy.wm.edu/view/Entry/160404?redirectedFrom=Redneck#eid (accessed June 26, 2017).

9. Jeffrey Escoffier, "The Political Economy of the Closet: Notes Toward an Economic History of Gay and Lesbian Life Before Stonewall," in *Homo Economics: Capitalism, Community, and Lesbian and Gay Life,* ed. Amy Gluckman and Betsy Reed (New York: Routledge, 1997), 123–34.

10. Carol Mason, *Oklahomo: Lessons in Unqueering America* (Albany: State University of New York Press, 2015).

11. John D'Emilio, "Capitalism and Gay Identity," in *Making Trouble: Essays on Gay History, Politics, and the University* (New York: Routledge, 1992), 3–16.

12. John Howard, ed., *Carryin' On in the Lesbian and Gay South* (New York: New York University Press, 1997); Howard, *Men Like That: A Southern Queer History* (Chicago: University of Chicago Press, 1999).

13. D'Emilio, "Capitalism and Gay Identity." Margot Canaday, *The Straight State: Sexuality and Citizenship in Twentieth-Century America* (Princeton, N.J.: Princeton University Press, 2009). David K. Johnson, *The Lavender Scare: The Cold War Persecution of Gays and Lesbians in the Federal Government* (Chicago: University of Chicago Press, 2004).

14. Escoffier, "Political Economy of the Closet," 123.

15. Howard, *Men Like That,* 78–124. See also John Howard, "Place and Movement in

Gay American History: A Case from the Post–World War II South," in *Creating a Place for Ourselves: Lesbian, Gay, and Bisexual Community Histories*, ed. Brett Beemyn (New York: Rutledge, 1997, 211–26.

16. David Harvey, *The Urban Experience* (Oxford, U.K.: Basil Blackwell, 1989), 83.

17. "Report on discussion at the meeting on problems of homosexuality in Florida," January 22, 1962, FLIC Records, ser. 1486, carton 1, folder 11, p. 3.

18. Gary R. Mormino, *Land of Sunshine, State of Dreams: A Social History of Modern Florida* (Gainesville: University Press of Florida, 2005), 1.

19. Braukman, *Communists and Perverts*. Judith G. Poucher, *State of Defiance: Challenging the Johns Committee's Assault on Civil Liberties* (Gainesville: University Press of Florida, 2014). James A. Schnur, "Closet Crusaders: The Johns Committee and Homophobia, 1956–1965," in *Carryin' on in the Lesbian and Gay South*, ed. Howard, 132–63.

20. Braukman, *Communists and Perverts*, 71.

21. Matt Houlbrook, *Queer London: Perils and Pleasures in the Sexual Metropolis, 1918–1957* (Chicago: University of Chicago Press, 2006), 5.

22. John Howard set out this strategy in *Men Like That* (307–8), and I believed it necessary here as well.

Chapter 1. Selling "The Sunshine State"

Epigraph source: "Selling the Florida Story," *All Florida Magazine*, October 6, 1957, *Panama City News-Herald*.

1. Mormino, *Land of Sunshine, State of Dreams*, 150.

2. Alistair Cook, *One Man's America* (New York: Knopf, 1952), quoted in Anthony J. Stanonis, *Faith in Bikinis: Politics and Leisure in the Coastal South Since the Civil War* (Athens: University of Georgia Press, 2014), 162.

3. Jackson, *Rise and Decline of the Redneck Riviera*, 13.

4. Phil Tiemeyer, *Plane Queer: Labor, Sexuality, and AIDS in the History of Male Flight Attendants* (Berkeley: University of California Press, 2013), 73–74. Fred Fejes, "Murder, Perversion, and Moral Panic: The 1954 Media Campaign Against Miami's Homosexuals and the Discourse of Civic Betterment," *Journal of the History of Sexuality* 9, no. 3 (July 2000): 305–47.

5. Stanonis, *Faith in Bikinis*, 133.

6. Ibid.

7. Jackson, *Rise and Decline of the Redneck Riviera*, 68. Beach access showcased the absurdity of racial segregation since whites and African Americans shared the same water (sometimes within a few yards of each other), yet black beachgoers could not cross the imaginary line in the sand.

8. Stanonis, *Faith in Bikinis*, 125.

9. "Warren Urges Continuous Drive for Tourists," *Panama City News-Herald*, October 21, 1954.

10. "Down to Earth Answers to Searching Questions about Florida's Tourist Advertising," Florida Development Commission, folder "Tourism 1940s–1950s," Pensacola Historical Society.

11. Jackson, *Rise and Decline of the Redneck Riviera*, 76.

12. Harvey, *The Urban Experience*, 83.

13. Mormino, *Land of Sunshine, State of Dreams,* 6.

14. Mayor Vince Whibbs Sr., Pensacola's longest-serving mayor, popularized the phrase during his term in the 1970s. Heather Carroll, "Pensacola: City of Five . . . nicknames" blog post on visitpensacola.com, June 9, 2016.

15. Jackson, *Rise and Decline of the Redneck Riviera,* 2. See also Mormino, *Land of Sunshine, State of Dreams.*

16. Jason Henderson, "Secessionist Automobility: Racism, Anti-Urbanism, and the Politics of Automobility in Atlanta, Georgia," *International Journal of Urban and Regional Research* 30, no. 2 (June 2006): 293–307.

17. "Eighth and Moving Up," *Panama City News,* October 31, 1961, 4.

18. Ford Cook, "Florida Makes Sure Travelers Are Welcome," *Mobile Press-Register*, September 11, 1965, folder "Tourism 1960s–1970s," Pensacola Historical Society.

19. Ibid., September 11, 1966, folder "Pensacola Tourism, 1960s–1970s," Pensacola Historical Society.

20. Ibid., September 11, 1965, folder "Tourism 1960s 1970s," Pensacola Historical Society.

21. F. Elgin Bayless to Sanderford Jarman, October 4, 1946, folder "Tourism 1940s–1950s," Pensacola Historical Society.

22. Cook, "Travelers Are Welcome."

23. "Welcome Station Opens," *Pensacola Journal*, February 22, 1954, folder "Tourism 1940s–1950s," Pensacola Historical Society.

24. Betty Parker, "At New York Show, Pensacola Girl to Tell of State," *Pensacola News*, February 26, 1955, folder "Tourism 1940s–1950s," Pensacola Historical Society.

25. James Brock and Gerri Reeves, "Signing the Sunshine State Or, The Prophylactic Guide to a Safe Miami," *Studies in Popular Culture* 20, no. 1 (October 1997): 1–28.

26. Ruby Parker, "City Housekeeping to Attract Tourists," April 16, 1961, folder "Tourism 1960s–1970s," Pensacola Historical Society.

27. "Great White Way," *Panama City Herald*, April 5, 1962, 4.

28. Jackson, *Rise and Decline of the Redneck Riviera,* 79.

29. Stanonis, *Faith in Bikinis,* 86.

30. Olan C. Volner, "Letter to Editor: Those Pesky Skeeters," *Panama City News-Herald,* April 26, 1962, 4.

31.Earle Bowden, "Gulf Beaches: Discovery Pays Off," folder "Tourism 1960s–1970s," Pensacola Historical Society.

32. Tim Hollis, *Florida's Miracle Strip: From Redneck Riviera to Emerald Coast* (Jackson: University Press of Mississippi, 2004); Jackson, *Rise and Decline of the Redneck Riviera.*

33. William Gober Jr., "Crime Must Go; Courtesy Must Be Polished," *Panama City News-Herald*, May 28, 1950, 10.

34. Andrew R. Broun, "Spot for Winter Vacation," *Panama City Herald,* March 2, 1962, 4.

35. "City Favorite Visiting Spot of Army Unit," *Panama City Herald*, May 2, 1956, 1.

36. *Bay Biz,* Autumn 1994, Local History Room, Bay County Public Library, Panama City.

37. "Over 3,000 Visitors View Local Exhibit in New York," *Panama City Herald*, March 23, 1962, 1.

38. "Caravan Takes Off," *Panama City News-Herald*, March 31, 1968, newspaper clipping, Bay County Local History Room, Bay County Public Library.

39. "Sign of Our Growth," *Panama City News*, March 13, 1962, 4.

40. Braukman, *Communists and Perverts*, 25.

41. "Brighter Day for Panama City," *Panama City Herald*, October 18, 1961, 4.

42. W. J. Hughes to Judge Earnest Mason, December 13, 1948, Mason Collection, box 10, folder 11, Special Collections, John C. Pace Library, University of West Florida, Pensacola.

43. Kevin M. Kruse, *One Nation Under God: How Corporate America Invented Christian America* (New York: Basic Books, 2015).

44. John T. Carlton, "Crime Prober Calls Public Hearings in Miami July 13–14," *Miami Sunday News*, July 2, 1950, 1. Associated Press stories carried nationally dating back to 1949 link Miami with national crime.

45. Mormino, *Land of Sunshine, State of Dreams*, 278.

46. William Gober Jr., "Crime Must Go; Courtesy Must Be Polished," *Panama City News-Herald*, May 28, 1950, 10.

47. Ibid.

48. Ibid.

49. Fejes, "Murder, Perversion, and Moral Panic."

50. Gober, "Crime Must Go," 10.

51. J.R., Letter to ONE, Inc., March 25, 1963, ONE Editorial Correspondence, 1956–1965, box 46, folder 29.

52. Allen Morris, "Probing Crime in Florida," *Panama City News-Herald*, July 23, 1950, 4.

53. "Report on discussion at meeting on problems of homosexuality in Florida," January 22, 1962, FLIC Records, ser. 1486, carton 1, folder 11, p. 9.

54. "Distasteful Medicine," *Panama City News*, April 25, 1962, 4.

55. Braukman, *Communists and Perverts*, 22.

56. "The 'Lid' Is On: Gambling Hits Virtual Standstill in Florida," *Panama City News*, February 24, 1950.

57. "Warren Insists He's Trying to Curb Gambling: Calls on People to Aid in Fight on Organized Crime," *Panama City News-Herald*, June 11, 1950, 1A.

58. Braukman, *Communists and Perverts*, 4.

59. Ibid., 2.

60. Ibid., 3.

61. Ibid., 12.

Chapter 2. Queer Circulation and the Economics of a Moral Panic

1. Jackson, *Rise and Decline of the Redneck Riviera*.

2. "Retiring in June," *Panama City News-Herald*, May 22, 1975, 4A. "Obituary," *Panama City News-Herald*, May 4, 1988, 8A.

3. John Howard, "The Library, the Park, and the Pervert: Public Space and Homosexual Encounter in Post–World War II Atlanta," in *Carryin' On in the Lesbian and Gay South*, ed. Howard, 107–31.

4. Gayle S. Rubin, "Thinking Sex: Notes for a Radical Theory of the Politics of Sexuality," in *Culture, Society and Sexuality*, ed. Richard Parker and Peter Aggleton (New York: Routledge, 1999), 143–78.

5. Stuart Lavietes, "C. Farris Bryant, 87, Governor of Florida at Turning Point," *New York Times*, "Obituaries," March 6, 2002.

6. "Ex-Detective Led Exposé That Won Pulitzer Prize: Reporter on 3-Man Crusading Team; Conspiracy Trial Soon," *Editor & Publisher*, May 12, 1962, 11, 78, Local History Room, Bay County Public Library.

7. Jackson, *Rise and Decline of the Redneck Riviera*, 47.

8. Ibid., 11.

9. Tom Baker, interview by author, July 9, 2011.

10. "Courageous Action," *Panama City Herald*, May 13, 1961, 4.

11. Duke Newcome, "Sheriff's Department Rolls Up Perfect Score," *Panama City Herald*, August 22, 1961, 1.

12. Duke Newcome, "City Court Tries Suspects of Local Prostitution Rings," *Panama City Herald*, August 15, 1961. "10th Person Arrested in Prostitution Ring," *Panama City News*, August 11, 1961. "Cabbie Found Guilty in Prostitution Case," *Panama City News*, August 15, 1961. "Shine Dealers Hit By Raid," *Panama City News*, April 7, 1962.

13. This information was gathered from multiple interviews, correspondence, and telephone conversations with Tom Baker throughout the course of this project.

14. Tom Baker, letter to author, February 22, 2011.

15. Duke Newcome, "Homosexual Ring Rounded Up by City, County, State Officials," *Panama City Herald*, October 5, 1961, 1.

16. Ibid., October 6, 1961, 1.

17. "Let's Finish The Job," *Panama City News-Herald*, October 8, 1961, 4.

18. "Airman Given 10 Days in 'Pick Up' Try," *Panama City News*, August 15, 1961, 2.

19. Newcome, "Homosexual Ring."

20. Fejes, "Murder, Perversion, and Moral Panic," 305–47.

21. Dave Moylan, "Exposition, Convention Begin Simultaneously," *Panama City News*, October 10, 1961, 1.

22. FLIC Records, ser. 1486, carton 9, folder 27, p. 4.

23. Ibid., folder 26, p. 18.

24. Tom Baker, letter to author, February 22, 2011. See also Howard, "The Library, the Park, and the Pervert."

25. Laud Humphreys, *Tearoom Trade: Impersonal Sex in Public Places* (New York: Aldine, 1975).

26. Tom Baker, letter to author, February 22, 2011.

27. Laud Humphreys offers the best description of the way men's restrooms were typically constructed and the organization of them. Lee Edelman offers an analysis of restroom construction by linking the restroom's layout to broader discourses of cleanliness and male display in his "Men's Room" in *Stud: Architectures of Masculinity*, ed. Joel Sanders (New York: Princeton Architectural Press, 1996), 152–61.

28. Tom Baker, letter to author, February 22, 2011.

29. Humphreys, *Tearoom Trade*, 104–30.

30. Newcome, "Homosexual Ring."

31. Tom Baker, interview by author, July 19, 2011.

32. Newcome, "Homosexual Ring." "Police Make 21st Arrest in Sex Case," *Panama City Herald*, October 9, 1961, 1. "22nd Suspect Charged Here In Sex Cases," *Panama City Herald*, October 12, 1961, 1.

33. Howard, "The Library, the Park, and the Pervert," 112–13.

34. John Howard, "Southern Sodomy; or, What the Coppers Saw," in *Southern Masculinity: Perspectives on Manhood in the South Since Reconstruction,* ed. Craig Thompson Friend (Athens: University of Georgia Press, 2009), 196–218.

35. FLIC Records, ser. 1486, carton 9, folder 28, p. 4.

36. Mark W. Turner, *Backward Glances: Cruising the Queer Streets of New York and London* (London: Reaktion Books, 2003), 35.

37. Howard, *Men Like That*; "The Library, the Park, and the Pervert"; "Southern Sodomy." See also Brock Thompson, *The Un-Natural State: Arkansas and the Queer South* (Fayetteville: University of Arkansas Press, 2010).

38. "Eighth, and Moving Up," *Panama City News*, October 31, 1961, 4.

39. FLIC Records, ser. 1486, carton 9, folder 27, p. 4.

40. Hayner, "Hotel Life and Personality," 784–95.

41. Eric G. E. Zuelow, *A History of Modern Tourism* (New York: Palgrave Macmillan, 2016), 73.

42. Tom Baker, interview by author, July 9, 2011.

43. FLIC Records, ser. 1486, carton 9, folder 28, p. 12.

44. Newcome, "Homosexual Ring."

45. FLIC Records, ser. 1486, carton 9, folder 30, p. 4.

46. Ibid.

47. Ibid., folder 27, p. 3.

48. Ibid.

49. Ibid., folder 28, p. 6.

50. Tom Baker recalled that he was asked by investigators to call several men while in their presence to arrange a "date." Baker remembered that he was in such shock about his arrest that it was difficult to sound convincing, and therefore his calls were ineffective.

51. FLIC Records, ser. 1486, carton 9, folder 27, p. 7.

52. Tom Baker, interview by author, July 15, 2011.

53. "Beach Roundup," August 1958, and "Bang Bang," March 1959, *ONE: The Homosexual Viewpoint* (Los Angeles: ONE, Inc.), ONE National Gay and Lesbian Archives, Los Angeles.

54. Handwritten caption accompanying article "Books Seeded Library Growth." Library scrapbook, Local History Room, Bay County Public Library.

55. Martin Meeker, *Contacts Desired: Gay and Lesbian Communications and Community, 1940s–1970s* (Chicago: University of Chicago Press, 2006), 20.

56. "Homosexuality and Citizenship in Florida: A Report of the Florida Legislative Investigation Committee," Archival Library and Museum Materials, purl.flvc.org/fcla/tc/fhp/UF00004805.jpg.

57. "Report on discussion at meeting on problems of homosexuality in Florida," FLIC Records, January 22, 1962, ser. 1486, carton 1, folder 11, pp. 4–5.

58. John Gerassi, *The Boys of Boise: Furor, Vice, and Folly in an American City* (Seattle: University of Washington Press, 2002), 4.

59. Newcome, "Homosexual Ring."

60. "3 Church Figures—20 Men Arrested on Sex Charges," *Pensacola News*, October 5, 1961, 14A.

61. "20 Arrested on Perversion Charge in PC," *Tallahassee Democrat*, October 6, 1961, 2. "Guilty Pleas Made in PC Morals Case," *Tallahassee Democrat*, October 7, 1961, 2.

62. John Egerton, *Speak Now Against the Day: The Generation Before the Civil Rights Movement in the South* (Chapel Hill: University of North Carolina Press), 1995. Fejes, "Murder, Perversion, and Moral Panic."

63. "Report on discussion at meeting on problems of homosexuality in Florida," January 22, 1962, FLIC Records, ser. 1486, carton 1, folder 11, pp. 7–8.

64. Ibid., p. 9.

65. "Now It's Our Move," *Panama City News-Herald,* November 6, 1961, 4.

66. *Panama City News-Herald,* March 20, 1962, and January 5, 1962. *Tallahassee Democrat,* January 5, 1962.

67. "Let's Finish the Job," *Panama City News-Herald,* October 8, 1961, 4.

68. Mary Benedict, "What Can I Tell My Children?" *Panama City News-Herald,* October 8, 1961, 4.

69. Karen Graves, *And They Were Wonderful Teachers: Florida's Purge of Gay and Lesbian Teachers* (Chicago: University of Illinois Press, 2009), 120–43. See also Rubin, "Thinking Sex."

70. "Brighter Day for Panama City," *Panama City Herald,* October 18, 1961, 4.

71. Ibid., 4.

72. Ibid., 4.

73. "Let's Finish The Job," *Panama City News-Herald,* October 8, 1961, 4.

74. "No Time for Leniency," *Panama City News,* July 31, 1961, 4.

75. ONE, Inc. Records, box 40, folder 9, Col2011.001, ONE National Gay and Lesbian Archives.

76. Tom Baker, letter to author, February 22, 2011.

Chapter 3. Cruising and Boundary Crossing

1. John Howard, "Place and Movement in Gay American History: A Case from the Post–World War II South," in *Creating a Place for Ourselves: Lesbian, Gay, and Bisexual Community Histories,* ed. Brett Beemyn (New York: Routledge, 1997), 211–226.

2. Ibid., 221.

3. David L. Lewis, "Sex and the Automobile: From Rumble Seats to Rockin' Vans," in *The Automobile and American Culture,* ed. David L. Lewis and Lawrence Goldstein (Ann Arbor: University of Michigan Press, 1996), 123–33.

4. Ibid., 124.

5. Marsha E. Ackerman, *Cool Comfort: America's Romance with Air Conditioning.* (Washington, D.C.: Smithsonian Institution Press, 2002).

6. FLIC Records, ser. 1486, carton 9, folder 47, p. 3.

7. Tom Baker, interview by author, July 19, 2011.

8. Tim Retzloff, "Cars and Bars: Assembling Gay Men in Postwar Flint, Michigan," in *Creating a Place for Ourselves,* ed. Beemyn, 227–52.

9. Tom Baker, interview by author, July 19, 2011.

10. FLIC Records, ser. 1486, carton 10, folder 82, p. 5.

11. Humphreys, *Tearoom Trade,* 75.

12. FLIC Records, ser. 1486, carton 11, folder 47.

13. Ibid., carton 9, folder 11, p. 20.

14. Ibid., carton 11, folder 47, p. 4.

15. Ibid., folder 31, p. 6.

16. Ibid., p. 2.

17. Turner, *Backward Glances.*

18. FLIC Records, ser. 1486, carton 11, folder 31, p. 3.

19. Ibid., 3.

20. Ibid., p. 7.

21. Ibid., p. 10.

22. Glenda Alice Rabby, *The Pain and the Promise: The Struggle for Civil Rights in Tallahassee, Florida* (Athens: University of Georgia Press, 1999).

23. Ibid.

24. FLIC Records, ser. 1486, carton 1, folder 12.

25. Ibid., carton 13, folder 34. Here I have assumed that the two men listed as "C" are African American ("Colored"), given that the only other racial designations are "w" and "cauc," for "white" and "Caucasian."

26. Ibid.

27. E. Patrick Johnson, *Sweet Tea: Black Gay Men of the South* (Chapel Hill: University of North Carolina Press, 2011), 6.

28. Braukman, *Communists and Perverts,* 87–120.

29. FLIC Records, ser. 1486, carton 9, folder 11, p. 9.

30. Ibid., p. 7.

31. Jennifer Jones, "Queering an American Dilemma: Sexuality and Gender in African American Political Organizing, 1945–1993" (in progress).

32. "Leon County: Jail Terms, Fines Levied in Sex Cases," *Panama City Herald* (final edition), January 4, 1962, 1.

33. Stanley Cohen, *Folk Devils and Moral Panics* (New York: Routledge, 2011). See also Gerassi, *Boys of Boise.*

34. FLIC Records, ser. 1486, carton 13, folder 34.

35. Because of restrictions placed on the FLIC's records, it is often difficult to definitively connect most interrogations with names and address. However, the interrogations of men arrested at the bus station illuminate behaviors and activities of these particular men.

36. FLIC Records, ser. 1486, carton 13, folder 34.

37. Ibid., carton 9, folder 76, p. 1.

38. Ibid., folder 60, p. 4.

39. Ibid., folder 77, p. 3.

40. Ibid., p. 4.

41. Ibid., carton 9, folder 49, p. 7.

42. Humphreys, *Tearoom Trade,* 12–14.

43. "Leon County: 70 Arrested as Suspected Sex Deviates," *Panama City Herald* (area edition), January 4, 1962, 1.

44. Ibid.

45. FLIC Records, ser. 1486, carton 9, folder 60, p. 1.

46. Ibid., pp. 1–2.

47. Ibid., pp. 2–3.

48. Ibid., p. 3.

49. Ibid., p. 5.

50. Ibid., carton 13, folder 34.

51. Ibid., carton 11, folder 8, p. 15. Names used in FLIC interrogations are redacted as a

condition of their early release. Other references in the text lead me to believe that Pierson was one of the men, though this cannot be definitively proven.

52. "College Boys in Florida Used to Arrest Deviates," *LA Times*, December 29, 1965, subject files "Films—Florida," folder "Florida 2001 and before," ONE National Gay and Lesbian Archives.

53. Howard, *Men Like That*, xvi.

54. Lusharon Wiley, "An Agent for Change: The Story of Reverend H. K. Matthews," PhD diss., University of West Florida, 2007, 115.

55. James T. Sears, *Growing Up Gay in the South: Race, Gender, and Journeys of the Spirit* (New York: Harrington Park Press, 1991), 338.

56. Thomas A. Foster, "The Sexual Abuse of Black Men Under American Slavery," *Journal of the History of Sexuality* 20, no. 3 (September 2001): 445–64.

57. FLIC Records, ser. 1486, carton 10, folder 139.

58. Ibid., p. 4.

59. Ibid., carton 11, folder 6, p. 7.

60. Ibid., carton 10, folder 139, p. 4.

61. Schnur, "Closet Crusaders," 132–63.

62. FLIC Records, ser. 1486, carton 10, folder 139, p. 6.

63. George Chauncey, *Gay New York: Gender, Urban Culture, and the Making of the Gay Male World, 1890–1940* (New York: Basic Books, 1995), 72. Sears, *Growing Up Gay in the South*, 159–66.

64. Gerassi, *Boys of Boise*, 5, 61–72.

65. FLIC Records, ser. 1486, carton 10, folder 139, p. 13.

66. Chauncey, *Gay New York*.

67. FLIC Records, ser. 1486, carton 11, folder 34, pp. 1–2.

68. Ibid., folder 30, 6.

69. Barry Reay, *New York Hustlers: Masculinity and Sex in Modern America* (Manchester, U.K.: Manchester University Press, 2010).

70. Howard, *Men Like That*, 105, 275–78.

71. Ibid., 276. Howard writes here about Mississippi residents' reactions to a congressman's racial transgression in 1981. How much more shocking would such an act have been in 1962 as racial tension exploded throughout the South?

72. Johnson, *Sweet Tea*, 485.

73. Ibid., 483.

74. FLIC Records, ser. 1486, carton 10, folder 82, pp. 5–6.

75. Ibid., pp. 7–8.

76. Ibid., folder 132.

77. Ibid., folder 81.

78. Gerassi, *Boys of Boise*. David M. Halperin, *How to Do the History of Homosexuality* (Chicago: University of Chicago Press, 2002).

79. FLIC Records, ser. 1486, carton 10, folder 132, p. 3.

80. Ibid.

81. David Richbourg, interview by author, November 28, 2014.

82. For further discussion of automobile cruising by circling a designated thoroughfare, see Retzloff, "Cars and Bars," 227–52.

83. FLIC Records, ser. 1486, carton 11, folder 29.

84. Ibid., p. 1.

85. Ibid., p. 3.

86. Ibid., p. 4.

87. Ibid., p. 6.

88. Ibid., pp. 5, 8–9.

89. Randy Mann, "Pensacola, Florida and Nearby Gulp Coast Playgrounds," *Steam* 2, no. 2 (Spring 1994): 201, subject files "Films—Florida," ONE National Gay and Lesbian Archives.

90. Allan Bérubé, *Coming Out Under Fire: The History of Gay Men and Women in World War Two* (New York: Free Press, 1990), 107.

Chapter 4. Drinkin' and Carryin' On in Search of Community

1. Escoffier, "Political Economy of the Closet," 123–34.

2. Lynn M. Homan and Thomas Reilly, *Tallahassee* (Mt. Pleasant, S.C.: Arcadia, 2005), 56.

3. Ibid.

4. Gordon E. Wilkinson, letter to ONE, Inc., July 25, 1960, ONE Editorial Correspondence 1954–1964, box 46, folder 9.

5. Fejes, "Murder, Perversion, and Moral Panic," 305–47.

6. Gordon E. Wilkinson, letter to ONE, Inc., July 25, 1960, ONE Editorial Correspondence 1954–1964, box 46, folder 9, p. 4.

7. Bob Damron, compiler, *The Address Book* (San-Francisco: Pan-Graphic Press, 1966), ONE National Gay and Lesbian Archives.

8. Chauncey, *Gay New York,* 331–54.

9. Howard, "Southern Sodomy," 196–298.

10. FLIC ser. 1486, carton 9, folder 45, p. 2.

11. Ibid., p. 6.

12. The correspondence files that remain at ONE National Gay and Lesbian Archives contain only five files of people with Tallahassee addresses. It is certain that the readership was much broader than these five, given the sharing of copies of the magazine.

13. Kingwood, letter to ONE, Inc., November 19, 1962, box 29, folder "Kingwood," ONE, Inc. Correspondence, ONE National Gay and Lesbian Archives.

14. FLIC Records, ser. 1486, carton 9, folder 47, p. 5.

15. Ibid., p. 6.

16. Ibid., folder 59.

17. Ibid., folder 48.

18. Lizabeth Cohen, *A Consumers' Republic: The Politics of Mass Consumption in Postwar America* (New York: Vintage Books, 2003). Elaine Tyler May, *Homeward Bound: American Families in the Cold War Era* (New York: Basic Books, 1988).

19. Kevin M. Kruse, *White Flight: Atlanta and the Making of Modern Conservatism* (Princeton, N.J.: Princeton University Press, 2005).

20. Howard, "Place and Movement in Gay American History," 211–26.

21. Bérubé, *Coming Out Under Fire,* 155–60. Howard, "Place and Movement in Gay American History."

22. FLIC Records, ser. 1486, box 11, folder 8, p. 12.

23. Ibid., p. 17.

24. Ibid.

25. Ibid., box 8, folder 29, p. 11.

26. Ibid., box 9, folder 47, p. 4.

27. Ibid., folder 8, p. 17.

28. Ibid., box 11, folder 39.

29. Ibid., box 9, folder 59, p. 22.

30. Humphreys, *Tearoom Trade,* 11.

31. Lisa Montagne, "Playground of the Deep South and Industrial Center of Florida," *Florida Opportunity Journal*, June 1956, 20, folder "Tourism 1940s–1950s," Pensacola Historical Society.

32. Deborah Dunlap and L. S. Boyles, *Pensacola: 1950s & 60s* (Pensacola: Deborah Dunlap, 2008), 40–41.

33. In 1948, the U.S. Congress established the WAF, which replaced the World War II designation of Women's Auxiliary Air Force (WAAF). In 1976 the gender designation was dropped (www.aerofiles.com/wafs.html).

34. Kendra Ann Kennedy, "Between the Bayous: The Maritime Cultural Landscape of the Downtown Pensacola Waterfront," PhD diss., University of West Florida, 2002), 186.

35. Alecia P. Long, *The Great Southern Babylon: Sex, Race, and Respectability in New Orleans, 1865–1920* (Baton Rouge: University of Louisiana Press, 2005).

36. Jackson, *Rise and Decline of the Redneck Riviera,* 30.

37. Ibid., 30.

38. Buddy to Judge Ernest Mason, October 28, 1949, Ernest E. Mason Collection, box 10, folder 1944–1954, University of West Florida Special Collections, Pensacola.

39. Ibid., p. 2.

40. FLIC Records, ser. 1486, carton 11, folder 10, p. 1

41. Ibid, p. 3.

42. Ibid.

43. Benton Abby, "In Pensacola, The Gayest 4th is Emma's," *Figaro* (New Orleans), July 1, 1972, 4.

44. Fred Brown, *Trader Jon* (Memphis: Castle Books, 1986). Because the book I consulted does not have page numbers, all numbers given in the following notes are the result of my numbering and are therefore approximate.

45. Ibid., 15.

46. Ibid., 16.

47. Dunlap and Boyles, *Pensacola.*

48. Brown, *Trader Jon,* 16.

49. Liz Watkins, director, *The Life and Times of Trader Jon* (Pensacola: Watkins Productions), DVD, 1999.

50. Ens. Carter Edman, "Trader Jon, Unofficial Curator of Naval Aviation Mementos," *Gosport*, folder "Trader Jon's, Pensacola Historical Society, Pensacola.

51. Brown, *Trader Jon,* 29.

52. "Trader Jon's Named Historic Site," *Pensacola News-Journal*, July 18, 1992, folder "Weisman, Martin Trader Jon," Pensacola Historical Society.

53. Brown, *Trader John,* 41.

54. Troy Moon, "History Clings to the Walls in This Pensacola Landmark, Where Everybody Knows Your Name. But Now an Era Comes to a Close," *Pensacola News-Journal*, folder "Pensacola Restaurants Trader Jon's," Pensacola Historical Society.

55. Taylor Hackford, director, *An Officer and a Gentleman* (USA: Paramount, 1982).

56. Matt Hilburn, "Trader Jon's Closes After 50 Years," blog post, November 17, 2003, www.matthew-hilburn.com/index.php?itemid=80 (accessed February 18, 2012).

57. John Waite, "Women and Cigars and Ultra-Violet Light," *Pensacola News-Journal*, September 7, 1969, folder "Pensacola Restaurants Trader Jon's," Pensacola Historical Society.

58. Brown, *Trader Jon*, 54.

59. Watkins, *Life and Times of Trader Jon*, 1999.

60. Tomek Mossakowski, "Queer Climates at the Poles: Cross-Dressing and Same-Sex Relations During Nineteenth Century Arctic and Antarctic Exploration," PhD thesis, King's College, London, 2015.

61. Tom Baker, interview by author, July 19, 2011.

62. Ibid., January 7, 2013.

63. Shaw, "Discreet Lovers of Emma Jones," 3.

64. Brown, *Trader Jon*, 69.

65. Howard, "The Library, the Park, and the Pervert," 107–31.

Chapter 5. Emma Jones: Queering the Fourth of July

Epigraph source: J.R., letter to *ONE* magazine, March 25, 1963, ONE Editorial Correspondence, 1956–1965, box 46, folder 29.

1. Craig M. Loftin, *Masked Voices: Gay Men and Lesbians in Cold War America* (New York: State University of New York Press, 2012), 153.

2. David K. Johnson, "Physique Pioneers: The Politics of 1960s Gay Consumer Culture," *Journal of Social History* 43, no. 4 (Summer 2010): 867–92. Meeker, *Contacts Desired*, 32.

3. Loftin, *Masked Voices*, 8.

4. L. Ewing Esch, letter to *ONE* magazine, November 6, 1961, ONE, Inc. Records, COL2011.001, box 24, folder "L. Ewing Esch," ONE National Gay and Lesbian Archives.

5. L. Ewing Esch, letter to *ONE* magazine, February 8, 1962, ONE, Inc. Records, COL2011.001, box 24, folder "L. Ewing Esch," ONE National Gay and Lesbian Archives.

6. Loftin, *Masked Voices*, 39.

7. Marc Stein, "Birthplace of the Nation: Imagining Lesbian and Gay Communities in Philadelphia, 1969–1970," in *Creating a Place for Ourselves*, ed. Beemyn, 253–88.

8. Loftin, *Masked Voices*, 231.

9. Unsigned letter to ONE, Inc., December 16, 1960, ONE, Inc. Records, COL2011.001, box 46, folder "1960–1974," ONE National Gay and Lesbian Archives.

10. John Loughery, *The Other Side of Silence: Men's Lives and Gay Identities: A Twentieth-Century History* (New York, Henry Holt and Co., Inc., 1998), 273.

11. Bill Rushton, "The Killing of Emma Jones—III: Only Memories Remain for Once-Gay Pensacola," *Advocate* 155 (January 15, 1975): 10, 16, ONE National Gay and Lesbian Archives.

12. Stein, "Birthplace of the Nation."

13. Howard Ealey to Don Slater, June 30, 1963. box 24, folder "Ealey, Howard," ONE, Inc. Records, COL2011.001, ONE National Gay and Lesbian Archives.

14. For a discussion of the national "imagined" community of homosexuals see Meeker, *Contacts Desired*; and Loftin, *Masked Voices*.

15. Howard Ealey to Don Slater, June 30, 1963. box 24, folder "Ealey, Howard," ONE, Inc. Records, COL2011.001, ONE National Gay and Lesbian Archives.

16. Howard, "Southern Sodomy," 196–298.

17. Dr. Donald Barberi to The Mattachine Society, May 1, 1954, Mattachine Society Project Collection COLL2008-016, box 6, folder 6:21, ONE National Gay and Lesbian Archives.

18. Ibid.

19. Bill Rushton, "The Killing of Emma Jones—III: Only Memories Remain for Once-Gay Pensacola," *Advocate* 155 (January 15, 1975): 10, 16, ONE National Gay and Lesbian Archives.

20. Shaw, "Discreet Lovers of Emma Jones," 14.

21. Robert D. Shaw Jr., interview with the author, February 26, 2015.

22. Shaw, "Discreet Lovers of Emma Jones."

23. One source close to the couple has stated that Henry made up the adoption on the spot and that the pair had met as adults. Unable to independently confirm this series of events, I have chosen to use their story as they relayed it to the public. Being brothers or other forms of kinship such as adoption were common tactics for gay men wishing to circumvent legal and societal strictures.

24. Braukman, *Communists and Perverts*. Johnson, *Lavender Scare*.

25. Wesley Chenault and Stacy Braukman, *Gay and Lesbian Atlanta, Images of America* (Mt. Pleasant, S.C.: Arcadia, 2008).

26. Interview of Henry Hillyer by Joshua Jones, June 2010. This information was conveyed in conversation with the author.

27. Shaw, "Discreet Lovers of Emma Jones," 1.

28. Ibid., 1.

29. Carson Weaver, letter, October 27, 1961, ONE, Inc. Correspondence, box 39, folder "Weaver," ONE National Gay and Lesbian Archives.

30. Dick McConchie, letter, January 28, 1959, ONE, Inc. Correspondence, box 31, folder "McConchie," ONE National Gay and Lesbian Archives.

31. Meeker, *Contacts Desired*.

32. Shaw, "Discreet Lovers of Emma Jones," 1.

33. Richbourg, David. Interview with author, November 28, 2014.

34. Howard, *Men Like That*.

35. Shaw, "Discreet Lovers of Emma Jones," 3.

36. Bill Rushton, "The Killing of Emma Jones—2: Who Is Responsible," *Advocate* 154 (January 1, 1975): 36, ONE National Gay and Lesbian Archives.

37. Shaw, "Discreet Lovers of Emma Jones," 2.

38. Ibid.

39. Rushton, "The Killing of Emma Jones—1," 4.

40. Shaw, "Discreet Lovers of Emma Jones," 2.

41. The date and number of original founders vary depending on who is telling the story.

42. "Florida, Inquisitionland, Not Vacationland," *ONE* 11, no. 6 (June 1, 1963).

43. Tommie Shields, friend of Hillyer, interview by author, August 13, 2016.

44. Shaw, "Discreet Lovers of Emma Jones," 8.

45. Loughery, *Other Side of Silence*, 279.

46. Joan Fleischman, Philadelphia activist, interview by Marc Stein, May 31, 1994, OutHistory.org.

47. Shaw, "Discreet Lovers of Emma Jones," 3.

48. Barbra Gittings, quoted in Stein's "Birthplace of the Nation," 259.

49. Stein, "Birthplace of the Nation," 259.

50. Mormino, *Land of Sunshine, State of Dreams,* 312.

51. Loughery, *Other Side of Silence,* 280.

52. Ibid.

53. The number of invitations varies depending on who is telling the story. John Loughery says twenty-five, yet other histories and remembrances use a figure of fifty.

54. Bill Rushton, "The Killing of Emma Jones—III: Only Memories Remain for Once-Gay Pensacola," *Advocate* 155 (January 15, 1975): 16, ONE National Gay and Lesbian Archives.

55. Ibid.

56. Shaw, "Discreet Lovers of Emma Jones," 3.

57. Bill Rushton, "The Killing of Emma Jones—III: Only Memories Remain for Once-Gay Pensacola," *Advocate* 155 (January 15, 1975): 16, ONE National Gay and Lesbian Archives.

58. Shaw, "Discreet Lovers of Emma Jones," 12.

59. Bill Rushton, "The Killing of Emma Jones—1: Gay Pensacola Becomes a Nightmare of Corruption and Bigotry," *Advocate* 153 (December 15, 1974): 8.

60. Shaw, "Discreet Lovers of Emma Jones," 4.

61. Loughery, *Other Side of Silence,* 274.

62. Benton Abby, "In Pensacola, The Gayest 4th is Emma's," *Figaro* (New Orleans), July 1, 1972, 4.

63. Emma Jones Convention Advertisement/Invitations, 1972 and 1973, Hillyer scrapbook, author's collection, courtesy of Kurt Young.

64. Loughery, *Other Side of Silence,* 275.

65. Bill Rushton, "The Killing of Emma Jones—III: Only Memories Remain for Once-Gay Pensacola," *Advocate* 155 (January 15, 1975): 16, ONE National Gay and Lesbian Archives.

66. Ibid.

67. Shaw, "Discreet Lovers of Emma Jones," 3.

68. Bill Rushton, "The Killing of Emma Jones—III: Only Memories Remain for Once-Gay Pensacola," *Advocate* 155 (January 15, 1975): 16, ONE National Gay and Lesbian Archives.

69. Ibid.

70. Shaw, "Discreet Lovers of Emma Jones," 12.

71. Ibid., 12.

72. "Beauty Contest Winner Wouldn't Give His Name," *Pensacola Journal,* July 6, 1972, 1C.

73. "A Gay Time in Pensacola," *Advocate* 91 (August 15, 1972): 14.

74. Ibid.

75. Ibid.

76. "Emma Jones Rises Again," *Advocate* 118 (August 15, 1973): 15.

77. Liz Highleyman, "What Is the History of the Advocate," *Letters from CAMP Rehoboth* 17, no. 13 (September 14, 2007), web.archive.org/web/20080518032727/http://www.camp-rehoboth.com/issue09_14_07/past_out.htm.

78. Fred Fejes, "Advertising and the Political Economy of Gay/Lesbian Identity," in *Sex & Money: Feminism and Political Economy in the Media,* ed. Eileen R. Meehan and Ellen Riordan (Minneapolis: University of Minnesota Press, 2002), 196–208.

79. Burke Williams, quoted in Shaw's "Discreet Lovers of Emma Jones," 10.

80. Escoffier, "Political Economy of the Closet," 123–34.

81. Shaw, "Discreet Lovers of Emma Jones," 28

82. Bill Rushton, "The Killing of Emma Jones—III: Only Memories Remain for Once-Gay Pensacola," *Advocate* 155 (January 15, 1975): 16, ONE National Gay and Lesbian Archives.

83. Ibid.

84. Jessica Clawson, "Queers on Campus: LGBTQ Student Visibility at Three Public Universities in Florida, 1970–1985," PhD diss., University of Florida, 2014.

85. Shaw, "Discreet Lovers of Emma Jones," 28.

86. "Homosexual Arrests Here Reach 19," *Pensacola News-Journal*, July 7, 1974, 1C.

87. "13 Plead Innocent in Morals Cases," *Pensacola Journal*, May 11, 1974, 4B.

88. "Homosexual Arrests Here Reach 19," *Pensacola News-Journal*, July 7, 1974, 1C.

89. Ibid.

90. Bill Rushton, "The Killing of Emma Jones—2: Who Is Responsible," *Advocate* 154 (January 1, 1975): 8, ONE National Gay and Lesbian Archives.

91. Ibid., 8.

92. Shaw, "Discreet Lovers of Emma Jones," 28.

93. Bill Rushton, "The Killing of Emma Jones—1: Gay Pensacola Becomes a Nightmare of Corruption and Bigotry," *Advocate* 153 (December 15, 1974): 4.

94. David Richbourg, interview with author, November 28, 2014.

95. Pat Jennings, "In Defendant's Day: Florida Holiday Not So Gay," *Womanews* 2, no. 6, p. 10, Lesbian Herstory Archives, New York City.

96. Ibid.

97. Bill Rushton, "The Killing of Emma Jones—1: Gay Pensacola Becomes a Nightmare of Corruption and Bigotry," *Advocate* 153 (December 15, 1974).

98. M.G., "Pensacola Nightmare Recalled," *Distaff* 3, no. 4 (April–May 1975): 18.

99. Ibid.

100. Bill Rushton, "The Killing of Emma Jones—III: Only Memories Remain for Once-Gay Pensacola," *Advocate* 155 (January 15, 1975): 16, ONE National Gay and Lesbian Archives.

101. Loughery, *Other Side of Silence*, 275.

102. Bill Rushton, "The Killing of Emma Jones—III: Only Memories Remain for Once-Gay Pensacola," *Advocate* 155 (January 15, 1975): 10, 16, ONE National Gay and Lesbian Archives.

103. Benton Abby, "In Pensacola, The Gayest 4th is Emma's," *Figaro* (New Orleans), July 1, 1972, 4.

104. Obituaries, Ray Hillyer, June 4, 2010; Henry Hillyer, March 30, 2011, *Pensacola News-Journal*.

105. Bill Rushton, "The Killing of Emma Jones—III: Only Memories Remain for Once-Gay Pensacola," *Advocate* 155 (January 15, 1975): 10, 16, ONE National Gay and Lesbian Archives.

Chapter 6. From Redneck to Gay Riviera

1. Jerry T Watkins III, "Underneath the Rainbow: Queer Identity and Community Building in Panama City and the Florida Panhandle, 1950–1990," M.A. thesis, Georgia State University, 2008.

2. Tom Baker, interview by author, July 12, 2011.

3. Ibid., January 2, 2013.

4. Watkins, "Underneath the Rainbow," 63.

5. A person's level of outness is always/already mediated by his or her own circumstances. Some individuals may park blocks away to hide their cars while others may walk in proudly. The Fiesta gives the opportunity for all of those expressions.

6. Watkins, "Underneath the Rainbow," 71.

7. Rictor Norton, e-mail conversation with the author, August 18, 2015.

8. Ibid., August 18, 2015.

9. Ibid.

10. Clawson, "Queers on Campus."

11. Hiram Ruiz, "News: Tallahassee GLF"; "GLF Meets," *Flambeau*, May 27, 1970, 9.

12. Rictor Norton, e-mail conversation with the author, August 18, 2015.

13. Clawson, "Queers on Campus," 60–61.

14. Bart Church, "I'll be back—I always come back," *Flambeau,* June 28, 1979.

15. Information gathered from conversations with several men at a gathering of the Tallahassee Prime Timers, August 22, 2015.

16. Escoffier, "Political Economy of the Closet," 123–34.

17. Chenault and Braukman, *Gay and Lesbian Atlanta,* 71.

18. Richard Kavanaugh, "It's Hot! Hot! Hot! This Summer on the Gay Gulf Coast," *Cruise: The Guide to Gay Entertainment in the South* 2, no. 8 (July 1977): 57–61, box 4, folder 3, Lesbian, Gay, Bisexual, and Transgender History Serial Collection, Atlanta History Center, Atlanta.

19. Ibid., 58.

20. Ibid.

21. Ibid., 58–59.

22. In addition to Robert Bosch, John Howard documents that a particular set of gay and lesbian southerners from Birmingham, Alabama, routinely spent their vacations in Panama City and other locations along the Gulf Coast in his "Place and Movement in Gay American History," 211–26.

23. Watkins, "Underneath the Rainbow," 81.

24. Ibid., 81–84.

25. Kavanaugh, "It's Hot! Hot! Hot!" 57.

26. Jessica Forbes, "Queer and Here: The Long History of Gay Tourists on Pensacola Beach," *Independent News* 14, no. 22 (May 23, 2013): 1–13, inweekly.net/wordpress/?p=15308.

27. Mike Cazalas, "Historic Building Burns," *Panama City News-Herald*, April 10, 1987, 2A.

28. Ibid.

29. Mike Cazalas, "Original Bricks Adorn 'New' La Royale," *Panama City News-Herald,* January 31, 1988, 2A.

30. Kavanaugh, "It's Hot! Hot! Hot!"

31. Steven F. Philipp, "Gay and Lesbian Tourists at a Southern U.S.A. Beach Event," *Journal of Homosexuality* 37, no. 3 (1999): 69–86.

32. Stanonis, *Faith in Bikinis,* 173.

33. Paul Wilborn, "Slaying on beach reflects gays plight," *Tampa Tribune,* July 7, 1991, Nation section, 1.

34. Ibid.

35. Steven Handelman, "America's Holy War," *Toronto Star,* August 13, 1994, B1.

36. William Rabb, "Gays wonder: will violence strike here?" *Pensacola News-Journal,* February 7, 1993, 1B.

37. Steve Hatch, interview by author, July 2016.

38. Forbes, "Queer and Here."

39. Tanya Dewhurst and Hannah Thompson, "Fahrenheit: Where the Girls Are," *Our World,* November 1993, 36–44, Canadian Lesbian and Gay Archives, Toronto.

40. "South in Brief," *Atlanta Journal-Constitution,* May 23, 1993, A3.

41. Philipp, "Gay and Lesbian Tourists," 84.

42. Amy Driscoll, "Gay-Friendly Label Polarizes Pensacola; Political Fight Looms," *Palm Beach Post,* June 13, 1993, 1A.

43. "Proffitt, Mayor out of line," *Pensacola News-Journal,* May 24, 1993, 6A.

44. Janelle Popp, "Seek Out Truth," *Pensacola News-Journal,* May 11, 1993, Letters, 7A.

45. J. W. Steele, "Proffitt, Maygarden OK," *Pensacola News-Journal,* June 5, 1993, 12A.

46. Andy Anderson, "Not Going Away," *Pensacola News-Journal,* May 29, 1993, 13A.

47. Lisa Pennãloza, "We're Here, We're Queer and We're Going Shopping: A Critical Perspective on the Accommodation of Gays and Lesbians in the US Marketplace," *Journal of Homosexuality* 31, nos. 1–2 (1996): 9–41.

48. "Gays heading to Pensacola, but what welcome's in store?" *Atlanta Journal-Constitution,* May 23, 1993, A3. Jim Yardley, "Southern Scenes—Pensacola, Fla.—Around the South—Gay Tourism divides Pensacola—Thousands are expected for holiday," *Atlanta Journal,* May 28, 1993, E10. Associated Press, "Will 'Gay Riviera' tourism slump?—Pensacola unsure how visitors will react to publicity," *Orlando Sentinel,* July 12, 1993, A1. Amy Driscoll, "Gay-friendly label polarizes Pensacola; political fight looms," *Palm Beach Post,* June 13, 1993. "Gay Money in Circulation: Pensacola Split over Image," *Sun-Sentinel,* Jun 5, 1993, 16A.

49. "'Gay Riviera' Coming Out of the Closet," *Stonewall News,* July 26, 1993, 12.

50. Stephen Handelman, "America's Holy War," *Toronto Star,* August 13, 1994, B1.

51. Duwayne Escobedo, "Marchers, join global praise day," *Pensacola News-Journal,* May 28, 1995, 1B.

52. Ginny Graybiel, "NOW Volunteers, prep as march, rally near," *Pensacola News-Journal,* May 7, 1993, 1A.

53. Brad Barnes, "Nails along roadside deflate holiday for some," *Pensacola News-Journal,* May 30, 1993, 1B.

54. Dewhurst and Thompson, "Where the Girls Are," 43. This longer version of Proffitt's quote appears here, but shorter variations of the quote and the sentiment are expressed in a number of other publications around the time.

55. Steve Hatch, interview by author, June 20, 2016.

56. Andy Anderson, "About the Cover," *Christopher Street South Quarterly* 2, no. 6 (February 1994): 3.

57. Dewhurst and Thompson, "Where the Girls Are."

58. Forbes, "Queer and Here."

59. Steve Hatch, interview by author, June 20, 2016.

60. Melissa Gabriel, "Pensacola's LGBT Memorial Day History has a place," *Pensacola News-Journal,* May 27, 2016.

61. Andy Anderson, "From the Editor and President of Christopher Street South," *Christopher Street South Quarterly,* February 1994, 7.

62. A number of scholars have theorized and researched the pink-dollar, pink-capitalism, and LGBTQ niche markets. A good place to start is Nadia Guidotto's "Cashing in on Queers: From Liberation to Commodification," *Canadian Online Journal of Queer Studies in Education* 2, no. 1 (2006), jqstudies.library.utoronto.ca/index.php/jqstudies/article/view/3286/1414 (accessed July 11, 2017).

63. Randy Mann, "Pensacola, Florida and nearby Gulp Coast Playgrounds," *Steam* 2, no. 2 (Spring 1994): 201–4, subject files "Films—Florida," ONE National Gay and Lesbian Archives.

64. Don Schwamb, "Steam Magazine," from "History of Gay and Lesbian Life in Milwaukee, Wisconsin," www.mkelgbthist.org/media/print/steam.htm (accessed April 1, 2013).

65. Randy Mann, "Pensacola, Florida and nearby Gulp Coast Playgrounds," *Steam* 2, no. 2 (Spring 1994): 201, subject files "Films—Florida," ONE National Gay and Lesbian Archives.

66. Ibid., 203.

67. Ibid., 202.

68. Ibid., 203.

69. Ibid., 203–4.

70. Brad Barnes, "Vandals, bomb threat reported at street party," *Pensacola News-Journal,* May 31, 1994, 1B.

71. Winnie Hu, "Holiday Crowds Big Business for Beach," *Pensacola News-Journal,* May 28, 1995, 1A, 8A; Winnie Hu, "Sparkling Sand, Relaxed Atmosphere Main Draw," *Pensacola News-Journal,* May 28, 1994, 8A.

72. Ted McCrary, quoted in "Queer and Here" by Jessica Forbes.

73. "What's our image? Better all the time," *Pensacola News-Journal,* May 29, 1994, 20A.

Epilogue

1. John Henderson, "Panama City Beach Spring Break not the party students expected," *Panama City News-Herald,* March 20, 2016; "Panama City Beach businesses suffering: New laws blamed for 50 to 80 percent drop in sales," *Panama City News-Herald,* March 19, 2016.

2. Bill Kaczor, Associated Press, "Online bank for lesbians and gays reports business brisk," *Stuart News,* November 15, 1999, D4.

3. "Florida briefs: Pensacola-based internet bank to close," *Celebrate! Key West,* March 7–20, 2002, 9. Archives of Sexuality and Gender: LGBTQ History and Culture Since 1940, Part II, www.gale.com/c/archives-of-sexuality-and-gender-lgbtq-part-ii.

4. Doug Landreth, interview by author, March 8, 2017. Jennie McKeon, "Gay Pride Celebrated in Panhandle," nwfdailynews, June 26, 2017, www.nwfdailynews.com/news/20170626/gay-pride-celebrated-in-panhandle.

5. Annie Utterback, "The Capitalist Appropriation of Gay Pride," *The Establishment,* June 30, 2016, theestablishment.co/the-capitalist-appropriation-of-gay-pride-150fc6111326.

6. Perry Stein and Lynh Bui, "Capital Pride parade disrupted by protestors; revelers rerouted," *Washington Post,* June 10, 2017, www.washingtonpost.com/local/public-safety/captial-pride-parade-disrupted-by-protesters-revelers-rerouted/2017/06/10/97053aa6-4e28-11e7-9669-250d0b15f83b_story.html?utm_term=.1e31a9022e88.

BIBLIOGRAPHY

Ackerman, Marsha E. *Cool Comfort: America's Romance with Air Conditioning*. Washington, D.C.: Smithsonian Institution Press, 2002.

Arsenault, Raymond. "The Cooling of the South." *Wilson Quarterly* 8, no. 3 (Summer 1984): 150–59.

———. "End of the Long Hot Summer: The Air Conditioner and Southern Culture." *Journal of Southern History* 50, no. 4 (November 1984): 597–628.

Baker, Blanche M. "Introduction." Will Fellows and Helen P. Branson, *Gay Bar: The Fabulous, True Story of a Daring Woman and Her Boys in the 1950s*. Madison: University of Wisconsin Press, 2010.

Bartlett, Neil. *Who Was That Man? A Present for Mr. Oscar Wilde*. London: Serpent's Tail, 1988.

Beemyn, Brett, ed. *Creating a Place for Ourselves: Lesbian, Gay, and Bisexual Community Histories*. New York: Routledge, 1997.

Bell, David. "Perverse Dynamics, Sexual Citizenship and the Transformation of Intimacy." In *Mapping Desire: Geographies of Sexualities*, ed. David Ball and Gill Valentine. New York: Routledge, 1995, 304–17.

Bérubé, Allan. *Coming Out Under Fire: The History of Gay Men and Women in World War Two*. New York: Free Press, 1990.

Boag, Peter. *Same-Sex Affairs: Constructing and Controlling Homosexuality in the Pacific Northwest*. Berkeley: University of California Press, 2003.

Brasell, R. Bruce. "Greetings from Out Here: Southern Lesbians and Gays Bear Witness." In *Out in the South*, ed. Carlos L. Dews and Carolyn Leste Law. Philadelphia: Temple University Press, 2001.

Braukman, Stacy. *Communists and Perverts Under the Palms: The Johns Committee in Florida, 1956–1965*. Gainesville: University Press of Florida, 2012.

Brock, James, and Gerri Reaves, "Signing the Sunshine State Or, The Prophylactic Guide to a Safe Miami." *Studies in Popular Culture* 20, no. 1 (October 1997): 1–28.

Brown, Fred. *Trader Jon*. Memphis: Castle Books, 1986.

Canaday, Margot. *The Straight State: Sexuality and Citizenship in Twentieth-Century America*. Princeton, N.J.: Princeton University Press, 2009.

Chanel, Rose. "The 'Jewel' of the South: Miami, Florida and the NAACP's Struggle for Civil Rights in America's Vacation Paradise." *Florida Historical Quarterly* 86, no. 1 (Summer 2007): 33–69.

Chauncey, George. *Gay New York: Gender, Urban Culture, and the Making of the Gay Male World, 1890–1940*. New York: Basic Books, 1995.

Chenault, Wesley, and Stacy Braukman. *Gay and Lesbian Atlanta, Images of America.* Mt. Pleasant, S.C.: Arcadia, 2008.

Clawson, Jessica. "Queers on Campus: LGBTQ Student Visibility at Three Public Universities in Florida, 1970–1985." PhD diss., University of Florida, 2014.

Cocks, H. G. *Classified: The Secret History of the Personal Column.* London: Random House, 2009.

Cohen, Lizabeth. *A Consumers' Republic: The Politics of Mass Consumption in Postwar America.* New York: Vintage Books, 2003.

Cohen, Stanley. *Folk Devils and Moral Panics.* New York: Routledge, 2011.

Cook, Alistair. *One Man's America.* New York: Knopf, 1952.

Cook, Matt. *London and the Culture of Homosexuality, 1885–1914.* Cambridge, U.K.: Cambridge University Press, 2003.

Corber, Robert J. *Homosexuality in Cold War America: Resistance and the Crisis of Masculinity.* Durham, N.C.: Duke University Press, 1997.

Creadick, Anna G. *Perfectly Average: The Pursuit of Normality in Postwar America.* Amherst: University of Massachusetts Press, 2010.

Daniel, Pete. *Lost Revolutions: The South in the 1950s.* Chapel Hill: University of North Carolina Press, 2000.

———. *Standing at the Crossroads: Southern Life in the Twentieth Century.* Baltimore: Johns Hopkins University Press, 1996.

D'Emilio, John. "Capitalism and Gay Identity." In *Making Trouble: Essays on Gay History, Politics, and the University.* New York: Routledge, 1992, 3–16.

———. "Homophobia and the Trajectory of Postwar American Radicalism: The Career of Bayard Rustin." *Radical History Review* 62 (Spring 1995): 81–103.

———. *Sexual Politics, Sexual Communities: The Making of a Homosexual Minority in the United States 1940–1970.* Chicago: University of Chicago Press, 1998.

———, and Estelle B. Freedman. *Intimate Matters: A History of Sexuality in America.* Chicago: University of Chicago Press, 1997.

Duberman, Martin. *About Time: Exploring the Gay Past.* New York: Meridian, 1991.

———. *Stonewall.* New York: Plume, 1993.

Dunlap, Deborah, and L. S. Boyles. *Pensacola: 1950s & 60s.* Pensacola: Deborah Dunlap, 2008.

Edelman, Lee. "Men's Room." In *Stud: Architectures of Masculinity,* ed. Joel Sanders. New York: Princeton Architectural Press, 1996, 152–61.

Egerton, John. *Speak Now Against the Day: The Generation Before the Civil Rights Movement in the South.* Chapel Hill: University of North Carolina Press. 1995.

Escoffier, Jeffrey. "The Political Economy of the Closet: Notes Toward an Economic History of Gay and Lesbian Life Before Stonewall." In *Homo Economics: Capitalism, Community, and Lesbian and Gay Life,* ed. Amy Gluckman and Betsy Reed. New York: Routledge, 1997, 123–34.

Faderman, Lillian. *Odd Girls and Twilight Lovers: A History of Lesbian Life in Twentieth-Century America.* New York: Penguin, 1991.

Fejes, Fred. "Murder, Perversion, and Moral Panic: The 1954 Media Campaign Against Miami's Homosexuals and the Discourse of Civic Betterment." *Journal of the History of Sexuality* 9, no. 3 (July 2000): 305–47.

Forbes, Jessica. "Queer and Here: The Long History of Gay Tourists on Pensacola Beach." *Independent News* 14, no. 22 (May 23, 2013): 1–13.

Foster, Thomas A. "The Sexual Abuse of Black Men Under American Slavery." *Journal of the History of Sexuality* 20, no. 3 (September 2001): 445–64.

Foucault, Michel. *Discipline and Punish: The Birth of the Prison*. London: Vintage Books, 1979.

———. *The History of Sexuality*. Vol. 1: *The Will to Knowledge*. Trans. Robert Hurley. London: Penguin Books, 1998.

Freedman, Estelle B. "Uncontrolled Desires: The Response to the Sexual Psychopath, 1920–1960." *Journal of American History* 74, no. 1 (June 1987): 83–106.

Gallo, Marcia M. *Different Daughters: A History of the Daughters of Bilitis and the Lesbian Rights Movement*. Emeryville, Calif.: Seal Press, 2007.

Gerassi, John. *The Boys of Boise: Furor, Vice, and Folly in an American City*. Seattle: University of Washington Press, 2002.

Ginzburg, Carlo, John Tedeschi, and Ann C. Tedeschi. "Microhistory: Two or Three Things I Know About It." *Critical Inquiry* 20, no. 1 (Autumn 1993): 10–35.

Graves, Karen. *And They Were Wonderful Teachers: Florida's Purge of Gay and Lesbian Teachers*. Chicago: University of Illinois Press, 2009.

Gray, Mary L. *Out in the Country: Youth, Media, and Visibility in Rural America*. New York: New York University Press, 2009.

Halperin, David M. *How to Do the History of Homosexuality*. Chicago: University of Chicago Press, 2002.

Harvey, David. *The Condition of Postmodernity: An Enquiry into the Origins of Cultural Change*. Oxford, U.K.: Blackwell, 1990.

———. *The Urban Experience*. Oxford, U.K.: Basil Blackwell, 1989.

Hayner, Norman S. "Hotel Life and Personality." *American Journal of Sociology* 33, no. 5 (1928): 784–95.

Henderson, Jason. "Secessionist Automobility: Racism, Anti-Urbanism, and the Politics of Automobility in Atlanta, Georgia." *International Journal of Urban and Regional Research* 30, no. 2 (June 2006): 293–307.

Herring, Scott. *Another Country: Queer Anti-Urbanism*. New York: New York University Press, 2010.

Hollis, Tim. *Florida's Miracle Strip: From Redneck Riviera to Emerald Coast*. Jackson: University Press of Mississippi, 2004.

Homan, Lynn M., and Thomas Reilly. *Tallahassee*. Mt. Pleasant, S.C.: Arcadia, 2005.

Houlbrook, Matt. *Queer London: Perils and Pleasure in the Sexual Metropolis, 1918–1957*. Chicago: University of Chicago Press, 2006.

Howard, John. "The Library, the Park, and the Pervert: Public Space and Homosexual Encounter in Post–World War II Atlanta." In *Carryin' On in the Lesbian and Gay South*, ed. Howard, 107–31.

———. *Men Like That: A Southern Queer History*. Chicago: University of Chicago Press, 1999.

———. "Place and Movement in Gay American History: A Case from the Post–World War II South." In *Creating a Place for Ourselves*, ed. Beemyn, 211–26.

———. "Southern Sodomy; or, What the Coppers Saw." In *Southern Masculinity: Perspectives on Manhood in the South Since Reconstruction*, ed. Craig Thompson Friend. Athens: University of Georgia Press, 2009, 196–298.

———, ed. *Carryin' On in the Lesbian and Gay South*. New York: New York University Press, 1999.

Humphreys, Laud. *Tearoom Trade: Impersonal Sex in Public Places*. New York: Adline, 1975.

Jackson, Harvey H., III, *The Rise and Decline of the Redneck Riviera: An Insider's History of the Florida-Alabama Coast*. Athens: University of Georgia Press, 2012.

Johnson, David K. *The Lavender Scare: The Cold War Persecution of Gays and Lesbians in the Federal Government*. Chicago: University of Chicago Press, 2004.

———. "Physique Pioneers: The Politics of 1960s Gay Consumer Culture." *Journal of Social History* 43, no. 4 (Summer 2010): 867–92.

Johnson, E. Patrick. *Sweet Tea: Black Gay Men of the South*. Chapel Hill: University of North Carolina Press, 2011.

Jones, Jennifer. "Queering an American Dilemma: Sexuality and Gender in African American Political Organizing, 1945–1993." Manuscript in progress.

Kavanaugh, Richard. "It's Hot! Hot! Hot! This Summer on the Gay Gulf Coast." *Cruise: The Guide to Gay Entertainment in the South* 2, no. 8 (July 1977): 57–61, box 4, folder 3, Lesbian, Gay, Bisexual, and Transgender History Serial Collection, Atlanta History Center, Atlanta.

Kennedy, Elizabeth Lapovsky, and Madeline D. Davis. *Boots of Leather, Slippers of Gold: The History of a Lesbian Community*. New York: Routledge, 1993.

Kennedy, Kendra Ann. "Between the Bayous: The Maritime Cultural Landscape of the Downtown Pensacola Waterfront." PhD diss., University of West Florida, 2002.

Kirby, Jack Temple. *Media-Made Dixie: The South in the American Imagination*. Athens: University of Georgia Press, 1986.

Krahulik, Karen C. *Provincetown: From Pilgrim Landing to Gay Resort*. New York: New York University Press, 2007.

Kruse, Kevin M. *One Nation Under God: How Corporate America Invented Christian America*. New York: Basic Books, 2015.

———. *White Flight: Atlanta and the Making of Modern Conservatism*. Princeton, N.J.: Princeton University Press, 2005.

Leap, William. *Public Sex/Gay Space*. New York: Columbia University Press, 1999.

LeVay, Simon, and Elisabeth Nonas. *City of Friends: A Portrait of the Gay and Lesbian Community in America*. Cambridge, Mass.: MIT Press, 1995.

Lewis, David L. "Sex and the Automobile: From Rumble Seats to Rockin' Vans." In *The Automobile and American Culture*, ed. David L. Lewis and Lawrence Goldstein. Ann Arbor: University of Michigan Press, 1983, 123–33.

Loftin, Craig. *Masked Voices: Gay Men and Lesbians in Cold War America* New York: State University of New York Press, 2012.

Long, Alecia P. *The Great Southern Babylon: Sex, Race, and Respectability in New Orleans, 1865–1920*. Baton Rouge: University of Louisiana Press, 2005.

Loughery, John. *The Other Side of Silence: Men's Lives and Gay Identities: A Twentieth-Century History*. New York, Henry Holt and Co., Inc., 1998.

MacCannell, Dean. *The Tourist: A New Theory of the Leisure Class*. 1999. Rev. ed. Berkeley: University of California Press, 2013.

Mason, Carol. *Oklahomo: Lessons in Unqueering America*. Albany: State University of New York Press, 2015.

May, Elaine Tyler. *Homeward Bound: American Families in the Cold War Era*. New York: Basic Books, 1988.

Meeker, Martin. *Contacts Desired: Gay and Lesbian Communications and Community, 1940s–1970s*. Chicago: University of Chicago Press, 2006.

Mormino, Gary R. *Land of Sunshine, State of Dreams: A Social History of Modern Florida*. Gainesville: University Press of Florida, 2005.

Mossakowski, Tomek. "Queer Climates at the Poles: Cross-Dressing and Same-Sex Relations During Nineteenth Century Arctic and Antarctic Exploration." PhD thesis, King's College, London, 2015.

Payton, Sallyanne. "Disability Benefits for Sexual Psychopaths." *Stanford Law Review* 20, no. 1 (November 1967): 118–35.

Philipp, Steven F. "Gay and Lesbian Tourists at a Southern U.S.A. Beach Event." *Journal of Homosexuality* 37, no. 3 (1999): 69–86.

Pittman, Craig. *Oh, Florida! How America's Weirdest State Influences the Rest of the Country*. New York: St. Martin's Press, 2016.

Poucher, Judith G. *State of Defiance: Challenging the Johns Committee's Assault on Civil Liberties*. Gainesville: University Press of Florida, 2014.

Rabby, Glenda Alice. *The Pain and the Promise: The Struggle for Civil Rights in Tallahassee, Florida*. Athens: University of Georgia Press, 1999.

Reay, Barry. *New York Hustlers: Masculinity and Sex in Modern America*. Manchester, U.K.: Manchester University Press, 2010.

Retzloff, Tim. "Cars and Bars: Assembling Gay Men in Postwar Flint, Michigan." In *Creating a Place for Ourselves*, ed. Beemyn, 227–52.

Revels, Tracy J. *Sunshine Paradise: A History of Florida Tourism*. Gainesville: University Press of Florida, 2011.

Rubin, Gayle S. "Thinking Sex: Notes for a Radical Theory of the Politics of Sexuality." In *Culture, Society and Sexuality*, ed. Richard Parker and Peter Aggleton. New York: Routledge, 1999, 143–78.

Schnur, James A. "Closet Crusaders: The Johns Committee and Homophobia, 1956–1965." In *Carryin' on in the Lesbian and Gay South*, ed. Howard, 132–63.

Sears, James T. *Growing Up Gay in the South: Race, Gender, and Journeys of the Spirit*. New York: Harrington Park Press, 1991.

———. *Rebels, Rubyfruit, and Rhinestones: Queering Space in the Stonewall South*. New Brunswick, N.J.: Rutgers University Press, 2001.

Segrest, Mab. *My Mama's Dead Squirrel: Lesbian Essays on Southern Culture*. Ithaca, N.Y.: Firebrand Books, 1985.

Serlin, David. *Replaceable You: Engineering the Body in Postwar America*. Chicago: University of Chicago Press, 2004.

Shaw, Robert D., Jr. "The Discreet Lovers of Emma Jones." *Miami Herald, Tropic* supplement, March 16, 1975.

Stanonis, Anthony J. *Faith in Bikinis: Politics and Leisure in the Coastal South Since the Civil War*. Athens: University Press of Georgia, 2014.

———. "Introduction: Selling Dixies." In *Dixie Emporium: Tourism, Foodways, and Consumer Culture in the American South*, ed. Anthony J. Stanonis. Athens: University of Georgia Press, 2008.

Stein, Marc. "Birthplace of the Nation: Imagining Lesbian and Gay Communities in Philadelphia, 1969–1970." In *Creating a Place for Ourselves*, ed. Beemyn, 253–88.

Stockton, Kathryn Bond. *Beautiful Bottom, Beautiful Shame: Where "Black" Meets "Queer."* Durham, N.C.: Duke University Press, 2006.

Sullivan, Andrew. *Virtually Normal: An Argument About Homosexuality*. New York: Vintage Books, 1996.

Tafoya, Terry. "M Dragonfly: Two-Spirit and the Tafoya Principle of Uncertainty." In *Two-Spirit People: Native American Gender Identity, Sexuality and Spirituality*, ed. Sue Ellen Jacobs, Wesley Thomas, and Sabine Lang. Urbana: University of Illinois Press, 1997, 192–200.

Thompson, Brock. *The Un-Natural State: Arkansas and the Queer South*. Fayetteville: University of Arkansas Press, 2010.

Tiemeyer, Phil. *Plane Queer: Labor, Sexuality, and AIDS in the History of Male Flight Attendants*. Berkeley: University of California Press, 2013.

Turner, Mark W. *Backward Glances: Cruising the Queer Streets of New York and London*. London: Reaktion Books, 2003.

Watkins, Jerry T., III. "Underneath the Rainbow: Queer Identity and Community Building in Panama City and the Florida Panhandle, 1950–1990." M.A. thesis, Georgia State University, 2008.

Watkins, Liz. *The Life and Times of Trader Jon*. Watkins Productions, Pensacola. DVD, 1999.

Wiley, Lusharon. "An Agent for Change: The Story of Reverend H. K. Matthews." PhD diss., University of West Florida, 2007.

Williams, Raymond. *The Country and the City*. Oxford, U.K.: Oxford University Press, 1973.

White, C. Todd. *Pre-Gay LA: A Social History of the Movement for Homosexual Rights*. Urbana: University of Illinois Press, 2009.

Winsboro, Irvin D. S. *Old South, New South, or Down South: Florida and the Modern Civil Rights Movement*. Morgantown: West Virginia University Press, 2009.

Zuelow, Eric G. E. *A History of Modern Tourism*. New York: Palgrave Macmillan, 2016.

INDEX

Page numbers in *italics* refer to illustrations.

JERRY WATKINS holds a PhD from King's College London in American studies. He is a historian of sexuality who focuses on southerners who are gay, lesbian, or otherwise queer. He continues to research, write, and work with community history projects that seek to diversify the archive. His teaching focuses on the twentieth-century United States, social justice, and the modern South.